Dear Reader:

If you're contemplating or already planning an
outdoor wedding, then congratulations are in order!
Planning any wedding is both a challenge and
a joy. While outdoor events present some added
considerations, they also provide an opportunity to
display your personal sense of style and your unique
romantic flair. You can't be overprepared when you
include the always unpredictable Mother Nature on
your guest list. I planned my wedding for a full moon
night, but as insurance against cloudy, starless skies,
I had my florist create an indoor moon of golden
chrysanthemums surrounded by glitter-painted starfish.

This book will help you decide whether an outdoor
wedding is right for you. It also provides inspiration
and guidance as you plan your event and offers the
encouragement and reassurance you need to design
the day of your dreams. I hope Mother Nature gift-
wraps a glorious day for you, but remember that it is
your love and the magic between you that will truly
make your celebration shine.

Best of luck on your special day,

Kim Knox Beckius

The EVERYTHING® Series

Editorial

Publishing Director	Gary M. Krebs
Associate Managing Editor	Laura M. Daly
Associate Copy Chief	Brett Palana-Shanahan
Acquisitions Editor	Kate Burgo
Development Editor	Katie McDonough
Associate Production Editor	Casey Ebert

Production

Director of Manufacturing	Susan Beale
Associate Director of Production	Michelle Roy Kelly
Cover Design	Paul Beatrice
	Erick DaCosta
	Matt LeBlanc
Design and Layout	Colleen Cunningham
	Holly Curtis
	Erin Dawson
	Sorae Lee
Series Cover Artist	Barry Littmann

THE
EVERYTHING®
OUTDOOR
WEDDING
BOOK

Choose the perfect location, expect
the unexpected, and have a beautiful
wedding your guests will remember!

Kim Knox Beckius

Adams Media
Avon, Massachusetts

To my parents, and to all who say "I do" to love.

An Everything® Series Book.
Everything® and everything.com® are registered trademarks of F+W Publications, Inc.

Published by Adams Media, an F+W Publications Company
57 Littlefield Street, Avon, MA 02322 U.S.A.
www.adamsmedia.com

ISBN: 1-59337-371-6
Printed in the United States of America.

J I H G F E D C B A

Library of Congress Cataloging-in-Publication Data
Beckius, Kim Knox.
The everything outdoor wedding book : choose the perfect location, expect the unexpected, and have a beautiful wedding your guests will remember! / Kim Knox Beckius.
p. cm.
Includes index.
ISBN 1-59337-371-6
1. Weddings--Planning. I. Title. II. Series: Everything series.

HQ745.B433 2005
395.2'2--dc22
2005026439

This book is available at quantity discounts for bulk purchases.

For information, please call 1-800-872-5627.

Contents

Top Ten Reasons to Choose an Outdoor Wedding xii
Introduction xiii

1 Why Wed Outdoors? 1
Your Day in the Sun 2
A Place That's Near and Dear 3
Spectacular Photography 4
Advantages of an Outdoor Event 7
Costs of an Outdoor Event 8
Trends in Outdoor Weddings 11

2 Weather Concerns 15
Conquering Your Biggest Fear 16
Long-Range Weather Forecasting 17
Selecting a Season 21
Anecdotal and Statistical Evidence 23
Rain Is Not the Only Enemy 25
Let a Smile Be Your Umbrella 27

3 Potential Pitfalls 29
Transportation 30
Creepy Critters 33
Uninvited Guests 35
Guest Comfort 37
Dirt, Sweat, and Tears 40
Sound Effects 41

4 Contingency Planning 43
Foul-Weather Gear 44
The Tent Question 46
Alternate Sites 49
Scheduling a Rain Date 51
Photography Flexibility 52
Communicating with Guests 54
Prepare for the Worst 57

5 Selecting the Setting 59
Beach Weddings 60
Garden Weddings 63
Historic Properties 65
Public Places 67
Getting Permissions 69
The Right Questions 71

6 Weddings at Home 75
Advantages of At-Home Weddings 76
Should You Do It All Yourself? 78
Parking Issues 82
A Big Job 83
Liability 84
When the Party's Over 86

7 Weddings Away from Home 91
A Wedding "On Location" 92
Selecting a Destination 95
Cruise-Ship Weddings 97
Will They Come? 99
Planning from Afar 100
Pre- and Post-Wedding Events 103
Making a Distant Place Your Own 104

8 A Built-In Theme 107
A Locale That Speaks to You 108
Incorporating the Place into the Planning 108
Local Lore, Language, and Libations 111
Adding Theme Elements 113
Avoiding Thematic Conflicts 115
Sneak Preview and Welcome Ideas for Guests 117

9 Dressing the Setting 121
Outdoor Wedding Design 122
Arches and Other Architectural Elements 124
Seating 125
The Aisle and Altar 127
Where's the Sun? 129
Seasons Change 130
Embracing Natural Elements 132

10 The Ceremony 137
Selecting an Officiant 138
A Service That Fits the Setting 141
Keeping the Focus on You 144
Sound Issues 144
Music 146
Involving Guests 149

11 Outdoor Receptions 153
Shelter 154
Restroom Facilities 156
An Intimate Atmosphere 158
Music and Dancing 161
When Darkness Falls 165
Bringing the Outdoors In 168

12 Catering Considerations 169
Dining Al Fresco 170
Interviewing Caterers 172
Menu Do's and Don'ts 175

Seating Arrangements 178
Wind Concerns 178
Carting in the Cake 179

13   Photography 183
Selecting a Photographer 184
Before or After? 188
Out of the Shadows 190
Makeup Touchups 191
Creative Effects 192
A Shot List for the Photographer 195
Videography 196

14   The Invitations 201
Save the Date 202
Themed Invitations 204
Instructions for Guests 208
Directions to Hard-to-Find Places 212
RSVP with Contact Information 213
Something Fun 213

15   Outdoor Attire 217
Bridal Gown Selection Tips 218
How to Wear Your Hair 222
Bridesmaids' Attire 225
The Groom's Garb 228
Communicating Correct Dress to Guests 232
Changing Attire Midstream 233

16   The Final Countdown 235
What Can Go Wrong 236
Things to Do One Week Before 238
Watching the Weather 243
Rehearsals 243
Assembling an Emergency Kit 247
Keeping Guests in the Loop 249

17 The Day Dawns 251
Last-Minute Decision-Making 252
Your Communications Plan 255
Getting Ready 256
Smile for the Camera 259
Schedule Private Moments 259
When It's Not What You Hoped For 261

18 A Grand Entrance 263
Transporting Guests 264
Your Transportation 266
Together or Separately? 269
Horses and Other Antiquated Modes of Transportation . . . 269
Limo Limits 273
Aerial Arrivals 274

19 Cleanup 277
Delegate Responsibilities 278
Clean As You Go 280
Do No Harm, Leave No Trace 281
Functional Favors 282
Saying "Farewell" to People and Place 285
Final Practicalities 288

Appendix A:
State-by-State Directory of
Suggested Outdoor Venues 289

Appendix B:
Wedding Day Emergency Contact Sheet 307

Photo Credits 311
Index 313

Welcome to the *EVERYTHING*® series!

These handy, accessible books give you all you need to tackle a difficult project, gain a new hobby, comprehend a fascinating topic, prepare for an exam, or even brush up on something you learned back in school but have since forgotten.

You can read an EVERYTHING® book from cover-to-cover or just pick out the information you want from our four useful boxes: newlywed know-how, rain or shine, piece of cake, and ask the wedding planner. We literally give you everything you need to know on the subject, but throw in a lot of fun stuff along the way, too.

We now have over 300 EVERYTHING® books in print, spanning such wide-ranging topics as weddings, pregnancy, wine, learning guitar, one-pot cooking, managing people, and so much more. When you're done reading them all, you can finally say you know EVERYTHING®!

newlywed know-how

Essential information

piece of cake

Quick handy tips

rain or shine

Helpful warnings

ask the wedding planner

Solutions to common problems

Acknowledgments

I am grateful to my parents, George and Carol Snyder, for encouraging me to love words and books at an early age and for reviewing and editing this manuscript.

Special thanks to Mark Sinatro, who answered my questions about insurance, and to Chef Jake Jacobus of Cape Cod's Ocean Edge Resort, who chatted with me about food choices for outdoor receptions. Thanks, as well, to the hundreds of public relations professionals and property owners who responded to my requests for information about outdoor wedding venues.

My sincere appreciation goes to my agent, Barb Doyen, and to Adams Media acquisitions editor Kate Burgo for presenting me with the opportunity to write this practical guide for couples hoping to marry outdoors.

My husband, Bruce, and daughter, Lara, cope admirably with a sometimes "absentee mommy," and I am fortunate to have their love and support for my creative endeavors.

Top Ten Reasons
to Choose an Outdoor Wedding

1. Celebrate your love in a place that holds special meaning for the two of you.

2. Take advantage of a spectacular natural backdrop for your wedding photographs.

3. Invite spontaneity and unexpected drama to color your event.

4. Host an affair that is as elegant or as casual as you desire.

5. Set your wedding apart from other celebrations. By selecting a unique and scenic location, you will overlay your event with a distinctive theme, look, and style.

6. Intertwine spiritual traditions and customs from multiple faiths and cultures in a nondenominational setting.

7. Hold your ceremony and reception in one location, allowing the party to start immediately, and increase the amount of time available to share with loved ones.

8. Save money and time on decorations. Mother Nature will do the decorating for you.

9. Infuse your wedding with personality, originality, and creativity in a space that provides unparalleled freedom to design the event of your dreams.

10. Begin your wedded life in a place of incomparable beauty that you will remember fondly and can revisit throughout your years together.

Introduction

Many couples dream of an outdoor wedding in an unforgettable setting, but often the logistics of planning such an event and the potential pitfalls are powerful deterrents. This book evaluates the risks and rewards of various types of outdoor ceremonies and receptions and provides practical tips and strategies for ensuring a beautiful outdoor wedding event.

This is not a general wedding-planning guide. You won't find a list of who pays for what or instructions for tipping your limousine driver. What you will discover is realistic, down-to-earth advice on selecting a location, planning an outdoor event, preparing for contingencies, and making the most of a celebration in a beautiful, open-air environment. You'll also learn more about portable toilets than most brides and grooms.

Keep in mind that not every tip in this book will apply to you. If you intend to marry in an outdoor gazebo behind the hotel where your indoor reception will follow, you will have far fewer worries than the couple that chooses to hike with guests to a mountaintop for an exchange of vows at sunrise. In a garden setting, bees might be a concern, whereas at the beach, noisy seagulls may be enemy number one.

Though this book necessarily points out the things that can go wrong, it is really meant to encourage you in your pursuit of the wedding of your dreams. An optimistic outlook will go a long way toward ensuring that your wedding day is spectacular. The months ahead will be filled with anticipation, preparation, and collaboration as you work together to design this special day in your lives. Once you decide to embrace the idea of marrying outdoors, go forward with confidence. No rain cloud can dampen your enthusiasm when you look into each other's eyes and declare, "I do."

Why Wed Outdoors?

Nature is quite a fine decorator, and for many couples, the most compelling reason to wed outdoors is to celebrate this special day in a place of unparalleled beauty. Outdoor weddings have a special air of romance and surprise, and they allow you to share a cherished spot or a dream locale with loved ones. Though the two of you will shine in any setting, a lovely location can set your event apart and provide a dramatic and colorful backdrop that will be captured forever in both photographs and memories.

Your Day in the Sun

You awake to a sparkling day and throw open the windows to let in the breeze as you don your wedding-day attire. As you prepare to meet your beloved on the mountaintop, in the garden, by the sea, at the farm, or in your backyard, the only clouds that dare to dot the sky are a few wispy white accent pieces. Sunlight warms your faces and reflects from the shining rings you exchange as you profess your eternal love. As the party stretches into the evening, you hold each other close and dance under a velvet sky glittering with stars.

newlywed know-how

Yuma, Arizona, is America's sunniest city. On average, Yuma boasts a 93-percent sunshine rate. That means Yuma sees a mere 267 hours of overcast or rainy weather out of the 4,400 hours of sunshine possible each year.

Contemplating an outdoor wedding usually begins with an idealized vision of the possibilities. Close your eyes, and conjure up an image of the perfect wedding scene. Invite your partner to do the same. Did you both picture joining hands, exchanging vows, and sharing a kiss in a space without a roof and walls? Hold tightly to those images. It is only natural that one or both of you will have a few second thoughts as you consider everything that can go wrong with an outdoor wedding. If you truly desire to tie the knot in a scenic spot, your vision will sustain you as you embrace the added complexities and reassure concerned family members and friends who question your sanity.

Yes, there are risks, but the odds are tremendous that your outdoor wedding will be absolutely gorgeous. Vow to prepare for potential problems, to maintain your sense of humor, and above all to remember that, sun or no sun, the day will glow with your love for each other. If you're up for the unique challenges and unpredictable elements inherent in an outdoor wedding, there's a good chance you're ready for what lies ahead—marriage.

A Place That's Near and Dear

For many brides and grooms, the decision to wed outdoors is driven by a desire to gather family and friends in a place that is special for one or both of them. It may be a cherished childhood play place, a spot that holds significance in their romantic history, a family home, or a favorite vacation destination. If the perfect place doesn't immediately come to mind, or if the site you initially select can't accommodate your event, you can still enjoy an open-air wedding. With a bit of creative thinking, you can identify other romantic locations that match your vision of the ideal environment in which to express and celebrate your love.

Start in Your Backyard

There is certainly something alluring about a fairy-tale wedding in an exotic, faraway land. The costs and logistics of a destination wedding can be daunting, though, so before you scan the globe, start your search closer to home. These questions may spark your thinking as you compile a list of locations to consider:

- Where do we live?
- Where do our family members and closest friends live?
- Where and how were we engaged?
- What is our favorite restaurant?
- When we want to get away from it all for an afternoon, where do we go?
- What is our favorite picnic spot?
- What local attractions or historic sites have we visited and enjoyed together?
- Where have we attended great outdoor events in the past?

rain or shine

Before you set your heart on marrying in a public place, such as a park, it is important to determine which governmental agency or organization manages the facility and what specific policies and fees apply to its use for private gatherings.

Widening the Search

You may find that your extraordinary setting simply doesn't exist within the realm of your everyday experience. If you live in Minnesota, for example, but dream of a lush, tropical wedding by the sea, you will definitely need to widen your search. As you contemplate options further afield, ask yourselves these questions:

- Where did we enjoy vacationing as children?
- Where have we traveled together?
- What is our ethnic and cultural heritage?
- What languages do we speak?
- Where were our parents or grandparents married?
- What movie locations have captivated us?
- In what type of environment do we feel most at ease?

Whether it is as close as your own backyard or as distant as the other side of the world, the outdoor wedding location you select should ultimately reflect who you are as individuals and as a couple. Allow your imaginations to freely roam during this initial brainstorming stage. Although some of your ideas may prove impractical, a true sense of the place that fits will emerge as you put your heads together and ponder the possibilities.

Spectacular Photography

Scan the pages of any bridal magazine, and you're unlikely to find even a single photograph that could have been part of your grandparents' or even your parents' wedding album. There are no pretty bridesmaids all in a row, no serious grooms standing shoulder-to-shoulder with proud parents, no stiffly posed brides with shy smiles and trains neatly splayed.

While traditional wedding shots aren't complete dinosaurs, a photojournalistic approach to capturing wedding memories on film is increasingly popular. Because these images focus on people and place, rather than pomp and posing, a wedding's setting is receiving increasingly prominent billing. Glossy candids of newlyweds scampering through fields of flowers, emblazoning their footprints across a sandy beach, or kissing passionately as mountain breezes tousle veils and coattails may have kindled your own yearnings for a natural backdrop for your nuptials.

piece of cake

Weddings are one of the few occasions that bring together generations of family members from near and far. Even if you're not planning to pose for traditional family portraits, make plans with your photographer to gather significant family groupings for informal photos.

Natural Light

Take a moment to flip through the pages of your own photo albums. Compare photographs of people taken indoors and outdoors. You'll likely notice that, as a rule, snapshots taken with natural light tend to be brighter, more three-dimensional, and more flattering, whereas indoor shots are grainier and may be marred by shadows, flash reflections, or the dreaded "red eye." Though squinting subjects, long shadows, and gray skies can certainly spoil outdoor photos as well, it is fair to say that most amateur photographers fare better when they point and shoot under open skies.

Of course, you will probably hire a professional to photograph your wedding, and your photographer should have the experience and expertise to capture stunning images under any lighting conditions. (Often enthusiastic friends and family members capture the images newlyweds end up cherishing most—after all, they know not only the bride and groom but everyone else at the wedding.) The professional photographer you engage is likely to find, too, that your outdoor wedding presents more variety, potential angles, good color, and dramatic light than a typical indoor event.

rain or shine

Couples marrying outdoors may want to consider a photographer with digital photography capabilities and experience. Not only does digital imaging allow for quicker delivery of proofs, many digital cameras enable photographers to adapt more quickly to changing light conditions.

Weddings under the sun also allow professional photographers to use their creativity and their equipment with few or no restrictions. While some houses of worship may prohibit use of a flash or even ban all photography during a marriage ceremony, outdoor venues usually enable the photographer to capture loving moments as they unfold. A photographer can frequently move about to take advantage of more angles in an outdoor setting, as well, and can be much more unobtrusive by avoiding the use of a flash.

Unexpected Drama

A sea swells; a butterfly alights; clouds part; a flower girl plucks a dandelion and tucks it behind her ear. While an interior space might seem to be a controlled environment, in the open air, there is a sense that anything can happen. Those unanticipated, charming surprises are the makings of one-of-a-kind wedding photographs.

For spontaneous couples with a sense of adventure, there's nothing scary about allowing natural forces to play a role in shaping the day. It is a way to introduce unexpected drama that may yield some of the event's most vivid impressions. If your photographer is on his toes, these chance occurrences may also inspire some of its most remarkable images.

Advantages of an Outdoor Event

Outdoor events have several additional benefits. For starters, it is frequently possible to host the ceremony and reception in a single location. This not only enhances the flow and intimacy of the event, it minimizes the "down time" that guests often experience between the marriage ceremony and the party that follows. Your wedding day will fly by quickly, and eliminating travel between two sites means more time you can share with your loved ones.

Blending Beliefs

For interfaith couples, an outdoor venue can provide a space in which spiritual traditions are easily intertwined. Free of the constraints that may be inherent in a house of worship dedicated to a single faith, you will have the latitude to design a ceremony that is truly your own. If you opt for multiple officiants, a nondenominational setting will help to ensure their comfort, as well as that of guests with differing beliefs and backgrounds.

newlywed know-how

According to Susanna Stefanachi Macomb, an ordained interfaith minister and the author of *Joining Hands and Hearts,* interfaith marriages are on the rise. In fact, the intermarriage rate is about 60 percent for Buddhists, 50 percent for Jews, 40 percent for Catholics and Muslims, and 30 percent for Mormons.

Something New

Even if you plan to don traditional bridal attire and exchange customary vows, a spectacular natural setting can set your special day apart. Engaged couples are increasingly driven to personalize their unions by adding unique elements. For those with an affinity for wide-open spaces, an extraordinary place can easily serve as a wedding's defining element.

Many brides and grooms select a thematic approach to differentiate their wedding and to create a unified thread. This theme can carry through from "save the date" cards and invitations to decorations, favors, and food. When you opt for a wedding in a unique location, you have a built-in theme. As you learn more about the place you have selected—its history, geologic features, and flora and fauna—you will likely find ways to incorporate a sense of this special locale into all of the components of your affair.

Costs of an Outdoor Event

Weddings can certainly cost a bundle. That may seem like a statement of the obvious, but as you make critical decisions about the type of function you'll host, it is only realistic to acknowledge any worries you have about cost. If you're considering an outdoor event, the good news is that it need not cost any more than a similar indoor event. While some additional expenses may be incurred, there are also potential savings.

Establishing a realistic budget should be one of your first wedding planning moves, regardless of where your event will be held. Allow yourselves to splurge a bit on one or two items that matter most to you. You can then work to control costs by comparison shopping, negotiating with vendors, taking on do-it-yourself projects, or eliminating components that are less important.

Outdoor Add-Ons

The first major category of additional costs to consider as you build your outdoor wedding budget is rental equipment. From tables and chairs to dance floors, tents, lighting, and port-a-potties, the list of items that may not be readily available at your wedding site can be lengthy. If the location is remote or difficult to access, transportation and delivery costs can mount, as well.

Transportation of bridal party members and guests to the celebration site can be part of the wedding budget. An offshore island may seem a romantic setting until the costs of ferrying guests are calculated. Be sure to consider accessibility issues, too, as they may apply to older relatives or guests with special needs.

Because weather can wreak havoc on outdoor events, you will need to consider your backup plan, which may be costly. If the site you select does not have a built-in, sheltered alternative, and if erecting a tent is not permitted or feasible, you may have to reserve and pay for an alternate site. If you opt for a rain-date approach, there may be additional expenses associated with holding two dates and with communicating a change of plans to guests. If you really fear the damage that might ensue in the event of a hurricane or other weather disaster, wedding insurance may even be something to consider.

Keep in mind that outdoor nuptials are essentially limited to the peak wedding months, when the weather is most likely to be cooperative. As such, you will pay premium prices for your site and for many of your vendors. Choosing to hold your event on a Friday afternoon or Sunday may help you to combat high prices. You might also decide to gamble on a shoulder season date, as long as an indoor backup facility is available.

If your reception will also be outdoors and you must contract with an independent caterer, be sure to ask whether additional charges apply for outdoor food preparation, storage, and serving equipment. Keep in mind that, without convenient refrigeration, your event may generate quite a bit of waste. The costs of site cleanup and trash disposal must also be considered.

newlywed know-how

The average cost of a wedding in the United States now exceeds $20,000. That's about $67 per minute for a five-hour affair. As more brides and grooms are shouldering some, if not all, of that big tab, they are more determined than ever to have a wedding that reflects who they are as a couple.

Savings Strategies to Offset Added Costs

Now that you have considered an outdoor event's potential negative impact on your wedding budget, it's time to focus on something more pleasant—potential savings. For starters, you may be able to cross decorations right off your budget worksheet, as most outdoor settings provide more than enough visual splendor. Aisle runners, pew bows, floral arrangements, balloons, candles, and other decorations may actually detract from the natural beauty of the environment.

If you are fortunate, you may discover that the site usage fee for your location is less than renting a hall or hosting your event at a restaurant or hotel. You may want to inquire about scheduling your event on a day other than Saturday, as that may also reduce fees. Be sure to ask if reduced site usage fees are available to members or supporters of sites owned and operated by not-for-profit organizations. A tax-deductible contribution may make sense if it reduces your costs.

Scheduling both the ceremony and the reception in the same open-air location can also reduce overall expenses. There is frequently a fee or suggested donation for use of a church, chapel, synagogue, or other house of worship. Concentrating everything in a single location can also help you rein in transportation costs for the bridal party.

Depending on the availability of electricity, your event may be limited to daylight hours. As a rule, daytime events are more casual and, thus, less costly. In fact, you may want to embrace the informality of the setting wholeheartedly and shave your expenses by opting for less fancy bridal party attire, beer and wine instead of a full bar, lighter reception fare, ice cream or watermelon instead of cake, and outdoor games instead of a DJ or band and dancing.

Trends in Outdoor Weddings

Weddings infused with personality, originality, and creativity are all the rage these days. The growth in the number of weddings held in outdoor settings is part of a much larger trend. It used to be that brides were shaking things up by opting for Pachelbel's *Canon* instead of Wagner's traditional "Wedding March" and by having both parents escort them down the aisle. Today, however, couples are finding new ways to imprint the occasion with their own style, from the moment invitations are mailed until the evening's final farewell.

ask the wedding planner ?

How common are outdoor weddings?

According to Conde Nast Bridal InfoBank's American Wedding Survey, 15 percent of weddings are held outdoors. That number may seem small at first glance, but when you consider that 2.3 million marriages occur annually in the United States, you'll be in the company of about 345,000 other couples if you opt to wed outdoors.

Outdoor weddings aren't really anything new. For decades, brides and grooms have tied the knot in her parents' backyard or sought to be outrageous by marrying on a ski slope, underwater, or in a hot air balloon. What has changed is that outdoor weddings are no longer solely the domain of the daring or the financially limited. An outside event, even one held in the backyard, can be every bit as elegant and moving as one that occurs within a traditional venue, and outdoor locations are frequently selected not for shock value but with a sense of reverence for the spirituality and beauty of nature's gifts.

Who Marries Outdoors?

There is no hard and fast rule that says you have to love hiking, camping, and boating to be inclined to marry in the great outdoors. Couples who choose the scenic route are a diverse lot, but one thing most have in common is confidence in what appeals to them and in how they would like their wedding to unfold. If you feel apprehensive or uncertain about choosing this path, an outdoor wedding may not be for you.

Finding yourself engaged at the same time as your college roommates, your sister, and your next-door neighbor may be what stimulates you to think outside the traditional wedding box. There can be competition among people whose weddings are close together. Here's a word of caution: Don't simply pick an outdoor spot because it is different from what your friends are doing. You must be completely committed to the concept of marrying outdoors and passionate about the place you have chosen in order to gracefully shoulder the additional complexities inherent in planning this type of event.

Because a wedding's location can help make it more dramatic, outdoor weddings are more common when the bride or groom or both have been married before. Some second-time brides and grooms try to make this event as different from their first wedding as possible, particularly if the guest list includes many of the same family members and friends. A more informal celebration may also be warranted, and an outdoor setting can offer flexibility and set a relaxed tone for the event. Once again, while doing something completely different may be a valid reason to consider this approach, only marry outdoors if both you and your spouse-to-be feel comfortable with and inspired by the idea.

More Places with Open Spaces

Outdoor weddings are also on the rise, in part because more and more facilities are catering to this trend. Weddings are big business, and owners of banquet halls, inns, restaurants, and other traditional wedding reception sites realize they need to stay attuned to the desires of brides and grooms in order to compete for bookings. As the demand for picturesque settings has grown, many facilities have added outdoor options by installing gazebos, landscaped gardens, charming water features, or arches. Often, they can offer the best of all worlds—a lovely outdoor environment if the weather cooperates and a nearby sheltered backup should storm clouds darken the day.

Also fueling the outdoor wedding movement is the expanding number of historic sites, museums, aquariums, zoos, botanical gardens, and public parks that now open their gates for private functions. For many nonprofit groups, hosting weddings has become a much-needed source of income. It is also a means of building goodwill within a community and recruiting new supporters and members, who may be introduced to the organization's offerings for the first time as the result of a wedding invitation. The availability of these properties opens up a colorful spectrum of possibilities for couples in search of a unique outdoor setting.

Weddings That Go On and On

It is rare these days to marry the boy or girl next door. Communications technologies and modern mobility have made it possible for couples to connect in new and unpredictable ways. Combine that with the fact that both men and women are marrying later in life, and the upshot is that just about any bride-and-groom combo will likely want to share their special day with friends and family across the nation—maybe even around the globe.

As weddings have increasingly evolved into travel events instead of hometown affairs, they have also mushroomed in many instances into much more than a five-hour party on a Saturday. Celebrations that incorporate pre- and post-wedding activities are becoming quite common. This is particularly true in the case of destination weddings, when even the bride and groom are visitors from out of town.

When an outdoor ceremony or reception is the centerpiece of several days of fun and merry-making rather than the main event, there is a bit less pressure for everything to be perfect. If rain does fall or an untimely cold front moves through, it will only put a small damper on days filled with loving moments, happy memories, and sunny interludes. With a days-long celebration, it is unlikely that your entire event will be a washout. If you crave all of the beauty and freedom of an outdoor celebration but feel compelled to hedge your bets, you may find that spreading the celebration over several days is a way to alleviate some worry and boost your confidence.

Weather Concerns

The threat of foul weather is enemy number one to the outdoor wedding. No matter how sure you are that an outdoor wedding is the choice for you, you can't help but worry about whether storms and other weather calamities might mar your day. Most couples who are contemplating an outdoor event wonder, "Is there anything we can do to stack the odds in our favor so that the date we select will be radiant with sunshine?"

Conquering Your Biggest Fear

Weather is a legitimate concern for anyone planning an outdoor event. The key is to approach this potential hazard logically and to rationally assess your ability to cope with circumstances beyond your control. The first step in conquering any fear is to accept and verbalize the anxiety that you are feeling. Talk to your partner, parents, or friends about the specific things that are worrying you. Try to tap into the true source of your fears. "I want to hold my wedding outdoors, but it might rain," is a starting point, but from there, ask yourself what troubles you most. It could be any of a number of things, such as, "My hair gets really frizzy when it rains," or "Our photos might be dark and dreary," or "Our guests might feel uncomfortable if the weather is damp and chilly."

piece of cake

Mark Twain once quipped, "Everybody talks about the weather, but nobody does anything about it." It is important to accept that the weather is not within your realm of control. Instead of agonizing, focus your energy on preparing a celebration that will be wondrous, whatever the weather. Then everybody will talk about how splendid your wedding was, rain or sun aside.

Once you have identified the specific causes for your greatest concerns, step back a bit and think through whether opting for an indoor venue completely eliminates all of your worst weather nightmares. You are likely to realize that a torrential downpour or other unfortunate weather event could create some havoc, even if you plan to be mostly inside. One distinct advantage of an outdoor wedding is that you will entertain the possibility of bad weather from the outset and will be prepared to cope with whatever nature sends your way. If storms brew, instead of scrambling to find oversized umbrellas at the last minute and fretting about how you will keep your eight-foot cathedral train from dragging in the mud, you'll have all of your foul-weather gear and a backup location in place, and you'll know that you've selected attire that will hold up under the rigors of outdoor wear. Worst case, you will wind up inside or under cover, rather than in the outdoor setting you preferred.

Though weather can certainly alter your plans, it doesn't have to ruin the day. Only you, however, can judge how well you are likely to handle any disappointment that stems from having to go with Plan B. Remember that emotions can run high on your wedding day, and even if you have coped gracefully in the past with washed-out plans for beach parties or backyard barbecues, you might not feel quite as unfazed on this particular day. It is not always easy to accept that some things are completely out of your control. If you are likely to spend the night before your nuptials wide awake and in tears because meteorologists are forecasting storms, you won't look and feel your best, even if the rain never materializes.

Long-Range Weather Forecasting

You're ready to select a wedding date that is six months, a year, or even further away. As you look at a calendar and contemplate possible dates, you can't help but wonder—what will the weather be like? Is there any way to know this far in advance?

Weather Technology

Admittedly, weather forecasting technology has come a long way. Super computers, mathematical models, space satellites, Doppler radar, and other instruments provide enhanced atmospheric data, improved storm monitoring, and greater understanding of the weather we experience. News outlets now rely on scientists with degrees in meteorology instead of weather reporters with attractive features to provide the public with dependable weather-prediction services.

If you want to know what to wear tomorrow, chances are the forecast you hear on the nightly news will be quite accurate. Modern technology makes even the three-day forecast a reliable indicator. Studies have shown that today's three-day forecast is as accurate as the one-day forecast was twenty-five years ago. According to the American Meteorological Society, there have also been dramatic improvements in the past two decades in the accuracy of medium-range (three- to seven-day) forecasts.

Accuracy at Long Range

What happens when weather predictions are made for more than a week in advance? The short answer is that the accuracy drops substantially, with precipitation forecasts less reliable than temperature predictions. Though it is certainly frustrating, unless you are searching for a day in the next week or so to spontaneously elope with your sweetheart, the weather for your wedding day will remain a mystery until your "I do's" are just days away.

piece of cake

According to the American Meteorological Society's policy statement on weather analysis and forecasting, "There has been a revolution in the accuracy and utility of weather forecasts in the past several decades." However, "no verifiable skill exists or is likely to exist for forecasting day-to-day weather changes beyond two weeks. Claims to the contrary should be viewed with skepticism."

Why is it practically impossible to forecast the weather far into the future? Without delving too deeply into a discussion of chaos theory, the conceptual explanation stems from the fact that Earth's atmosphere is subject to an infinite number of variables. No matter how advanced computers and modeling systems become, most meteorologists concur that while short-range forecasts may improve in accuracy, dependable predictions beyond two to three weeks will remain forever elusive.

That said, the National Weather Service's Climate Prediction Center does offer seasonal outlooks that attempt to analyze whether rainfall and temperatures will be above, below, or near normal in various U.S. regions for the year ahead. These long-term forecasts can be accessed online at *www.cpc. ncep.noaa.gov*. While this trend data may provide a few clues as to whether the season you are contemplating will be excessively wet or unusually warm, keep in mind that these are generalizations that do not necessarily apply to any given date in any selected location. Also, the reliability of these outlooks varies with the region and the season. For example, accuracy is known to be lower during transition times, such as during the months of April, May, and June, when weather can fluctuate dramatically from day to day.

Folklore and Other Fun Prognosticators

Though they lack sophisticated forecasting equipment, animals have been given a lot of credit over the years for their weather prediction abilities. When cows lie down in a field, it is going to rain. If the groundhog sees his shadow, it means that spring is still six weeks away. If an owl hoots on the east side of a mountain, it foretells bad weather. The shorter the middle brown band on a woolly bear caterpillar, the more severe the impending winter.

Is there any scientific basis for trusting these animal indicators? Not really. Nor is there any evidence that other common weather folklore is any more reliable, though it is fun to consider old weather sayings, such as "A summerish January, a winterish spring" or "When the stars begin to huddle, the Earth will soon become a puddle."

If you decide to consult the *Old Farmer's Almanac,* you certainly won't be the first couple to seek wedding date input from North America's oldest continuously published periodical, a source of long-range regional forecasts since 1792. The almanac's first editor, Robert B. Thomas, devised a secret weather-forecasting formula based on sunspots and solar cycles that is still kept under lock and key at the publication's New Hampshire offices. While the *Old Farmer's Almanac* claims its predictions are 80-percent accurate, and it certainly won't hurt to see what the forecast is for the dates you're considering, it's important not to rely too heavily on this information. Keep in mind that these predictions cover rather large regions. While it may be true that heavy rain will fall somewhere in New England on a forecasted date, the chances that there will be heavy rain everywhere in the region are slim.

newlywed know-how

Wedding weather superstitions are many. You may hear that rain is a sign that you will have many children. Since wedding lore from various cultures is contradictory as to whether rain is a good or bad omen on your wedding day—think positive! As one encouraging old saying goes, "A wet knot is more difficult to untie," so a long married life may await those who marry under rain clouds.

Since precipitation is a primary concern for those planning an outdoor wedding, you may also be intrigued by a system that claims an 85-percent accuracy rate in predicting dry weather days as much as 18 months in advance. Ruch Weather Services of Santa Ana, California, claims its DRYDAY Planning Forecast system is mathematically tuned to identify days that will be free of rainfall. Monthly DRYDAY forecasts for specific cities and towns in the continental United States are available for purchase at *www.dryday.com.* The company makes its thirty-day reports available free online, so you can evaluate their validity before you buy.

If you're inclined to read your daily horoscope, you may also want to pay a visit to *www.weathersage.com.* Carolyn Egan's Web site is devoted to astrometeorology—the practice of divining the long-range forecast via the stars. Egan provides her forecast for the season ahead, and you can learn more about astrological techniques used since the seventeenth century to predict future storms and other weather events.

Selecting a Season

Winter is romantic. Spring is lively. Summer is sensual. Fall is colorful and passionate. The season a couple selects for a wedding is usually a matter of personal preference and convenience. For celebrations taking place in an open space, however, the time of year becomes something to consider quite carefully.

Summer Splendor

Summer is the most popular season for outdoor weddings, and it is easy to understand why. Temperatures are most reliably warm. Everything is green. The sun lingers in the evening sky. Long holiday weekends give guests time to travel. And picnics, barbecues, and other outdoor festivities are already a summertime ritual.

ask the wedding planner ?

Why is June the most popular month for weddings?

While weather is certainly a factor, the tradition of June weddings actually dates back to ancient Rome, when it was believed that Juno, goddess of marriage, would protect those who wed during her namesake month.

There are a few drawbacks to this bright season, though. For starters, in some locations, summer is simply too hot. In other places, humidity can make cavorting outdoors unbearable at worst and moist and uncomfortable at best. Summer is also the season for bugs, surprise thundershowers, and vacations and other family commitments that may keep some guests from attending your event. During the busiest wedding months, you will also need to compete with many other couples for everything from ceremony and reception locations to the services of DJs, florists, seamstresses, and limousine drivers.

Spring and Fall

In many locales, spring and fall have the advantage of lending natural beauty to an outdoor event as new blossoms awaken or trees turn vibrant shades of crimson and gold before shedding their leaves. Bouquets, bridesmaids' gowns, table linens, and other accents can all coordinate with the vibrant pastels of spring or the rich, warm tones of autumn. Temperatures are most often moderate. And the competition from other events is a bit less intense.

newlywed know-how

Interest in fall weddings has been on the upsurge in recent years. According to TheKnot.com, 20 percent of all weddings occur in September and October. An added plus of an autumn honeymoon is that resorts are less crowded and more tranquil, since children have returned to school.

The one hurdle presented by these otherwise desirable seasons is unpredictability. The degree of seasonal variation is more dramatic in some geographical regions than others, so if you are marrying away from home, it is important to familiarize yourselves with the potential range of weather conditions. How likely is an April heat wave or an October frost? When does hurricane season begin and end? Take into consideration, as well, that it is impossible to predict precisely when spring flowers will erupt in full bloom or when fall foliage will reach its peak color.

Winter Warmth

In northern climes, an outdoor winter wedding is largely out of the question unless you and your sweetie dream of a somewhat novel celebration at a skating pond or a ski slope. The key, then, to marrying outdoors between

November and March is to plan the event for a southerly spot where snow is rare and winter temperatures remain warm. Alternatively, if you must marry in winter and travel beyond cold, northern regions is not an option, explore interior settings that offer the flavor of the outdoors, such as an atrium, greenhouse, aquarium, butterfly conservatory, indoor water park, or even a casual seafood or barbecue restaurant.

Keep in mind that even in areas where conditions are relatively mild year-round, winter can be a season of temperature fluctuations and increased precipitation. Warm weather destinations are also subject to price spikes and crowded conditions in winter as snowbirds and vacationers flee the frigid North. While the holiday season may seem a romantic time to embark on your journey as husband and wife, keep in mind that this is also a terribly hectic period for your invited guests. For those who must travel, high fares, unpredictable weather, and packed planes and trains can all be deterrents.

Anecdotal and Statistical Evidence

There is no way to know what kind of weather you will have for your wedding day. However, a bit of research can still shed some light on what conditions are probable. Before you make your final date selection, ask around and check some data.

Talk About It

The weather is a favorite topic of conversation, so it is easy to do some investigative research and to gather anecdotal evidence. Talking to locals is of particular importance if your wedding will occur in an unfamiliar location where you do not live year-round. Chat with the people who manage the property where your wedding will be held. Pop into a diner or coffee shop and talk to employees and regulars. Seek out a local gardener or farmer who may be particularly attuned to weather happenings, or call the local department of agriculture or cooperative extension.

While you will need to keep in mind that memories are not perfect and that past weather does not guarantee a repeat performance, you may be surprised to hear similar advice from several individuals. Unlike popular but unsubstantiated weather sayings and lore, what you learn from the locals is based on experience in the exact location where you intend to hold your event. You may just discover some interesting things, such as, "It's always hottest around the Fourth of July," or "It never rains around here in August," or "We always seem to have one last snowstorm in early spring," or "The leaves really don't start changing until the first of October." Though not scientific by any measure, you may do well to heed the counsel of those who are kind enough to share their recollections and observations.

Finding Weather Data

Regardless of whether the location for your wedding is familiar, it may be sensible to take a look at weather statistics that indicate what is normal and the range of potential deviation. A good starting place is the local newspaper, which may feature an almanac section that includes information about such things as normal precipitation and temperatures for the month as well as record highs and lows set on specific dates. You may need to visit the local library to look at back issues for a particular month.

piece of cake

Visit *www.weatherbase.com* for extensive, free summary statistics for cities and towns across America and around the world. You will find such helpful weather stats as monthly average high and low temperatures, highest and lowest recorded temperatures, average precipitation, average number of clear and cloudy days, and average probability of sunshine.

Rain Is Not the Only Enemy

Certainly, rain tops the list of unwelcome intruders at an outdoor wedding. It is important to keep in mind, though, that even if the clouds don't shed a drop, there are other weather demons that might rear their ugly heads and cause some mischief. Though you may not be able to foresee every foul-weather possibility, anticipating potential problems will help you to plan ahead for whatever surprises the atmosphere might have in mind.

Blowing in the Wind

A gentle breeze can ease the oppressiveness of a sweltering day, tickle petals and feathery grasses, coax colorful balloons into a jubilant dance, and infuse the air with an invigorating freshness. When the wind picks up a notch, though, trouble could be brewing. Even on a dry day, gusty, blustery winds can force outdoor revelers to head for cover.

newlywed know-how

In 1939, the International Meteorological Committee adopted a wind-speed scale that describes winds as follows: 0–7 mph, Light; 8–12 mph, Gentle; 13–18 mph, Moderate; 12–24 mph, Fresh; 25–38 mph, Strong; 39–54 mph, Gale; 55–72 mph, Whole Gale; 73 mph and higher, Hurricane.

What problems can wind whip up? On the level of mere annoyance, it can tousle the string quartet's sheet music, disrupt carefully styled hair-dos, blow napkins off tables, and flip the pages of the officiant's sermon notes. High winds become a serious problem when they are capable of overturning chairs and tables, tipping over candles and glass vases, sending bridesmaids' billowy skirts skyward, and knocking out electrical power. A beach wedding can be particularly problematic in the face of heavy gusts, as weddings are tear-inducing enough without sand stinging guests' eyes.

Heat Waves and Cold Snaps

If you've done your homework, you likely know what the average temperatures are for the month and place in which you intend to wed. The question is, how dramatically can temperature conditions vary from the norm? Some geographic locations will be more subject to fluctuations than others, but it is relatively safe to say that abnormal temperatures do occasionally occur just about everywhere.

A heat wave is generally defined as a period of uncomfortably hot and usually humid weather that can last for several days or even weeks. Whether or not your wedding day occurs in the midst of a wave or is simply subject to a sudden temperature spike that sends the mercury climbing, you will need to take the heat into consideration. Possible ill effects of heat include fatigue, dehydration, sunburn, sweat, heat cramps, fainting, overheated vehicles, heat exhaustion, and sunstroke. Sustained high temperatures can also tax the power grid and lead to brownouts and blackouts.

On the opposite end of the temperature spectrum, a cold snap can also make an outdoor celebration challenging. You can contend with a slight chill by making sure you've purchased a jacket or shawl that coordinates with your bridal gown. You might also rent outdoor propane heaters and have a few warm blankets on hand for elderly relatives or anyone who is particularly subject to shivering. On the rare day when it snows in May, though, you will likely need to activate Plan B and move the affair to shelter in order to avoid slipping on icy ground, forcing guests to huddle for warmth, and uttering vows through chattering teeth.

Extreme Weather

Though it is not an everyday occurrence, some brides and grooms do have to decide what to do when a severe weather event is forecast for their wedding day. The good news is that the science of meteorology and constant monitoring of atmospheric conditions have made it pretty tough for hurricanes, tornadoes, floods, and other extremes of weather to sneak up on us. Whether your wedding is planned for indoors or out, when you hear that really extraordinary weather is on the way, you need to heed advisories and evacuation orders and make safety your first priority.

rain or shine

The Atlantic hurricane season runs from June 1 until November 30, with most of history's worst storms occurring in the fall. The Eastern Pacific hurricane season begins May 15 and extends through November 30. The National Hurricane Center provides the latest information on hurricane activity (online at *www.tpc.ncep.noaa.gov*).

Though postponing your wedding may involve a certain amount of confusion, disappointment, and added expense, it is always better in the big scheme of things to be safe than sorry. On the bright side, you will have an interesting story to tell and an excuse to celebrate two anniversary dates for the rest of your lives.

Let a Smile Be Your Umbrella

If love does indeed conquer all, your joy and happiness will certainly chase away any gloom that might be cast by dark, leaky clouds. Vow to view the weather as neither a good thing nor a bad thing but as something that simply is. Every couple dreams of a perfect wedding day, but true perfection lies in being able to stand side by side, laughing and loving through the unpredictable and imperfect incidences of everyday life.

piece of cake

If you need additional incentive to smile as you confront a wet wedding day, keep in mind that rainy conditions mean longer-lasting bouquets; a dewy complexion; fresher makeup; passionate-kiss–concealing umbrellas; misty, romantic photographs; and extra excuses to cuddle.

Try to remember that rain *can* be exceedingly romantic. Ensconced safe and dry inside a tent or building, surrounded by those you cherish most dearly, you may even be glad for the focus and intimacy foul weather has brought to your day. A change of plans is always a bit difficult to swallow at first, but try to keep the weather in perspective. Years from now, wild winds, torrential rains, beating sun, or frost-nipped buds will be either completely forgotten or a treasured aspect of what made your "I do" day one you'll forever remember.

Potential Pitfalls

You may breathe a sigh of relief when your special day arrives complete with cloud-free skies and pleasant temperatures. You're not home free just yet, though. There are a few other potential pitfalls associated with outdoor celebrations, and though none is as intimidating as bad weather, you'll be wise to think through what else may go wrong long before your wedding day dawns. A bit of forethought will enhance comfort and safety for you and your guests and minimize unwelcome distractions.

Transportation

Your best man's flight is cancelled due to thunderstorms. The DJ's van gets stuck in the mud. Your plan to arrive in an antique, horse-drawn carriage is thwarted by rainy skies. Inclement weather can certainly cause transportation delays and issues. Even when the weather is perfectly cooperative, though, outdoor events require a bit of extra planning when it comes to getting everyone to the wedding site safely and on time.

How Do We Get There?

Providing guests and vendors with directions is a fairly simple task when a wedding is held at a church, synagogue, meeting house, town hall, restaurant, or banquet hall. However, getting your friends and the flowers and food to a specific spot at the beach, in a national park, or on a mountainside can be a different matter entirely. It isn't likely that you'll be allowed to post a plethora of signs indicating, "Wedding This Way." And instructing folks to walk 150 paces north or to turn left at the second oak tree may seem fun at first until the focus of your events shifts from you two to search and rescue.

newlywed know-how

It may not be prudent to rely on cell phones for communication and coordination, particularly if you have selected a remote outdoor site where signal strength can be unreliable. A good solution is to rent two-way radios or walkie-talkies for the day. Long-range radios allow you to stay in touch with key people at a distance of up to five miles.

Short of incurring the tremendous expense of enclosing satellite tracking units with your wedding invitations, how can you best direct everyone to a location that lacks a street number and address? For starters, it is a good idea to ask the site manager or wedding coordinator if a map of the property is available. If you are able to acquire a map, be sure to evaluate its accuracy before blindly making dozens of copies to send to guests. If you will need to mark the map yourselves to indicate the exact spot where you intend to congregate, ask for assistance from someone who knows the site well, if possible, before you make that big red X. Before distributing the map, it is a good idea to schedule a field test with a volunteer who has never been to the location to make sure that any potential sources of confusion are identified.

If a map isn't available, or even if one is, it may be helpful to enlist a few friends or family members to serve as guides or escorts. Position them at strategic spots where some might opt for the wrong fork in the path, or assign them to meet and greet guests at the parking area and to lead them to your wedding site in small groups. You may need to alert guests to seek out these escorts when they arrive, and you may want to make these helpers visible by asking them to wear a certain color or to tie red balloons around their wrists. Be sure to ask vendors what time they will arrive to make deliveries or begin setting up so that someone is available to meet them.

Limited Access

For some outdoor wedding sites, you may be faced with the added challenge of limited vehicular access or parking. It is important to find out what vehicles will be allowed where and at what time. Then you can coordinate a plan to get people and supplies to their destination.

Be candid with your caterer, DJ, tent rental company, and other suppliers about logistics and any restrictions that will be imposed. In some cases, they may be able to drive a vehicle in to unload but will need to park at a substantial distance from the celebration site. If tent poles, dance floors, speakers, tables, chairs, port-a-potties, or other equipment cannot be unloaded close to their ultimate destination, vendors may need to make specific arrangements for extra help, and you may incur some additional costs.

If limited parking is available for guests, there are several strategies you might employ. First, consider paring down your guest list. Then, talk to those who plan to attend about the possibility of carpooling. If you will still have far more cars than the site allows, you may need to make arrangements to shuttle guests from an off-site meeting place. Keep in mind that this creates an extra burden on guests to arrive on time and to stay until the shuttle is available to return them to their vehicles, which may present a problem for those with small children or schedule conflicts. While renting a van or small bus and enlisting a volunteer driver may be your most affordable option, hiring a chauffeured van may prove to be a more flexible and less stressful solution.

rain or shine

The parking lot at a local shopping plaza or high school may seem a perfectly convenient meeting place for guests who will need to catch a shuttle to your shindig. Before you engrave directions to the lot on invitation enclosures, though, be sure to get permission. A joyful day can end in a horrible hassle if your guests' cars have all been towed.

Guests with Special Needs

Is it a long walk from the parking area to your celebration location? Is the path gravelly, sandy, or marred by potholes? Is it an uphill climb? While most of your guests won't be bothered at all by such things, it is important to think of those friends and loved ones with physical limitations as you make your plans.

If handicapped spots are not already marked in the parking area, you may want to designate an area for those who would benefit from being as close as possible to the action. Be sure that guests are alerted ahead of time to the availability of the reserved area or that someone is on site to direct them. If you will be shuttling guests from an off-site location, you may need to hire a van with a lift for wheelchair-bound guests.

If there is distance or difficult terrain between the parking area and the ceremony and reception location, first check to see if it may be possible to drive guests with limited mobility closer to the site. If not, you may want to inquire about the availability of a golf cart or look into renting one yourselves.

While you may be aware of the special needs of certain close friends and relatives and can communicate transportation arrangements directly with them, it is important to inform all guests about what to expect when they arrive. After all, anyone can break a leg between the RSVP and the advent of your big day. Also, if you have not personally met some guests' significant others or dates, you may not be able to anticipate every need for assistance. It is also a courtesy to all of your female friends and family members who might be debating between flats and stilettos to let them know if they're in for a rugged mile-long trek.

Creepy Critters

You can pretty much control who will arrive at your outdoor wedding on two legs. It's not nearly as easy, though, to dictate who might fly in, buzz by, or strut through on six, eight, or more legs. Without the benefit of windows, walls, doors, and a roof, the deterrents to unwelcome pests are few. Remember that while you are using this outdoor environment for your special day, a variety of creatures likely call it home no matter what the occasion. Your challenge is to identify potential intruders, then find ways to minimize the problems they might cause without seriously disturbing their habitat.

Buzzing Bees

The nectar in flowers attracts bees, so if you are marrying in a garden or carrying or decorating with an abundance of fresh flowers, these buzzing interlopers may be among your top concerns. In general, bees are attracted most to blue, purple, and yellow flowers, and they prefer single-blossom species. Spring and summer are peak bee seasons.

As a rule, bees, wasps, and hornets do not sting unless they are provoked, but it is possible that trespassing on their turf could ignite their fury. A sting can be painful, but that is the worst of it for most people. Only 4 percent of the population is allergic to bee stings, and most people who know their reaction to a sting might be severe carry a bee-sting or anaphylaxis kit for emergencies. If someone experiences considerable swelling, muscle cramps, headaches, difficulty breathing or swallowing, fever, nausea, or drowsiness following a bee sting, get to the emergency room immediately.

piece of cake

It is a good idea to prepare a bee sting and bug bite treatment kit and to have it available at your wedding site. It should contain alcohol swabs, antiseptic soap, tweezers, an ice pack, Benadryl, nonaspirin pain reliever, hydrocortisone cream, calamine lotion, and baking soda toothpaste.

Other Insects

Most other insects you're likely to meet up with in the great outdoors don't present much danger, but they can make a groom wish *he* was the one wearing a veil. Biting bugs can also force guests to spend more time slapping and scratching than feasting and dancing. Flies flitting around your lavish buffet can be rather unappetizing, too, even if guests don't notice the ones that have accidentally embedded themselves in the frosting on your cake.

The best defense against bugs is a good offense. Do some investigating to determine at what time of year and time of day mosquitoes, black flies, sand fleas, gnats, and other biting insects are most likely to be active. There may be certain insect seasons that you will simply need to completely avoid. In some locations, it is important to also be aware of the presence of such pests as fire ants and Lyme-disease–carrying ticks.

Next, discuss bug management strategies with those who operate your wedding site to see what may be allowed. Can you hire an exterminator to spray the area a day or two before your event? Can citronella candles or torches be lit? Can electronic or propane-powered bug control devices be used if purchased or rented?

newlywed know-how

If insects may present a problem, be sure to have a supply of bug repellant spray on hand for use by guests. Those that contain DEET are considered most effective. For something fun, look for glow-in-the-dark insect-repelling wrist bands at a drugstore or online.

Talk to your caterer, too, about protecting food from winged and crawling taste-testers. There may be ways to employ tents, netting, or other attractive bug barriers to keep pests away. If insects are likely to be more and more bothersome as dusk arrives, you may want to hold your ceremony and cocktail hour outside, then move the party indoors where the bugs won't be able to nibble on guests or the fine spread.

Uninvited Guests

Depending upon the location you choose, you could be faced with unpleasant animal encounters. At the shore, the prime risk lies with washed up remains of dead sea creatures, which are not only unsightly but can smell rather offensive. You'll want to appoint someone to patrol the beach just before your event. On rare occasions, shark sightings and beached marine mammals can lead to beach closings, which could send you scrambling for a backup site. In addition to animal encounters, you may also have to watch out for the occasional human interruptions.

Feathered Friends

If you recall the animated scene of sweetly chirping little birdies helping Cinderella dress for the ball, you may find it hard to believe that feathered onlookers might be a nuisance. Keep in mind that not all birds chirp melodiously. Some, like seagulls, can create quite a racket with their squawking. Others, like madly hammering woodpeckers, can also drown out vows, sermons, serenades, and toasts. And, to put it delicately, birds can also make quite a mess. Though the odds are slim of being "hit" by a bird flying overhead, those ducks, geese, and swans that you thought were lovely as they glided across a lake or pond can become much less attractive when they waddle ashore and leave sloppy deposits near the cocktail area.

piece of cake

As much as you love your own pets, for weddings at home, it may be smart to board them at a kennel or with friends. The excitement of the day may send them into a bit of a tizzy, and they are not likely to understand your imposition of restrictions on their usual levels of affection and playfulness.

Some birds that are accustomed to people can also be aggressive food scavengers. Though you can do little to combat bird chatter other than speaking loudly or turning the music up a notch, you *can* take action to reduce other undesirable bird effects. Note areas where birds gather and nest, and try to situate your event as far away as possible. There are also commercially available chemical products that may help you to keep meddlesome birds at bay.

While the snakes that might wriggle along a garden gate or across a lawn are probably harmless, they can still startle and upset you or one of your guests. You may want to ask about whether snakes are common. In more rugged environments, you definitely need to know if there is a risk of uncovering a poisonous or otherwise dangerous snake, scorpion, or lizard.

In a public place, such as a park, where dogs are welcome, you should once again enlist the help of a scout to check for any unscooped surprises. Though owners may be required to keep their dogs leashed, an overzealous hound might break free and come bounding your way, and muddy paws and pale silk gowns are not a good mix. Ask about the site's policies regarding dogs, and opt, if possible, for a location that is far away from popular dog-walking paths.

Passersby

Though uninvited humans aren't likely to fly up and sting you, walk all over the potato salad, screech loudly throughout your ceremony, or try to jump up and lick your face, the presence of onlookers can be intimidating or disquieting to some couples. Some outdoor wedding settings afford privacy, but others do not. If you are adamant about preserving the intimacy of your event, you will need to select a location that will not be open to the general public at the time of your union.

Even if you are perfectly comfortable in the spotlight, keep in mind that some of your attendants and guests may not be. If you decide to forego seclusion in order to marry in a cherished public place, try to create your own sense of focus and intimacy by having guests stand in a tight circle around you. Scheduling your wedding at an off-peak time may also help to minimize the number of spectators. If you do attract a few gawkers, remind yourselves that these folks are merely curious and likely enthralled by the scene. If your loving energy draws a few inquisitive looks, consider these strangers to be among those who sense the magic between you and wish you abundant happiness in your new life together.

Guest Comfort

Yes, it is your special day. However, unless you plan to elope, you need to think about more than just the two of you as you plan your wedding. Successful weddings are those at which guests feel welcome, comfortable, involved, and truly blessed to share in the festivities.

ask the wedding planner ?

How many people should you invite to your wedding?

Your budget will likely be the primary determining factor in how many invitations you extend. However, even if you have unlimited funds, in an outdoor setting, it is important to consider how many guests can be accommodated comfortably. Honestly evaluate the site's facilities and limitations before arriving at a final number.

Regardless of who is paying for the event, most brides these days assume chief responsibility for planning. Grooms are frequently involved in many aspects of the decision-making process, as well. That means it is your party, and in addition to looking radiant, smiling for the cameras, and dancing the night away, etiquette dictates that you also shoulder the responsibility of being gracious and thoughtful hosts.

Forewarning

It is important to advise guests that all or part of your celebration will be held outdoors. This will allow them to dress appropriately, whether that means a hat to provide protection from the sun or a sweater in crisp weather. It also allows those with allergies, sun sensitivity, or other health conditions impacted by weather to plan accordingly. And those who suffer from seasickness will really appreciate the heads-up if your wedding will take them out on the water.

Don't assume that because you have listed the location as Such and Such Gardens that everyone will know that you plan to be outside. Specify that an outdoor reception will follow an outdoor ceremony, or whatever the case may be. Providing detailed instructions about where the event will move in the event of inclement weather will serve as additional reinforcement.

Appropriate Dress

What should guests wear to an outdoor wedding? It is up to you to dictate the formality of the event and to communicate what is expected to guests. However, if you have your heart set on a black-tie affair in July, you really should rethink your selection of an outdoor site.

The setting, the season, and the amount of time you will spend without cover are all factors that should be taken into consideration. If you will head inside a grand mansion after a fifteen-minute service on the lawn, you can ask guests to dress to the nines. If your hour-long outdoor ceremony will be followed by a lakeside chicken barbecue that guests will eat from paper plates held in their laps, that is a different story.

piece of cake

Even if other party-goers are festively and informally dressed, that doesn't mean you can't set yourselves apart by choosing traditional, formal wedding attire. After the ceremony and photos are done, though, you may want to make a quick change and join the comfortable crowd.

Though many weddings are still lavish and elaborate, there is a trend toward less formality, and nowhere is this more apropos than at soirees held out of doors. Casual guests are happy guests. Remember that you most likely want to wed outdoors in order to break the bonds of tradition a bit and add color and beauty to the day. When men don Hawaiian shirts instead of stiff suits and women wear flouncy, colorful sundresses rather than somber black cocktail dresses, the mood can be much more lively and festive.

Comforting Gestures

Every good host knows that small gestures can make a big difference. Anticipating guests' needs can go a long way toward keeping everyone smiling. Make a list of small, yet thoughtful touches that might alleviate some potential discomforts of the outdoors. Here are a few ideas to get you started:

- Appoint a greeter who will welcome guests and point out the location of restrooms, shady areas, and indoor facilities available to those who need to escape the heat or cold.
- Stock a first-aid kit with supplies to care for anyone who is bit, stung, bruised, scraped, burned, or otherwise injured.
- On a sweltering day, provide large pitchers of ice water with slices of lemon, lime, or cucumber from the moment that guests arrive.
- If children will be in attendance, hire a teenager to organize games to keep them amused during the cocktail hour or dancing.
- Outfit port-a-potties with mirrors, towels, antibacterial liquid soap, and hand cream.
- Set up a sunglass stand with a few loaner pairs for those who left their shades at home or in the car.
- If the weather may be cold, windy, or damp, set up a comfort station with extra blankets, scarves, earmuffs, hats, and gloves for those who are a bit underdressed.
- Purchase a supply of functional yet attractive hand fans that guests can use to provide their own cooling relief on a warm day.

Dirt, Sweat, and Tears

You probably don't have to be reminded that it can be hot, sticky, and dirty in the great outdoors. Then again, your romanticized images of how the day will unfold may not have included all of the nitty-gritty realities. The truth is, it is hard for a groom to look his most dashing in a sweat-stained tuxedo, and a bride who doesn't shed a tear during the ceremony may sob openly when she looks down and discovers that the hem of her white gown is heavily soiled and her once-pristine shoes are encrusted in mud. And while tears may cause mascara to run, that may be the least of a bride's cosmetic worries on a steamy, makeup-melting day. Mud, dust, heat, humidity—all can make for unpleasant conditions for guests, as well.

piece of cake

There is no way to turn the outdoors into a temperature-regulated and antiseptic environment. The key is to accept this and to keep outdoor hazards in mind as you make decisions about what you will wear and how you will prepare for the day. For example, you'll be far less heartbroken to sully a dress that cost hundreds rather than thousands of dollars. You'll feel confident if you've packed a complete makeup repair kit. And your groom will look fresher, feel more comfortable, and remember why he adores you if you ensure there is an air-conditioned vehicle or building where he can await your arrival. You might even go one step further and assure him it's perfectly okay to skip the jacket and wear just a shirt or shirt and vest if the heat is truly unbearable.

Sound Effects

Walk into any music store, and you can purchase recordings of nature. That's because many people find the sounds of wind, waves, morning songbirds, babbling mountain streams, waterfalls, whales, or the woods at night to be soothing. For the most part, you are likely to be pleased by the background sound texture that the environment provides for your outdoor function.

Sound effects become a potential problem when they are too loud, harsh, or out of character with the surroundings. Vigorous, crashing surf can drown out the most experienced speaker. Shrieking birds or yapping dogs can grate on anyone's nerves. And if your peaceful garden wedding is constantly interrupted by the din of planes cruising overhead or trucks rumbling by, that will certainly detract from the overall atmosphere and mood.

Make a listening visit to the site where you hope to marry, and camp out for at least an hour at the time of day you intend to hold your ceremony to see what sounds you encounter. If the surf or the chatter of birds truly will be uproarious, you may need to rent a public address system. If the relaxing rhythms of nature are punctuated by the roar of airplanes or the clatter of trains, it may be a good idea to check timetables to see if you can schedule your ceremony at a time when interruptions are least likely. If noise is a problem in one area of the property, you may want to look into other spots that may be farther away from roadways, the oceanfront, or places where people and animals gather in order to reduce the potential for noise interference.

Contingency Planning

Just about every wedding Web site and bridal magazine includes a planning checklist of tasks to complete a year, six months, one month, and so forth before your big day. Those who intend to marry outdoors must add a few items to the standard to-do list in order to cover contingencies—those things that hopefully won't happen, but which you should prepare for just in case. For instance, the chance of bad weather certainly necessitates a backup plan.

Foul-Weather Gear

Anyone who enjoys spending time outdoors knows that the proper gear can make or break anything from a picnic in the park to a mountain hike. Having the right gear at your disposal can also affect how well you cope with inclement weather on your wedding day. Though you may not wind up needing any of the protective equipment that you line up, you will rest easier knowing that you are prepared for anything.

Gear Must-Haves

Umbrellas should be at the top of your must-have list. Small, flimsy umbrellas won't do. You will need to purchase, borrow, or rent large golf umbrellas. A 60-inch diameter is a good size.

Plan for ushers to each have an umbrella so that they can escort and shelter guests as they arrive. You will want to have oversized umbrellas for the bride, the groom, and other wedding party and family members, as well. Even if skies look bright, it is a good idea to keep your stash of umbrellas close at hand in case of a sudden sun shower. Umbrellas can also be used to provide shade on a clear day.

rain or shine

On a rainy day, umbrellas will show up in many of your wedding photographs. Keep this in mind as you make arrangements to acquire umbrellas for the day. You may want to coordinate colors, avoid those emblazoned with advertising logos, and be sure that the best-looking umbrella is reserved for the bride.

An umbrella alone may not be enough to protect your fancy attire from the elements, so it is important to prepare your personal foul-weather gear in advance. For the groom, a raincoat or poncho should suffice. Galoshes may be a good idea on muddy, wet days, or you can wear sneakers and tote your dress shoes to the ceremony site.

Brides should be prepared with a jacket or shawl that provides not only a barrier against the rain but a layer of warmth. If the gown you have selected is sleek and form fitting, a raincoat or poncho may work to keep the fabric dry and free of raindrop spots. Billowy skirts and flowing trains present greater challenges. You may need to enlist helpers to shield you with several umbrellas as you dash through a downpour. Wear backup shoes until storms subside or you're safely inside.

piece of cake

For any foul-weather gear you plan to rent, investigate not only pricing but the number of rental units available and the lead time required to reserve them for your use. If possible, you may want to wait until you've seen a reliable weather forecast before committing to big-ticket items, such as heaters or air conditioners for your tent.

It is worthwhile, as well, to invest in several large, waterproof tarps. Whether you string them from trees to create an emergency canopy shelter, use them to protect everything from food to gifts and cards, or lay them down to keep an area dry in the hopes that you'll still be able to dance outside when the clouds recede, there are many handy ways to put them to good use. Tarps made of heavy-duty canvas are the sturdiest and best quality. If you don't need them on your wedding day, you can always use them when you paint a new home someday.

Extras That May Save the Day

Whether the weather is cold, wet, or exceedingly warm, there are various ways to combat the elements and to make tents, pavilions, or other semi-enclosed shelters more comfortable. Be sure to check with your host site about restrictions on using certain equipment and on the availability and voltage rating of electrical power for those appliances that require it. Here is a list of items to consider, from the simple and practical to the more extravagant. While your budget and logistics will likely make it impractical to have all of these items on hand, those that you can manage to have available will potentially enhance everyone's comfort and help to alleviate problems associated with less-than-ideal weather conditions.

- Hairdryer
- Plastic aisle runner
- Mosquito netting
- Lighting
- Oscillating stand fans
- Electric, propane, or kerosene space heaters
- Portable air conditioning units
- Outdoor carpeting
- Kindling and firewood for a bonfire
- A four-wheel-drive vehicle

The Tent Question

When you schedule your wedding for an outdoor location, it is imperative to determine in advance exactly where you will relocate the event in case of bad weather. A tent has many advantages. A tent is not always a perfect solution, however, so it is important to be aware of the disadvantages, as well.

Advantages of Having a Tent

Should the weather necessitate a move indoors, a tent at the same location where you had planned to marry under blue skies can certainly streamline the transition from outdoors to in. Guests won't have to watch the forecast and call for updates, and you won't have to worry that everyone has received word of a change of plans. Best of all, you won't have to make a final decision whether to herd everyone in until the very last minute if the weather looks iffy.

Some sites that specialize in outdoor weddings may be able to provide a tent for your use. If not, tent rental companies are fairly abundant. You will want to place the responsibility for tent setup in the hands of professionals.

An improperly installed tent may not only fail to protect your event from the elements, it can be downright dangerous.

ask the wedding planner ?

What size tent do we need?

Your rental company will help you to determine the best tent size based on the number of guests; quantity, shape, and size of tables; the area required for a band or DJ and dance floor; and the style of meal you will serve—sit-down or buffet. As a starting point, either a 30' x 60' or 40' x 40' tent can hold about 120 people.

Remember the fun of pitching a tent in the backyard as a kid? Inside a tent, you can create your own secret wedding world. Lighting effects can create a warm, twinkling glow, and decorations can either mimic the outdoor setting from which you have retreated or conjure up a feel that is entirely unique.

If you opt for a tent as your backup plan, it needn't go to waste if the day shines and you are able to hold your celebration outdoors. Your caterer will likely welcome a space out of the sun in which to make preparations and perhaps even serve hors d'oeuvres or a buffet meal. Set up a cozy seating area inside the tent regardless of the weather for those who need a bit of shade or quiet and a break from the action. If the tent is large, you may even want to move portable toilets to one corner, where the beating sun won't turn them into smelly saunas.

The Disadvantages of Tents

Before you conclude that a tent is definitely the way to go, it is important to consider the drawbacks to this seemingly convenient backup site solution. For starters, there may simply be no good place to locate a tent. Tents require a level site of sufficient size to accommodate not just the structure but any exterior stakes and supports. The site should have good drainage and be clear of overhead and underground utilities, as well as trees and other plantings. Access to electricity is definitely important, as well.

You won't want to be scrambling for a tent at the last minute, so you will need to reserve one well in advance. A tent must also be set up well before your event—usually at least a day ahead. That means it will be part of your wedding backdrop, even if the weather cooperates. A large tent may detract substantially from the view and the natural beauty of the site, compromising the very aspects that led you to choose this location in the first place. Ask to see photos of tented events on the property if they are available so that you will have a sense of how the scene will appear.

Another disadvantage of relying on a tent is that although one can certainly keep you dry, it won't necessarily keep you warm. Wet days often tend to be cool and damp, and though your love may burn warmly, it can't put out enough BTUs to heat 1,600 square feet. During shoulder seasons, you will need to consider renting space heaters to make the tent a comfortable environment. At the height of summer, you probably won't need heaters—in fact, you may need to consider renting portable air conditioning units.

newlywed know-how

The American Rental Association Web site, *www.ararental.org*, is a good source for locating accredited rental companies across the United States and Canada and in other countries. Ask your site's manager and your caterer for recommendations, as well, and shop around to find the best deal and a vendor who can accommodate your needs.

A tent, space heaters or air conditioners—the costs are already mounting, and you only have an empty, climate-controlled tent thus far. For some, a tent may seem the perfect blank slate within which to create the layout and ambiance of your dreams. Even if you can envision great possibilities, though, keep in mind that outfitting the tent can quickly become a costly endeavor. In addition to tent rental, installation, and tear-down charges, plus special fees for such things as disinfecting mildewed tents, you may pay extra for such enhancements as windowed tent flaps, outdoor carpeting or other flooring material, and lighting. You will also need to rent tables, chairs, linens, china, flatware, stemware, and a dance floor, and perhaps invest in additional floral and decorative embellishments.

Alternate Sites

You may not be allowed to erect a tent at your chosen wedding site, or you may rule out a tent due to other logistical, aesthetic, or economic factors. Where, then, can you hold your event inside if the weather is frightful outside? Some facilities that host outdoor weddings have the distinct advantage of being large properties that also have a structure that might fill the bill if you need a backup. If there is no hall, lodge, barn, educational building, or other interior space available, though, you will need to widen your search for an alternate site.

Two Is Better Than One

You know that two can be better than one—you're getting married, after all! A secondary site totally apart from your preferred outdoor location may be a better option than trying to force things to work under less than optimum conditions. When thunder rolls and jet-black skies emit torrents of rain, wouldn't it be better to gather everyone in the cozy, well-lit basement of an Italian restaurant than to watch them sloshing across the lawn and shivering miserably under an eerily dim pavilion or tent?

The question likely foremost in your mind is whether two will cost more than one. It certainly can, but it doesn't necessarily have to. Start by accepting the fact that a backup plan must be part of your overall outdoor wedding budget.

Just as many traditional weddings use two sites—one for the ceremony and one for the reception—your event may require two sites, as well, and you will need to visit and book both as part of your planning process. Remember, too, that while a tent may enable you to stick to a single site, the total costs of a tent may exceed those associated with renting a hall, which may be better equipped with such necessities as tables, chairs, a dance floor, and heat or air conditioning.

As you explore various outdoor/indoor combinations, be candid with providers about your plans. If you will not be using the outdoor site at all on a rainy day, ask if fees might be waived or reduced. Likewise, see if charges might be scaled back if you opt not to move indoors, eliminating the need for setup, cleanup, electricity, and other services. If fees for use of one site are substantial, you may need to balance your budget by seeking economy on the other side of the equation. Be sure that your caterer and other vendors will be able to follow you to either site.

Where Do We Go from Here?

Try to select a backup facility that is within ten or fifteen miles of your outdoor site, if possible. Inevitably, some vendor or guest will get his signals crossed and wind up at the wrong location. If you strive for minimal distance between the two locations, you will reduce the potential for hassles and frustrations resulting from such a mishap.

piece of cake

At minimum, post a sign directing guests to the other location at whichever site you will not be using on your wedding day. Better still, station a volunteer there to assist anyone who has gone astray. Print copies of directions from each site to the other so that they can be provided to guests who need to find their way.

As you search for an alternate site, remind yourselves that the probability is high that you won't need it at all. Focus on finding an affordable place that is functional, not extravagant. You may even be able to use your home or that of a close family member if it can accommodate your expected number of guests. Also check into rental space at local fairgrounds, fire stations, community centers, hotels, universities, veterans' organizations, and membership clubs such as the Elks or Lions.

Scheduling a Rain Date

If you simply can't bear the thought of relocating your wedding to a place that lacks the aura of the outdoors, you might want to consider moving it to another date, instead. A rain-date strategy, however, is fraught with complexities and costs. It may also require you to make tough choices between the place of your dreams and the people who mean the most to you.

Setting up a rain date is actually a simple matter of double-booking everything from the location to the photographer, musicians, florist, caterer, and limo driver. While your costs for tangible goods, such as food and flowers, will likely remain unchanged, few vendors and sites will allow you to tie up two days without some additional compensation. Finding vendors and host facilities with availability on two separate dates may also be a challenge, particularly during peak wedding seasons.

rain or shine

If you decide to postpone your event until the rain date, you will need a plan for communicating this to all parties. It may be sunny where some guests are, so don't assume they will know not to make the trip. It is also critical to think through what you will do if it rains on your rain date.

You will want to announce the rain date in your save-the-date cards and invitations. While a rain date may allow you to fulfill your fantasies of the perfect outdoor wedding day, it can also be a major nuisance for any guest traveling from beyond driving distance. Keep this in mind, particularly as you decide whether your rain date will be the very next day or a week or more after the original date. If it is the following day, faraway visitors will only need to extend their travels by a day. If it is further into the future, some folks whom you would have liked to have present may simply be unable to attend.

Photography Flexibility

For many couples, a prime motivator for choosing an outdoor wedding setting is the hope of capturing stunning images. While you might not be terribly upset that the feasting and dancing had to be moved indoors, you may feel tremendous disappointment if you miss out on those coveted photographs of the two of you, lost in each other's loving gaze, against a spectacular natural backdrop. When foul weather threatens to interfere with your photos, it is time to be flexible.

Another Place

Your wedding will last just a few short hours, and whether it occurs indoors or out, it will be filled with intense moments of love, joy, and laughter. The best wedding photography captures these emotions. Wedding photographers are portrait photographers, not landscape photographers, and while cobalt skies and purple mountains might complement their work, their primary job is to catch images of radiant smiles, human interaction, and the new family that you have forged. The good news is that a talented photographer can click stunning photos wherever your event takes place.

newlywed know-how

Wedding photojournalism is a hot trend these days, and the best wedding photographers are indeed skilled at unobtrusively documenting events as they occur. However, you should also seek a photographer who has a knack for staging beautiful, formal portraits that don't appear posed, even if they were.

If your event will be moved to an indoor location in the event of bad weather, your photographer must be aware of this possible change of plans. Indoor and outdoor photography can require different equipment and films for optimum results. The photographer you select should visit both sites, if possible, in order to familiarize himself with lighting conditions, layout, and potential shooting locations. Be willing to listen to the photographer's suggestions, and, most of all, enjoy the day. Your wedding photographs will focus much more on how you were feeling than where you were.

Another Time

You will definitely want pictures of your ceremony and reception as they occurred. If you are unable to hold the event outdoors during the allotted time slot, however, you can still come away from this momentous day with something close to the fabulous outdoor photos you had envisioned. The key is to think outside the box and to hire a photographer who is willing to be flexible, as well.

ask the wedding planner?

Is it okay for the groom to see the bride before the ceremony?

Though some still consider this to be bad luck, the roots of this superstition date back to times of old when brides and grooms did not even meet before their arranged marriages. Thankfully, times have changed, so if it makes sense to take pictures before the ceremony, don't worry about this particular taboo.

Wedding photographers charge both for their time and for the prints they will sell to you after the wedding. Since you are paying for their time, and since few photographers book more than one wedding on any given day, you should be able to negotiate some flexibility into your contract, especially since it is in the photographer's best interest to deliver images that you will be inclined to buy. Ask if you can schedule the photographer for the duration of the event, plus one extra hour to be scheduled at the last minute once the forecast for the day is apparent. If your wedding is at 3 P.M. and afternoon showers are forecast, key cast members, or even just the two of you, can dress early and meet the photographer for a 10 A.M. outdoor shoot. If you wake up to dark skies, but the clouds should clear by nightfall, try to move the outdoor photo session to the early evening hours, even if most guests have headed for home.

Though there may be additional costs, if outdoor photos are important to you, there is also nothing to prevent you from hiring the same or a different photographer for another day. Will you have a rehearsal at the location the evening before? Though you probably won't be sporting your wedding day attire, you will be wearing a look of eager anticipation. Some photographers even offer a morning-after package designed to capture couples in the dreamy, blissful state of awakening after an incredible day to face the world for the first time as husband and wife. The morning after may just dawn a bit brighter. Though you may not relish leaping out of bed, you will cherish not only the new day but the images that result if you've hired a photographer to revisit that special outdoor setting with you.

Communicating with Guests

The to-do list for every wedding includes making a guest list, gathering addresses, and mailing invitations about eight weeks before the event. Some couples may also opt to send a save-the-date card further in advance. After the last envelope is stuffed and the last stamp is placed, communicating with guests can be crossed off most couples' lists. Not so for those who have extended an invitation to an outdoor affair.

Your Contact Database

Because outdoor weddings can involve a last-minute change of plans, it is important to be able to communicate with guests directly and efficiently. You certainly won't be able to let everyone know of a change of date or venue via mail, so your contact database must be much more extensive. In addition to a mailing address, try to assemble the following contact information for each guest:

- Home telephone number
- Work telephone number
- Cell phone number
- E-mail address

For guests traveling from out of town, it is important to gather some additional information. Include arrival dates and times and accommodation arrangements with the other contact data. A computerized database or spreadsheet program is the best tool for managing your wedding contact list. This allows you to make and save changes and additions rapidly, to print hard copies when needed, and to keep a backup copy on a disc or CD.

Keeping Everyone Informed

Well in advance of your event, you should decide exactly how to spread the news if weather or other unforeseen circumstances necessitate activation of a backup plan. In fact, it is a good idea to have this strategy in place before invitations are mailed. Much confusion can be eliminated if you provide clear instructions with your invitations.

As you develop your communications plan, there are a few key things to keep in mind. First, do not rely on one communications method. Not every guest will have an e-mail address, and even those who do may not check their e-mail regularly. Second, remember that severe storms can disrupt communications. If power is lost, you will be unable to use a computer and some telephones. Finally, even if you have developed a plan and enclosed detailed instructions with your invitations, don't count on guests to be able to locate this critical information when they need it most—on your wedding day.

No plan is foolproof, but some communications strategies will serve you better than others. For example, avoid the use of a phone tree that requires each guest to call the next guest on the list. These systems have a way of breaking down, and it will be impossible for you to determine at what point the chain collapsed. A much better idea is to have each member of your wedding party assume responsibility for a list of a dozen or so guests and to keep detailed notes of who they reach and who they do not.

rain or shine

Though e-mail probably won't work as a sole means of notification, you may want to have an e-mail distribution list ready to go so that you can speedily send a message out to many guests simultaneously. Ask guests to hit "Reply" and to type, "Got it." That will allow you to check them off your list and reduce the number of phone calls to be made.

You can count on receiving many, many phone calls if the weather looks questionable. Keep a guest list printout near the phone so that anyone who answers can check off those who have received updates. If you have not yet made a decision, be careful not to tell guests you are leaning one way or the other, as they may misunderstand and fail to check back. Keep in mind that in addition to calling you, guests may try to call your intended, your parents, your maid of honor, or any number of other people in your inner circle. Be sure that all key players are aware of how you intend to handle communications and kept abreast of any decisions.

If you are technology savvy and many of your guests are, too, you may want to post updates and final details to a wedding Web site or designate a special phone number that guests can call to hear a recorded message. With call identification such as Caller ID, you can even track who has called to listen to the recording. Send an e-mail a day or two before the event to remind folks of the Web address or the phone number they can monitor for updates, just in case they have lost the information you sent with invitations. In the midst of the chaos of preparing for the big day, you will be thankful for any system that can cut down on the number of calls you must answer.

For the sake of your guests, decide on a plan at least a few hours before the ceremony is scheduled to begin. Though you may want to cling to the hope that clouds will part, unless your backup location is on-site or just minutes away, you can wind up confusing and inconveniencing many people by being indecisive. Even with a timely decision and a detailed plan for communication, the chances are good that someone won't get the correct message. Post a sign, or station a volunteer at your outdoor site to instruct anyone who arrives there on how to find your alternate location.

Prepare for the Worst

"Prepare for the worst; hope for the best" may be an old cliché, but it is a fitting motto for those planning to marry outside. An optimistic attitude will help to keep you focused and upbeat as you handle the necessary, though not necessarily pleasant, tasks of considering and preparing for what can go wrong. What, really, is the worst thing that can happen? In the big scheme of things, postponing your outdoor event or moving it to an alternate location does not rate as a tragedy.

One way that people prepare for the worst is to purchase insurance. Though it is not yet prevalent, wedding insurance is definitely available. Because outdoor weddings are more prone to cancellation and the accompanying financial impacts, it may be something for you to consider. As a rule, the more coverage you require, the higher the premium. Though insurance is always a gamble, wedding insurance policies are quite affordable considering the costs of a typical wedding, and insurance may deserve a line in your budget if it buys you peace of mind.

newlywed know-how

Even if you do not purchase one of its policies, the Markel Insurance Company's Web site, *www.wedsafe.com*, offers a wealth of information about wedding insurance to help you to make an informed decision about whether to explore this option.

Be sure to examine the insurance policy carefully and to understand exactly what is and is not covered and what deductibles may apply. Wedding insurance can cover costs incurred when weather or other uncontrollable occurrences, such as military deployment, force you to relocate or postpone your wedding. It may also cover such things as damage to your wedding gown, loss of your wedding rings, theft of gifts, default by vendors who go out of business, and other potential financial losses. It does not, however, provide reimbursement when a wedding is called off due to a change of heart.

Selecting the Setting

Once you decide to wed outdoors, the next important decision is to figure out where. Though the possibilities may seem limitless, outdoor wedding settings actually tend to fall into a few broad categories. Which is right for you? Each presents its own set of benefits and challenges. Consider these pros and cons as your dreams of an open-air celebration become realities. Once you agree on the type of setting you prefer, visit potential sites armed with questions that will help you determine whether you have found the perfect fit.

Beach Weddings

A wedding beside the waves incorporates the tradition of "something blue" in a big way. Endless ocean vistas somehow seem the ultimate backdrop against which to pledge your deep and undying devotion. Beach weddings are definitely one of the most popular choices among those who wed outdoors, and entire enterprises have sprung up to cater to the needs of today's beach bride, selling everything from seashell tiaras to jeweled adornments for bare feet.

Beauty and the Beach

Unsurpassed beauty is but one of the advantages of a sandy wedding setting. Everyone loves the beach, it seems. Hordes of vacationers flock to coastal resorts, lakeside cottages, and quiet island hideaways each year to be soothed and re-energized by the water. You won't have to twist guests' arms too hard to get them jazzed about the prospect of kicking up their heels in the sand with you.

newlywed know-how

The "something blue" from the traditional English wedding rhyme has its origins in ancient times, when the color blue symbolized modesty, fidelity, purity, and love. Until 1828, when John Quincy Adams's son married a bride in white, blue was actually a common color for a wedding dress.

If you live near the shore or a picturesque lake, then you are blessed. Beach weddings frequently, though, are destination weddings. Exquisite seaside resorts the world over stand ready to cater to your every wedding day whim. If you are considering a honeymoon jaunt to a tropical paradise anyway, marrying there adds little to your travel expenses and enables you to jumpstart your fun. In fact, the term "weddingmoon" is now in common use to describe these types of combination getaways.

Beach weddings also have the advantage of being casual by nature. Guests may find this extremely appealing, and even the two of you may opt for the carefree and less costly strategy of trading formalwear for khakis and a billowy white sundress. A single vibrant flower tucked behind your ear may be more dramatic than any headpiece and veil, and light refreshments and frozen, fruity drinks may be all you need as you dance the night away to the sounds of a steel drum band.

Beach weddings have actually become so prevalent that you will find it easy to locate all of the themed extras you might desire. From sea-blue invitations featuring beach umbrella or lighthouse designs to favors such as sand-dollar sugar cookies and chocolate seashells, the array of options is stunning. It may seem more attractive, at least at first, to be blazing your own wedding trail. But as any bride will tell you who has searched in vain through invitation samples for the perfect complement to an obscure theme, the ability to effortlessly coordinate elements of your wedding is the way to go. This is particularly true if your timeline from engagement to wedding day is short.

Special Considerations for Beach Weddings

Hurricane rains and gale-force winds aren't the only natural calamities that could mar an oceanside affair. Brides and grooms must also consider uncontrollable forces as crashing surf and seagulls behaving badly. And that enraptured glint in your eyes and smile on your lips could be instantly erased when, while prancing barefoot through the sand to join hands with your beloved, you step squarely on the gelatinous mass of a half-dead jellyfish.

If possible, a private beach at a resort, inn, or waterfront restaurant is the way to go. If you simply must marry at a public beach, keep in mind that your uninvited guests may include much more than seagulls. Avoid throngs of unwanted onlookers by choosing an off-peak time; a sunrise wedding might be lovely and intimate, for example. Be sure, as well, to have scouts at the site long before you arrive to be sure the area where the service will be held is clear and free of unwanted debris. Assign these same helpers the job of cleanup when your ceremony is through.

Timing is also a major consideration for those planning to wed near the water, particularly for coastal locations. Be sure to check the tide tables for the date of your wedding. Discuss lighting conditions with your photographer, as the intense sun may reflect off the sand and water and wash out images. During peak heat months, be sure not to schedule your event for the hottest part of the day. And, of course, you should have several tubes of sunscreen available for all in attendance if the sun will be making an appearance.

piece of cake

Beach weddings necessitate a backup plan. Be sure there is a covered pavilion, tent, or building to provide shelter in the event of foul weather. Consider the needs of elderly relatives, who may not be surefooted on sandy slopes and who may need an umbrella or other source of shade.

Garden Weddings

Flowers and romance have a longstanding relationship, and it is difficult to imagine a wedding without some form of floral embellishment. It is only natural, then, that gardens are popular with couples who dream of a sweet and romantic outdoor environment in which to plant the seeds of their union. While a fragrant floral garden may seem the likely choice, other cultivated landscapes can also provide dramatic backdrops. You might consider an herb garden, arboretum, sculpture garden, vineyard, water garden, wildflower meadow, or even a zoological garden. Though you won't technically be outdoors, you can even pull off a winter garden wedding inside the warm confines of a greenhouse or conservatory.

Love in Full Bloom

If you have already talked to a florist about bouquets, nosegays, boutonnières, and centerpieces, you know that the cost of wedding flowers can add up quickly. If you love flowers and want to be surrounded by them on your wedding day, a garden wedding is an ideal way to add thousands of blooms in a rainbow of hues without breaking your budget. Your time, energy, and funds can be focused on other elements of your special day when you place the task of decorating in the hands of nature and a garden's caretakers.

piece of cake

Before you select wedding colors, it is important to know what flowers are likely to be in bloom at the time of your event. If possible, visit the garden a year in advance and take photographs. If that isn't possible, ask to see photos taken at about the same time of year, and talk to gardeners and groundskeepers to learn as much as possible about the garden's coloration.

Gardens frequently feature a layout that naturally lends itself to wedding ceremonies and receptions. A garden path might serve as a natural aisle for your processional. A lushly overgrown, arched arbor can set the stage for the marriage service. Rustic stone walls and garden gates will add visual variety to wedding photographs. Ornate benches can be welcome resting places for those who tire of circulating during the cocktail hour. And tables and chairs can be strategically arranged so that all guests dine with a garden view.

Perhaps the greatest advantage of a glorious garden is that it can be dressed up or dressed down to suit your tastes. The same plants and posies can serve as accents for an elegant high tea or a casual backyard jamboree. Whatever sense of style you bring to your event, be sure to carve out time for the two of you to savor a private garden stroll before the sun sets and guests bid adieu.

Special Considerations for Garden Weddings

Your favorite aunt declines your invitation due to her bee-sting allergy. You snag your delicate lace train on a thorny rose bush. The pollen activates Grandpa's hay fever, and his violent sneezes punctuate your entire wedding video.

Gardens can be good wedding settings, but they also present a unique set of possible evils. While the blossoms and foliage may welcome a burst of rain, you and your entourage won't find spring showers or summer storms nearly as refreshing. Even if clouds clear and the sun shines at the appointed hour, days of rain can leave you to contend with soggy grounds and puddled garden paths. Your alternate site, even if it is a nearby tent, may need to be outfitted with potted trees, plants, and flowers in order to mimic the atmosphere you had hoped to create.

A public garden may have the advantage of offering helpful amenities such as electrical outlets and restroom facilities. If the site will be open during your event, however, the intimacy of your celebration may be in jeopardy. Weigh the potential for invasion of privacy against the hefty costs that can be associated with renting portable toilets, along with chairs, tables, tents, sound and lighting equipment, a dance floor, and more. Keep in mind, as well, that the site you select may have specific policies that limit the size and placement of tents and other equipment in order to protect the plant life. Before you book your date, spend time walking the property with a member of its management team to familiarize yourselves with layout and any setup issues and to ensure you feel comfortable with any limitations.

rain or shine

Spring's arrival doesn't always adhere to a strict schedule. If your wedding fantasies include tiptoeing through the tulips or waltzing amid the daffodils, plan to have potted flowers available as a backup. Employ the same strategy if you are counting on other seasonal flowers.

Historic Properties

From Scottish castles to Southern plantations, historic properties are lowering the drawbridge or opening their ornamental iron gates to welcome wedding celebrations. Historic places can provide a movie-set backdrop for your event. They also allow you to establish a tone for the day, from the moment guests arrive until you head off to begin your happily-ever-after.

A Place in Time

If you are enchanted by the idea of playing prince and princess for the day, but there are no castles or even Disney theme parks nearby, you may need to consider a destination wedding. However, a wedding at a historic site close to home can offer many of the enticements of a destination wedding—without the expense and logistical concerns of a long-distance event. When you opt to travel to a different time rather than a different place, you can feel a world apart on your special day without also feeling jetlagged.

newlywed know-how

Historic properties provide the stage, and from there, you are free to be as creative as you dare with other thematic embellishments. Send parchment invitations with Gothic calligraphy for your Medieval-themed nuptials. Alight from a horse-drawn stagecoach or the rumble seat of an antique Ford. Wear period garb, and invite your guests to tailor their apparel to the event, as well. Opt for black-and-white photography. Your chosen location is likely to inspire dozens of fun and ingenious ideas.

Another great advantage of choosing a historic property is that most feature both beautiful grounds and a structure, whether a barn or an elegant mansion, that can provide cover should you face inclement weather or prefer an indoor setting for your reception. Because many operate as tourist attractions or as conference or retreat centers, they also usually offer adequate restroom facilities and handicapped access. They may also be well marked with highway signs, facilitating your guests' timely arrival.

Special Considerations for Weddings at Historic Properties

Historic properties tend to fall into three categories: those operated by governmental organizations such as the National Park Service, those operated by nonprofit historical societies and organizations, and those that remain in private hands. As a general rule, privately owned sites that book weddings are most likely to be in the business of hosting functions and may offer the greatest flexibility. These facilities usually employ a dedicated wedding coordinator who can help you plan the event of your dreams. While public historic sites may have separate areas or times for weddings in order to minimize the potential for disruptions, a privately owned property promises superior privacy and intimacy.

Be particularly aware that many historic sites have relationships with only one or a handful of caterers that are approved to work on site. If you have a specific caterer in mind, or a special menu (such as one that features many ethnic specialties), this limitation can prove to be a stumbling block. You may also discover that restrictions exist on erecting tents, serving alcohol, trucking in equipment, blaring music, and partying past a certain hour. Be sure to read contracts carefully and to ask about what is and is not allowed.

piece of cake

Choosing a period costume for bridal attire can certainly create glamour and drama, but it may also present unique challenges. Be sure to try on that heavy hoop skirt on a steamy afternoon before you commit to playing the part of a Southern belle on your wedding day, and don't plan to light candles in a Renaissance-style gown with long, flowing sleeves.

You don't have to be a history buff to embrace the idea of a wedding at a place imbued with a sense of yesteryear. However, you should feel an appreciation for the site and a level of comfort with the notion of molding your event to harmonize with this environment. Think through the various aspects of your event—attire, ceremony, food, music—to be sure there are no jarring thematic conflicts.

Public Places

You met while walking your dogs in the park, inline skating along a rail trail, waiting in line for concert tickets, or on your daily subway commute. Now you can't think of a more perfect place to wed than the very spot where your romance began. Can you trade "I do's" in a public place? Should you?

Public Displays of Affection

There is no single formula for finding the right life partner, but for many couples, it certainly seems as though unseen forces played a hand. Whether you call it fate, serendipity, or dumb luck, the place where you first connected on a chemical level may very well seem the most magical place on Earth. It may seem apropos to revisit that special spot as you embark upon your next chapter, even if the place happens to be a bustling public venue.

newlywed know-how

An often-overlooked plus to hosting an outdoor wedding in a public park is that the fees charged for usage are often incredibly low. Check your local city or town's government Web site to learn about available facilities in your area and permit fees charged for weddings.

While others may not consider a playground, bus stop, hotel lobby, or university library a particularly romantic place, the place where your paths first intersected it undeniable magic. Even if it is not the place where you met, another public location may hold special meaning for the two of you. Selecting a place that isn't ordinarily a wedding setting allows you to design an event that is truly one of a kind and deeply personal. Your guests' surprise at your choice will quickly turn to appreciation for the uniqueness of your celebration when they learn why you cherish this spot.

Special Considerations for Weddings in Public Places

Of course, the main drawback of a wedding in a public place is the pesky public. In most cases, you won't be able to shoo away curious onlookers. Even if you feel perfectly comfortable displaying your love to uninvited guests, there is always that one individual in the crowd who is not content to merely observe. Ask yourself if a stranger waving and mouthing, "Hi, Mom," in the background as you exchange vows will utterly ruin your wedding video or enhance its documentary quality. If you answered the former, you may need to go back to the drawing board and pick a more private wedding setting.

You will also need to carefully consider the size of your guest list. Can the site safely and comfortably accommodate your loved ones? Will they be charged an admission fee? As a rule, fewer guests make for an easier wedding in a public setting. If necessary, you might even consider limiting those present at the ceremony to the officiant, two witnesses, and the two of you. You can always invite additional guests to a reception at a second, larger facility.

Before you make a final decision, be sure to learn as much as possible about the site, the permissions required for its use, and the restrictions that may be imposed. Do not assume that because a site is open free to the public, you can use it for your event without permission or payment of fees. Check with the property's owner or manager, whether it is a private individual or organization, a municipality, or the state or federal government, to determine fees and rules for usage of the property. A public park may have ample space, a covered pavilion for inclement weather, and picturesque grounds for photo-taking, but if alcoholic beverages are not allowed on the premises, you may not be able to host the event you'd envisioned. If your event will generate significant added traffic and crowds, you may be required to pay for beefed-up security or even police support—a cost you may not have considered during your initial budgeting.

Getting Permissions

At some outdoor venues, weddings are routine, and making your arrangements should be a snap. However, if you select a location that does not typically host large private gatherings, you may need to do some legwork up front to obtain the necessary permissions and permits. It's usually easy to find the path to such approvals. But if you are unsure about who owns a particular swath of beach, park, or other open expanse, some sleuth work may be required. Good starting points are the city or town hall, the tourism office, or the chamber of commerce in the municipality where the site is located.

Is This Allowed?

Once you have determined that you will indeed be able to use the site for your event, there may still be obstacles in your way. It is important to determine at the outset exactly what is and is not allowed and what compromises you are willing to make. For starters, ask about limitations on the number of guests, the time and duration of the event, the equipment that can be brought in, and the food and beverages, particularly alcohol, that can be served on site.

You may have heard that throwing rice is often taboo because it's bad for the birds, but it may come as a surprise that birdseed is also a no-no in many instances—it is difficult to sweep up and may attract undesirable wildlife. Other things that may be forbidden include balloons, butterflies, doves, pets, confetti, glitter, feathers, flower petals, streamers, Silly String, candles, luminaries, sparklers, fireworks, amplified music, smoking, bug spray, bonfires, signs, and lighting. If any of these items *must* be part of your affair, it is important to ask about it early in the process in order to avoid disappointment.

Get It in Writing

Whether you are assembling a handful of loved ones to witness your vows on a rocky promontory overlooking the surf or inviting 200 guests to a grand garden soiree, it is important that you obtain some form of written documentation that confirms your rights to use the site for the purpose of your wedding. The permit, contract, or letter of agreement should stipulate the dates and times during which you will have access to the property for setup, the celebration, and cleanup. It should also spell out any fees involved and any restrictions or regulations that apply to the use of the property. If additional facilities will be made available to you in the event of foul weather, this should be specified. Finally, be sure your agreement covers procedures and penalties that will apply should you need to cancel or reschedule the event.

Read all paperwork carefully before you sign an agreement and make a deposit. Do not allow yourselves to be rushed or pressured into signing for fear of losing out on a preferred date or time slot. Even when you are sure you have found the right location, it is always a good idea to give yourselves twenty-four hours or more in case additional questions or concerns creep up.

piece of cake

Once you have secured your wedding setting, it is a good idea to research marriage license laws. In most cases, you must obtain a license in the town where the ceremony will transpire. Determine what is required and how far in advance you can or must apply for your license, then mark your calendar so that you won't overlook this important step.

Once you have finalized a contract, treat yourselves to a special dinner or other small celebration. You have completed one of the most challenging pieces of the wedding planning process—reserving the date and the place. Be sure to make an extra copy or two of any important documents, and store them in a safe place for easy reference. You may need to reread the fine print as you make other planning decisions.

The Right Questions

Honing in on your ideal wedding setting will likely require numerous phone calls and site visits. As you evaluate the possibilities, it is important to ask questions and keep careful notes about each potential venue. Wedding notes, clippings, brochures, contracts, and other paperwork can pile up fast. While it is not necessary to purchase a fancy wedding planner, it is critical to devise an organizational system that will work for you, whether it is a three-ring binder, an accordion folder, or a tabbed notebook.

Questions to Ask

General Questions

Use this list to guide your initial inquiries. These questions apply to all types of outdoor wedding venues:

• Can this site be used for a wedding ceremony and/or reception?

• Is it available on our preferred date? If not, what other dates are available?

• What is the cost for use of the facility, and what schedule and form of payment are required?

• How many guests can be accommodated?

• Are functions restricted to specific areas of the site?

• Are there any restrictions on our selection of a caterer and other vendors?

• What facilities are available, such as restrooms, kitchen, or covered pavilion?

• Will the site be open to the public during our event?

• Are there restrictions regarding timing? Tenting? Alcohol? Other equipment and decorations?

• Can we see photographs of weddings that have been held at the site?

Location-Specific Questions

Depending on the type of location you are considering, other questions may be pertinent. Consider the following:

Beach Weddings

* Is the beach cleaned and groomed on a regular basis?

* Will guests be charged an admission or parking fee?

* Is shade available for guests who need a break from the heat?

Garden Weddings

* What is the garden's typical blooming season? When is it at its best?

* Can flowers from the garden be purchased for use in bouquets and arrangements?

* Are bees and bugs more prevalent at certain times?

Historic Property Weddings

* Will guests be charged an entrance fee?

* Are tours of the property available to guests?

* Are special site rental rates available to donors?

Public-Place Weddings

* Is a special permit required for use of the site?

* Are we required to hire and pay for security or police support?

* Are there specific times of day when we may enjoy fewer interruptions?

Questions to Ask Yourselves

Choosing an outdoor wedding spot can be both exhilarating and overwhelming. Before you make a final decision, take a moment to regroup and to ask yourselves a few soul-searching questions:

- Does this place feel right?
- Is it a reflection of who we are?
- Is it a place we will enjoy sharing with our circle of friends and family, and will it accommodate them comfortably?
- Will this site allow us to have the event we envision?
- Can we picture ourselves happily beginning our married life in this space?

Don't be bashful about visiting a site more than once before you sign on the dotted line. In fact, it may be wise to see the places that are in contention under a variety of conditions. Definitely pay a visit after nightfall to determine whether guests will have difficulty finding their vehicles when the party is over. You may also want to visit in less-than-perfect weather or after a stretch of rain to get a sense of the property under adverse conditions.

Weddings at Home

Home can be a great place to host your outdoor wedding. Tying the knot in this comfortable and familiar spot has the advantage of allowing you to manage every detail and nuance, while most likely saving a few dollars, too. However, at-home weddings also come with a unique set of stresses, and not all of these can be controlled. It is important to remember that your single most important job is to star in the show. Other details will fall into place.

Advantages of At-Home Weddings

The idea of marrying at home usually arises when a couple is looking for ways to cut costs. Home can be your own place, a family vacation place, or the residence of a relative or close friend. Unless that home is used regularly for large, lavish parties, you may find that an at-home wedding is not as inexpensive as you had hoped. Still, there are some distinct advantages of marrying on your own turf that can't be valued in dollars and cents.

Backyard Bash

Can you really achieve substantial savings by holding your wedding at home? Possibly, but not always. It is true that costs associated with the ceremony and reception location can be one of the biggest line items in a wedding budget. However, if the site fee is hefty, it usually pays for more than just a beautiful backdrop. It may include many items you will need to rent for a wedding at home, from tables and chairs to restroom facilities.

There are three key considerations that will determine whether a wedding at home can be economical: size, setup, and swankiness. As a rule, the more guests you intend to invite, and the more elegance you hope to achieve, the more it will cost to transform a home into a wedding venue. You will need to carefully evaluate the property's possibilities and work within its limitations if you hope to keep costs under control. The truth is, a wedding can cost whatever you would like to spend, so it is up to you to decide whether you would be pleased to celebrate at home with twenty of your nearest and dearest over coffee and cake or if you must invite hundreds of guests to enjoy a fancy meal and revel until the wee hours.

rain or shine

As with any outdoor event, weddings at home require a backup plan in case weather is an issue. Unless you have ample space for and are prepared to rent a tent, only invite as many guests as you can comfortably accommodate inside your home.

If you keep your celebration small and casual, you can indeed pull off an affordable affair. In addition to eliminating site expenses, you can also reduce your outlay for such things as limo transportation, trash removal, and perhaps even a DJ if you own a good, programmable stereo system. Be careful not to focus too intently on how much you are saving by staying home, though, or you may find yourselves splurging in other areas.

Things Money Can't Buy

There are other motivations for marrying at home that have nothing to do with money. As you seek out that special place, it is certainly possible that your search will lead you home. After all, the place where you live and dream is not only a reflection of you, it is a cozy and intimate sanctuary from the world.

piece of cake

Be careful not to take on too many home-improvement projects in the midst of planning your affair. You will want a freshly mown lawn and a clean interior, but a wedding should not be used as an excuse for completing a total landscape overhaul, a kitchen remodel, or any other major renovation.

Marrying at home comes with certain conveniences, not the least of which is availability. If you find that popular wedding sites are booked a year or more in advance, you may be drawn to the idea of a place that is available on any date you choose, even one that is just a few months away. If you fancy appearing your absolute freshest throughout your outdoor soiree, what better place to primp between photo sessions than your own well-equipped bathroom? If a grandparent or parent is unable to travel, bringing a wedding home can ensure that those you cherish most are able to share your joy.

An at-home wedding also allows you to control every detail. There is no other place where you can overlay your personal touch on such minutiae as the color of the toilet paper. If you are keen on the idea of saving money and injecting personality by taking a do-it-yourself approach to your day, home is a familiar environment in which to unleash your creativity and to do things your way.

Should You Do It All Yourself?

Though some couples do entrust the majority of their wedding planning to parents or an event coordinator, most feel compelled to play an integral role in designing their special day. For those who intend to wed on the home front, the urge to take on even more than the typical bride and groom can be strong. A do-it-yourself approach can help you to further minimize the costs of your affair. However, it is important to evaluate the price you may pay in lost sleep, added anxiety, and diminished opportunity to simply savor and enjoy this new beginning.

newlywed know-how

According to the Holmes & Rahe Life Events Scale, there are only six events that can occur in life that are more stressful than marriage: death of a spouse or child, divorce, marital separation, detention in jail, death of a close family member, and major personal injury or illness.

Starring and Directed by You

If you have ever filled in for an absent coworker, you know that juggling two jobs can be quite a demanding feat. As you think through the various chores that go into planning and producing a wedding, it is important to limit the jobs that you assign to yourselves. Remember that your first obligation is simply to be the bride and groom. If you are going to perform your primary duties to the best of your abilities, you will need to delegate some tasks to others.

Know Your Limitations

If you have never sewn a stitch, it probably wouldn't even cross your mind to make your own wedding gown. However, as you page through the glossy spreads in bridal magazines, you may find yourself musing that a hand-tied bouquet of tulips doesn't look terribly tricky to create or that the three-tiered, rose-petal–adorned wedding cake you fancy will be a cinch to bake and decorate. When these thoughts arise, it is critical to honestly assess not only your talents but your available time.

A smart way to approach any do-it-yourself impulse is to ask yourself a simple question. If my best friend asked me to do this for *her* wedding, would I have enough confidence in my abilities and free time in my schedule to answer yes, immediately? If you can indeed respond affirmatively, then tackling this challenge for your own wedding may not be such a stretch. It is crucial, however, to take a hard look at all of the other items on your to-do list before you add to your wedding workload.

If you are undaunted by the fact that you have never designed an invitation, catered a party, arranged a centerpiece, crafted a headpiece, or built a dance floor, then by all means proceed, but proceed cautiously. Be sure to start time-consuming projects well in advance of the date on which they must be completed. For tasks that must be handled at the final hour, such as baking a cake or assembling a bouquet, be sure you have made a prototype or done a trial run ahead of time, and keep careful notes about exactly how you achieved the finished results you were seeking. Be sure to ask a friend or family member whose candid opinion you trust to participate in a taste test or to evaluate your creative efforts.

Whether you have substantial experience or are simply gutsy, before you commit to any cooking, decorating, or crafting project, you should consider the worst-case scenario. How will you handle any last-minute catastrophes such as burnt hors d'oeuvres, lumpy frosting, or wobbly centerpieces? Do you have a backup plan? Will you be able to distance yourself emotionally if faced with disappointing results? Though few weddings are worry-free, be sure that you haven't placed so many burdens on your own shoulders that you won't be able to feel happy and light-hearted on your momentous day.

rain or shine

Sometimes, a do-it-yourself undertaking can involve much trial and error. Keep in mind that if your foremost objective is to save money, it can actually be far less expensive to hire a professional than to experiment extensively on your own.

Finding Good Help

You will likely decide that you need assistance with some aspects of planning, preparing, and pulling off your at-home celebration. Even if you could do a phenomenal job on your own, delegation can allow you to feel pampered and to focus on those pieces of the party that cry out loudest for your personal touch. Finding good help is important regardless of where your wedding will be held, but it is particularly critical for weddings at home.

Any vendor or other helper whom you entrust with a key component of your celebration must be someone whose work you respect and whose references you have researched. When you invite a caterer, decorator, photographer, wedding planner, or other professional into your home, however, you need to seek a bit more than commendable, reliable service. Because these individuals will be invading your personal space in a sense, it is important to be able to establish a rapport with them. If you do not feel completely comfortable, you may find it difficult to communicate your expectations and to share your living and work space.

At-home weddings, particularly when they are hosted at the home of a family member or friend, can generate many offers to help that you will need to either accept graciously or tactfully decline. While a teenage nephew who offers to take charge of parking cars is a wonderful asset, you may need to redirect the energies of your overzealous amateur-photographer cousin. It is a practical idea to compile a list of basic, fairly straightforward tasks. Then, as well-intentioned offers come your way, you can politely say, "No, we have that covered, but we could really use your help with this, instead."

Renting Equipment

Weddings at home can mean a lot of rentals. From tents to tableware to toilets, you may need to outfit your place with some additional equipment if the crowd you intend to gather will be larger than what you might have over to watch football on a Sunday. The good news is that you will likely be able to find a rental company that offers one-stop shopping for practically everything you need. The bad news is that rental costs can be a real drain on your budget.

Before you rent, think about borrowing or buying. If you are a member of a church, synagogue, or civic organization, you may be able to borrow tables, chairs, and other necessities at little or no cost. If you might have future use for such items as large baking pans or a coffee urn, buying may be more sensible than renting.

As you call or visit rental centers, ask these questions:

☐ What is the rental price? What deposits are required, and when is full payment due?

☐ Does the price include delivery, setup, and retrieval? If not, exactly what additional charges apply?

☐ When will equipment be delivered?

☐ When must everything be picked up or returned?

☐ Do items such as china, silverware, glassware, cooking pans, and coffee pots need to be washed before they are picked up or returned?

☐ What charges will be assessed for items not returned due to loss or damage?

☐ Is the company insured?

☐ What is the cancellation policy?

☐ Can you provide any references?

newlywed know-how

Try to have one toilet available for every twenty to twenty-five people. When you are making calculations, don't forget that in addition to you and your guests, the number of folks in need of facilities will include band members, photographers, catering staff, and others you have employed for the day.

Parking Issues

While many of the things your home lacks can be rented or purchased, there is one that may be more difficult to acquire—parking space. If your home has a long, wide driveway or a flat, open expanse of lawn, you will likely be in good shape. Even still, you should think through the logistics of how you will arrange cars to ease guests' departures, as well as what you will do if the area you had intended to use as a lot becomes waterlogged following a stretch of rain.

If there is no readily available parking area on-site, there are several possibilities you might explore. Street parking may be an option, but it is wise to check with your town or whichever entity owns and maintains the road to ensure there are no restrictions of which you should be aware. It is also a kind gesture to forewarn your neighbors of your plans. In fact, if you are on friendly terms with your neighbors, and particularly if you plan to include them on your guest list, you may find they are willing to contribute their driveways or lawns as space for additional parking. If you are still strapped for space, you may need to encourage guests to carpool, operate a valet-type service to remove cars to another location, or shuttle guests from a nearby parking area that you have been granted permission to use.

If the parking arrangements are complicated, include an explanation with your invitations. You may also need to designate one or more volunteers to direct parking as guests arrive. For safety, be sure that clear access remains available so that emergency vehicles can reach you if needed.

A Big Job

Home may be where the heart is, but it can also be where the headaches are once you decide to marry there. Planning a wedding requires more mental energy and emotional investment than you may have anticipated at the outset. When home is at the epicenter of the wedding planning frenzy, it is sometimes difficult to step back and view the big picture. It can also feel impossible to escape from the overwhelming reminders of tasks that must be completed. If possible, try to keep all wedding paperwork in one place and to restrict wedding projects to one room or area of the house.

piece of cake

While you're in do-it-yourself mode, make something nice for you. It's easy to create your own exfoliating sugar scrub. Add enough olive, corn, or sunflower oil to a half-cup of sugar to create a paste. A dollop of scented body lotion adds a tantalizing scent. In the shower, massage in a circular motion from face to toes and rinse.

The months leading up to your union will be filled with excitement and joyful anticipation. They can also be loaded with stress if you get overly consumed with wedding details. Make a concerted effort not to neglect other responsibilities while you are organizing your event. Delegate as much as possible; your parents, attendants, and spouse-to-be are all likely eager to contribute to the overall success of the day. Even though the wedding hubbub may be exhilarating, you *can* have too much of a good thing. Schedule entire days when you will get out of the house and forget every wedding-related chore save one—spending time with the person you intend to cherish for life.

Liability

You are planning an outdoor wedding, so "Be prepared for anything" is already your mantra. Not all wedding chores are as pleasurable as trying on dresses, researching honeymoon destinations, and sampling cake flavors. One of the more mundane details you will need to handle for a wedding at home is a review of the insurance coverage for the property where the event will be held.

Accidents Happen

It is an unfortunate reality, but millions of accidents occur in the home each year. Common causes of fatalities and disabling injuries include poisons, falls, choking, and fires. Many of these accidents are preventable.

Are You Covered?

Accidents can impact both people and property. If individuals are involved, your thoughts, of course, will be focused immediately on attending to their needs, ensuring they receive any treatment necessary, and addressing any unsafe conditions that may have led to the mishap. Property damage may require you to cordon off dangerous areas or, in rare instances, to evacuate guests from the premises. If injuries or property damage are severe, it may ultimately be necessary to file an insurance claim.

rain or shine

Purchasing augmented property insurance coverage is not the same thing as purchasing wedding insurance. Most wedding insurance policies cover very specific losses and would not offer protection in the event that a guest or vendor is injured or that damage to your home occurs.

As you plan your event, it is an opportune time to review your existing homeowner's insurance policy or to ask those who own the residence where you will host your shindig to do so. The policy will likely provide coverage for injuries that occur on the property and any significant damage to the physical site. However, it is important to ascertain the level of coverage and any applicable deductibles. Also, be sure you discuss with your insurance company or agent whether it is advisable for you to purchase an additional rider covering your wedding day.

Emergency Precautions

Whether you are holding your gathering at your own home or that of a relative or close friend, there are measures you can take to enhance site safety and to ensure that you will be able to react quickly in the event of an emergency. Here are some precautions you should consider:

☐ Post emergency phone numbers beside every telephone.

☐ Test smoke detectors.

☐ Purchase fire extinguishers.

☐ Locate grills and other outdoor cooking apparatus at least three feet away from the house and any exterior structures.

☐ Be prepared with ashtrays for smokers.

☐ Ensure that all areas are well illuminated if guests will be departing after dark.

☐ Place candles only in locations where they can be observed at all times and where they are unlikely to be knocked or blown over or to come in contact with decorations or other flammable materials.

☐ Know of at least two guests who are certified in CPR and basic first-aid techniques, or learn these life-saving skills yourself.

The trickiest liability issue you will encounter relates to the dispensing of alcohol. Ask your insurer about the liquor liability coverage provided by your homeowner's insurance policy. It should be adequate to cover you if you intend to offer an open bar. If you intend to operate a cash bar, however, you will need to seriously consider purchasing a one-day liquor liability policy. If you are engaging a caterer who will assume responsibility for serving drinks and monitoring alcohol consumption, ask to see documentation of the business's insurance coverage, and ask to have your name and the homeowner's name added to the policy as an insured for the day of your event.

When the Party's Over

If you choose to wed at home as a means of making your event a very customized and singular affair, you may be surprised to realize that there is something your celebration will have in common with every other wedding. No matter how many months of preparation lead up to the big day, when the last guest says goodbye, you will scratch your heads and wonder, "How did it fly by so quickly?" While many newlyweds can head off into the sunset without a care as to who will clean up, those who tie the knot at home still have a bit of work ahead after the party is over.

piece of cake

In your list of wedding-day contacts, be sure to include a phone number for a local taxi company. You will want to be prepared just in case you need to make transportation arrangements for a guest who has consumed too much alcohol.

Saying Farewell

Even for small, informal gatherings, communicating to guests that it is time for them to mosey along can present an etiquette predicament. At most weddings, the bride and groom's departure is a signal that the affair is coming to a close. A home setting can present a unique challenge when it comes to bidding guests farewell.

Even if you will be returning to spend the night at home, you may want to stage a departure and simply spend a bit of quiet time with your new spouse while your wedding party handles the tasks of seeing guests off and cleaning up. Here are a few other strategies for ensuring a timely conclusion to your event:

- Indicate an end time in your invitations.
- Close the bar.
- Have the DJ or band announce the last song.

If you are planning a honeymoon, you may want to build in an extra day or more between your event and your departure. The aftermath of a wedding at home, particularly at your own place, can be a bit more involved than for one held at a site that is owned and maintained by others. You will feel more relaxed on your trip if you leave knowing that rental items have been returned, tents have been removed, and messes won't be awaiting your return.

Your Cleanup Crew

The old saying, "Many hands make light work," is one to embrace if you are marrying on your own turf. Though it is not a chore that anyone will relish following hours of dining, drinking, and dancing, the more folks you can convince to join your cleanup crew, the more quickly you'll be able to restore a sense of order and peace. Though you may be tempted to delay cleanup efforts until another day, you'll be much better off if you take advantage of the availability of many helpers to handle major undertakings, such as breaking down tables and chairs. If a family or wedding party member offers to oversee cleanup so that you don't have to trade your gown and tux for jeans and T-shirts, by all means accept this generous offer. Just be sure you provide detailed instructions about where cleaning supplies are located, when and in what condition rented equipment must be returned, and how to lock up the property, particularly if you won't be returning until after your honeymoon.

If you don't feel comfortable imposing on friends and family members to assist with cleaning duties, you may need to hire some help. Line up local teens to assist with any heavy lifting and loading jobs. You may want to engage a cleaning service to spruce up interiors both before and after your wedding so that you will be free to handle other details that require your attention.

newlywed know-how

Instead of giving away table centerpieces at random or providing favors for everyone, you may want to reserve special gifts for those who contribute to the cleanup effort. Be sure to express your gratitude for their assistance when you write your wedding thank-you notes, as well.

Contending with Leftovers

One universal law of feeding a crowd is that there are always more leftovers than anticipated. If you will be staying in town during your early hours as husband and wife, you may be delighted by the prospect of not having to shop or cook for a few days. However, if you'll be jetting off for a romantic escape, you'll need to plan ahead in order to avoid returning to a refrigerator teeming with green, fuzzy food.

If you own or rent a freezer, you may be able to preserve the excess from your nuptial feast for future dinners for two. Otherwise, leftovers will need a new home at the conclusion of your event. If you plan to send food home with guests, have a large supply of plastic bags and containers on hand. Be prepared, too, to break up any squabbles over who gets to claim those prime filets or that tray of delectable chocolate-dipped strawberries. If you fear that guests who have traveled a distance will feel slighted when the spoils are distributed, you may want to suggest they bring their own coolers along.

Better yet, rather than starting a food fight or allowing anything to go to waste, why not contact a local food pantry, soup kitchen, or shelter to see if they would welcome a donation? Your caterer may have suggestions. Be sure to ask about any limitations on the type and quantity of food the organization can accept. Keep in mind that you may need to make special arrangements in advance to have your edible extras picked up or delivered to the facility, particularly since your wedding will probably take place on a weekend day. Sharing your abundance with those who are less fortunate is a loving solution to the leftover dilemma.

Weddings Away from Home

From the glitz of Las Vegas, to the color of the Caribbean, to the Old World elegance and charm of Europe, wondrous outdoor wedding settings await those who have the adventurous spirit—and the budget—to plan a wedding away from home. Destination weddings can be complex and are not for every couple. Still, looking beyond the immediate environment opens up a realm of possibilities for those in search of a spectacular backdrop for their exchange of vows.

A Wedding "On Location"

Every wedding is an event, but there is undeniably an added level of excitement when a marriage celebration is merged with travel to a fabulous destination. Technological advancements in travel and communications continue to make the world a smaller place, opening new doors for those intrigued by the possibility of hosting a wedding on location. While faraway weddings present some additional challenges, they are increasingly popular with couples who dream of beginning their lives together in a place that holds special appeal, even if that happens to be a world away from their everyday lives. If you are contemplating a wedding away from your home turf, however, it is important to consider the potential rewards along with the possible drawbacks.

newlywed know-how

Statistics compiled by Conde Nast's Bridal Group Infobank and *Modern Bride* magazine indicate that destination weddings are on the rise. One in ten American couples chooses to begin married life away from home.

The Advantages of Getting Away

Depending on where you live and what type of outdoor wedding setting you agree is ideal, getting away from home may be the only way to fulfill your dreams. If you are willing to travel, chances are good that you can find the perfect place out there somewhere. Weddings held in exotic locations can be fun and exhilarating, and they offer a few other subtle advantages, too, not the least of which is that you'll enjoy a head start on your honeymoon.

Though increasingly popular, getaway weddings are still considered somewhat unconventional. This not only makes your event different, it frees you to dispense with tradition. For couples who have been married previously, a destination wedding can offer a different start that sets this new marriage apart.

If you prefer an intimate affair, holding your wedding away from home can be a strategic way to keep your event small. For starters, fewer guests may accept your invitation due to the travel expenses and time commitment required. You will also be justified in extending fewer invitations, as those who aren't invited will likely be more understanding than if they had been excluded from a nearby event. Destination weddings are particularly popular with those who want to limit their assemblage to just two. Eloping while on vacation is a way to avoid many of the hassles of planning a traditional wedding while still making your marriage celebration truly memorable.

piece of cake

If you have sent few or no invitations to your getaway wedding, you may want to consider mailing formal announcements to friends and family members after the event. If you think ahead, you can bring your announcements along to your destination so that the stamp and postmark commemorate the location of your nuptials.

Marrying away from home can even help you to curb costs, particularly if you would have felt pressure to host a large and elaborate affair back home. Many couples intend to book a honeymoon trip anyway, so the cost of travel frequently does not represent an added expense. More and more resorts in spectacular locations are recognizing the demand for outdoor weddings, and they provide exquisitely beautiful settings that need no embellishments. Many offer affordably priced, all-inclusive wedding packages for guests that also alleviate much of the stress of planning a wedding from afar. In many cases, you'll save by having a smaller event. If you do intend to share the day with others, you may even save them some money if you select a popular vacation destination with reasonable airfares and plenty of lodging options.

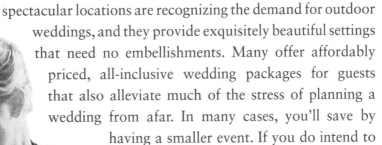

Things That Can Trip You Up

While the vision of saying "I do" in paradise may have tremendous appeal, it is important to think this option through carefully before you board a plane. A destination wedding *can* be pricey, not just in dollars but in the cost of lost relationships if your decision to take off results in hurt feelings. Start out by asking yourselves if a small celebration is really what you have in mind. If you would prefer to have every cousin, colleague, and college buddy present for your shindig, a destination wedding likely won't work.

For many couples, a wedding is first and foremost not about where but *who*. Infirmities, finances, work, and family commitments can all prevent people who would really like to share this day with you from attending an event that requires travel. Excluding friends and family, even from an event that is obviously out of their reach, can cause some people you care about to feel left out and hurt. Elopements may seem an easy option at the time, but they can cause bruised feelings on the part of parents and others who dreamed of celebrating this moment with you.

While it is possible to plan a reasonably priced destination wedding, a faraway event can also be expensive, particularly if you decide to pay for transportation and accommodations. Some destinations are affordable, but others are more exclusive, and cheap flights and budget lodgings may both be limited. When you have invited people to join you on a holiday, there is a tendency to schedule additional festivities before and after the wedding, which can tax your budget even further. While a resort's wedding package may be attractively priced, the options it offers may be too limited for your liking. However, finding reputable vendors when you don't live in the area can require many costly long-distance phone calls and even a visit or two to the destination if you really want to control the look and feel of your event.

Once travel becomes an integral part of your celebration, you also must contend with a layer of added intricacy. If your plane or train is delayed, your luggage is lost, or jetlag leaves you woozy, your celebration may not get off to the best start. If many guests will be converging on the destination, you may also have to worry about their safe and timely arrival.

Selecting a Destination

Once you have decided that the pros of traveling to find the perfect outdoor wedding setting outweigh the cons, the next step is to choose a destination. Web sites, books, magazines, and promotional brochures are all good resources for exploring possibilities. It's a big world out there, but you should be able to narrow the list of potential locations by first reviewing the basics of what you are seeking in an outdoor celebration site and then evaluating any specific logistical hurdles each destination might present.

The Wide World of Weddings

Weddings occur all over the world. All destinations, however, are not equal when it comes to attracting couples seeking to marry outdoors. Some places have a reputation for romance. Others have the distinct benefit of offering a temperate climate year-round. Each boasts its own unique visual allure.

newlywed know-how

Some of the most popular destination wedding locations include Alaska, Hawaii, Florida, California, Colorado, Las Vegas, New Orleans, Italy, Scotland, Greece, Mexico, Bermuda, and the Caribbean.

There is a good chance that you will be attracted to a place with which you have some familiarity—a vacation destination you have visited together or a family homeland that you've heard tales of since childhood, for example. Other destinations may be heavily advertised in magazines and other media, thus piquing your interest. The type of setting you desire will also influence your considerations. For historic flavor, you might turn to Europe, while would-be beach brides and grooms might focus their search on islands in the tropical seas.

Finding the Right Place

First and foremost, the right location for your wedding is one where you feel happy and at ease. You should be able to envision your ceremony and celebration occurring in this space. As with any outdoor wedding, you must also take into consideration such practical factors as accessibility, cost, climate, facilities, legalities, and availability of an indoor alternative should the weather be uncooperative.

rain or shine

There is a danger in planning your wedding at any destination sight-unseen. Brochures and Web sites don't always accurately portray a place. If you are unable to make a scouting trip, be sure to read any available reviews of the property. You should also ask for references from other couples who have married there.

As you evaluate potential wedding destinations, there are a few other important items to consider, such as these:

- Distance that you and important guests must travel (and potential for jetlag if crossing time zones)
- Distance from wedding site and the nearest available airport, ferry dock, or train station
- Passport, visa, and other entry and departure requirements
- Estimated travel expenses for you and guests
- Amount of time you have available for travel
- Suitability of the locale to also serve as your honeymoon destination
- Availability of a variety of lodging options for guests at a range of prices
- Local requirements for getting married and the availability of a local officiant
- Requirements for having your marriage legally recognized at home

If you find yourselves without time to adequately research potential wedding spots, or if you are overwhelmed by the sheer number of possibilities and logistical issues to consider, you may be wise to hire a wedding consultant with particular expertise in destination weddings. Once you provide a description of your ideal location, along with some distance and budget parameters, a qualified consultant will be able to offer precise recommendations. If the consultant is experienced in coordinating weddings at the destination you select, you may want to also engage this person throughout the planning process to assist with travel arrangements, accommodations, and securing the services of local vendors.

Cruise-Ship Weddings

If you are having trouble choosing just one destination, a cruise-ship wedding might be the answer to your dilemma. Whether you choose to marry on deck or on land at one of the ship's ports of call, a cruise can take you to a variety of dazzling places. It can also offer a continuous line-up of everything you might desire in both a wedding and a honeymoon, including entertainment, recreation, sightseeing, dancing, and glorious food. As vacations go, cruises can also be quite affordable, and all-inclusive wedding packages featuring everything from bouquet to cake are often available for a reasonable additional charge.

A Celebration of Love at Sea

If you have never taken a cruise, the first step is to familiarize yourselves with cruise lines and the routes they travel. Itineraries vary greatly in duration, number and location of ports visited, side excursions offered, and waters navigated. Cruise ships come in many sizes and levels of luxury. At the high end, they are akin to floating cities, offering amenities and services that rarely fail to amaze and delight passengers.

Already a popular honeymoon choice, cruises are a natural fit for the destination-wedding concept. Not only do they offer an out-of-the-ordinary setting for a wedding under open skies, they are almost always equipped to handle a large gathering if you are hopeful that many of your friends and relations will join you. Should inclement weather make it impossible to proceed with a wedding on deck or ashore, the ship will provide the shelter you require.

piece of cake

Thanks to advancements in storm tracking, cruises continue to operate even during hurricane season. Though safety is rarely a concern, a hurricane can force an ocean liner to alter its intended course. If you have your heart set on marrying at a specific port of call rather than on board, your wedding should be scheduled during a month when hurricanes are not a threat.

You will need to do some research in order to compare the prices and included features of wedding packages that various cruise lines offer. Be sure an officiant will be available to legally unite you in marriage and a photographer will be on hand to document your event. A travel agent or wedding consultant with special expertise in booking cruise weddings may be able to assist you, particularly if you have special needs or requests. Many cruise lines also offer the service of personal wedding coordinators who can answer your questions about options and legalities.

Setting Sail on a Smaller Scale

Luxury liners aren't the only boats you might consider for an outdoor wedding afloat. On many rivers and large lakes, paddlewheel or sightseeing cruise vessels can be chartered to take you and your guests out on the water for a scenic celebration. Most of these boats have the advantage of being outfitted with an enclosed cabin that can serve as your backup shelter for all but the most tumultuous weather conditions. For a smaller gathering, a wedding on a yacht or a sailing schooner might be an option.

The changing panorama as you motor or drift along can provide a kaleidoscopic background for your ceremony and reception on board. Marrying on a boat, however, also presents its own set of potential problems. Primary among them is that any guest who is late will literally miss the boat.

Also, choppy water can turn some guests green and make dancing and holding on to a dinner plate both tricky propositions. It is also important to ascertain whether you might still be able to host your event on board even if the boat must remain docked in bad weather.

Will They Come?

What if you threw a wedding and nobody came? Unless your intention is to elope with little fanfare, this can be a legitimate concern for those planning a destination wedding. If you can afford to cover travel and lodging expenses for all guests, your turnout will likely be excellent. However, most couples who marry on location must hope that guests will be willing and able to pay for their own travel and lodging bills.

rain or shine

Encouraging guests to make the trip for your wedding is only half the battle. If many decide to book extended stays at the same hotel or resort where you hoped to honeymoon, you may have to devise creative ways to convince them to leave you alone. Alternatively, consider relocating to another inn or hotel nearby so that you'll have more privacy.

For some guests, your destination wedding will be a welcome excuse to plan a vacation. You know your friends and family best. Do they enjoy travel and take several trips each year? Will the destination you have selected appeal to them? Are they located all over the country or even around the world, meaning that most guests will have to travel for your wedding anyway?

If you want to increase the odds that a high percentage of guests will accept your destination wedding invitation, consider the following tips:

- Select an easily accessible location with widespread appeal.
- Send a save-the-date card well in advance that includes detailed travel information.

- Negotiate with one or more hotels or resorts to reserve a block of rooms at a discounted rate for guests.
- Check with airlines for potential group savings programs. American Airlines, for example, offers a wedding event travel discount program—for information, search the airline's Web site (at *www.americanairlines.com*).
- Organize a line-up of events and activities in addition to the wedding that will be fun for guests.

If you know in advance that many of your closest friends and family members will not be able to join you for your wedding away, or if you are disappointed with the number of affirmative responses you receive, there are several ways to expand participation in your celebration. One is to hire a company that can facilitate a live wedding Webcast, making your celebration available via streaming video on the Internet. Another is to plan a reception or party when you return home.

Planning from Afar

Planning a wedding is an involved process, even when all of your vendors are a local phone call away and your ceremony and reception sites are close enough to visit whenever the need arises. The further from home you intend to venture, and the less familiar you are with the place, the more difficult it will be to coordinate arrangements. Unless you have the time and funds to make several visits ahead of time or to employ an on-location event coordinator, your best strategy may be to keep your celebration as simple as possible, bearing in mind that the setting itself will lend drama to your event.

Couples planning destination weddings must exercise a tremendous amount of forethought and be extraordinarily well organized. Your travel reservations must be made with care and confirmed both several weeks in advance and just before your scheduled departure. You must pack meticulously, knowing that you may not be able to easily acquire anything you've left behind and you certainly won't be able to race home to retrieve forgotten rings or paperwork. If you will be sharing the event with traveling guests, you must be prepared to serve as their travel agent and tour guide.

One of the easiest ways to communicate with service providers at a distance is via e-mail. Be sure to save all correspondence so that it can easily be retrieved and reviewed if questions arise. If the predominant language at your wedding destination is not one that you speak fluently, you may need to enlist the services of a translator to ensure that your wishes are understood. You should also ask a translator to review any foreign-language documents that you must sign.

piece of cake

One of your biggest logistical concerns may be how to transport your gown to your wedding destination. Consider shipping it in a protective box ahead of the event. Be sure to select a courier that offers package tracking, a guaranteed delivery date, and insurance. You should also make arrangements with a local cleaner to have the dress pressed just before the wedding.

Legalities

In the United States, each individual state makes its own laws regarding matrimony. If you have selected a domestic destination, you will need to research applicable state laws to find out what requirements must be met, what fees apply, how long the license is valid, and, in particular, whether a waiting period is required either between application for and granting of the license or between the time the license is issued and when the ceremony can take place. One of the reasons that Las Vegas is such a popular wedding destination is that there is no waiting period in the state of Nevada. You must get your license in the same locality where you marry, so a waiting period may mean you have to arrive at your destination several days in advance in order to ensure that you are properly licensed to wed.

newlywed know-how

If you choose to marry on foreign soil, you may face hurdles obtaining a license and ensuring that your marriage will be legally recognized when you return from your trip. One simple solution is to marry privately in a small civil ceremony at home before making your overseas journey.

If you marry anywhere within the United States, your marriage will definitely be legal in your home state. Marrying abroad is not always so cut and dried, however. You will need to do some legwork to see both if you are eligible to be formally married in a foreign land and if your marriage will be valid at home. Some nations require a period of residency, which may make obtaining a foreign marriage license prohibitive. The American embassy in a given foreign country (or that country's U.S. embassy) should be a good resource. Keep in mind that marriage does not automatically entitle a foreign national to live in or even to enter the United States, so if you are marrying a non-U.S. citizen in a foreign land, you will need to go through proper immigration channels if you both intend to live in the United States.

The Weather Over There

Just as you would research historic weather patterns before scheduling a wedding at home, you should familiarize yourselves with the conditions you are likely to experience at your intended destination during the month when you hope to marry. Keep in mind that seasons are reversed in the Southern Hemisphere, so when it is winter in the United States, it is summer south of the equator. While many destinations don't experience what you might think of as winter, there may be a rainy season that you will want to avoid. Some destinations, such as Hawaii, are comfortable year-round, but others can be unbearable during the peak heat of summer.

As your departure and wedding day loom closer, you will want to keep an eye both on local weather information that might affect your travel plans and on forecasts for your wedding destination that may force your celebration indoors. Weather forecasts for cities around the globe can be easily monitored online. You may also want to touch base with someone at the location, such as your venue's manager, a few days before your arrival to ask what local forecasters are predicting.

Pre- and Post-Wedding Events

The term "wedding day" is increasingly becoming a misnomer, as many nuptial events are expanding to encompass several days of festivities. Weddings on location are among those most likely to be weekend-long or longer affairs. If you have selected a fabulous destination, many guests will be tempted to view the trip as a vacation and to linger for a few days, rather than booking the first flight out after the last dance. With guests and bridal party members going out of their way to travel for the event, many couples feel compelled to provide a busy slate of activities from the moment guests begin to arrive until the time to say farewell draws near.

Come and Stay Awhile

Whether you intentionally set out to host a days-long event or you find your wedding mushrooming spontaneously, chances are good that your away-from-home marriage celebration will involve a span of days. This can be a definite plus, as many couples' biggest wedding day regret is that it all passed by too quickly, and they did not have adequate time to enjoy the company of their near and dear. By involving everyone in a variety of activities and experiences both before and after the main event, it is often possible to foster a bonding experience akin to going away to summer camp. New friendships will be made, two families will indeed become united, and all participants will leave with fond memories of days invested in sharing your celebration, rather than hours spent witnessing your wedding.

piece of cake

Appropriate favors for destination weddings include sample-sized containers of locally made food products, local handicrafts, photo frames and albums, and address books so that guests who have become friends can exchange contact information and keep in touch.

Of course, the more events you add on, the greater the overall expense of your event. However, your pre- and post-wedding schedule does not need to be loaded with such costly activities as a golf tournament, spa escape, chartered sightseeing cruise, champagne brunch, fireworks, or elaborate rehearsal dinner in order to be fun and memorable. Instead, invite guests to participate in guided walking tours, a hamburger and hotdog cookout, a bonfire marshmallow roast, an evening sing-along, or a simple afternoon tea with cookies or morning coffee hour with bagels.

Time Together and Time Apart

While add-on events can help everyone to feel a part of your celebration, be careful not to overschedule guests' time. Don't forget that they may see this as a vacation, and as such, they may want to have some control over their own itineraries so that they can see sights that interest them or simply relax. If a few folks refuse to play along, resist the temptation to chastise them for not wanting to participate in all group events. Some people simply are not joiners, and above all, you want your guests to feel at ease. Try to offer plenty of options so that participants can make choices, particularly if some events, such as a day of golf, carry an added expense for guests.

Making a Distant Place Your Own

While marriage customs and rituals around the world may differ, they are all inspired by common themes: love, commitment, romance, joy, and eternity. Embracing local traditions is a common desire of couples who wed away from home, but even when you are open to the adventure of marrying the way the locals do, you should still try to make your celebration deeply personal in many ways. The place you have chosen will exert a powerful influence upon your event. Still, your wedding is about something even more special than this unique environment; it is about a love that can only be shared by two.

Don't become so overwhelmed by the destination piece of the planning process that you forget about the wedding component. Write personal vows that you will exchange at your ceremony. Strike a balance between adopting local traditions and incorporating traditional elements of the wedding you would have had back home. Invite friends and family members in attendance to serenade you, to offer blessings, or to deliver speeches or toasts. Bring along your own CDs so that you can dance to the music you know and love.

A Built-In Theme

Theme weddings are increasingly popular with couples who want to differentiate their celebration from other events. Can you combine a theme wedding and an outdoor wedding? Yes. But it is important to select the theme carefully and to exercise some restraint as you add thematic elements. The outdoor space you have selected will already make your affair distinctive. Any thematic embellishments must coordinate with the ambiance of the place. You can either start with a theme as inspiration for your location or choose a theme that matches the site you've already picked.

A Locale That Speaks to You

The outdoor wedding location you have selected is hopefully one that matches your taste. As you begin to brainstorm possible wedding themes, you may discover that many of your ideas will work nicely in this setting. A theme, after all, should also be a reflection of your personality and passions.

newlywed know-how

Popular wedding themes include those inspired by historical eras, such as the medieval or Victorian periods; those related to heritage or culture, such as Irish or Hispanic weddings; those centered around a holiday or season; and those related to an area of interest, such as a favorite hobby, flower, fairy tale, or musical genre.

Of course, humans are multidimensional beings. It is quite possible that you and your beloved enjoy both garden strolls and rock concerts, historic house tours and football games, or days at the beach and nights of watching sci-fi films. When it comes to planning a wedding, however, it is important to hone in on one unifying motif that will lend a sense of focus and identity to the day.

If you have a theme in mind from the outset, you may want to allow it to guide your selection of a locale. For example, if you and your sweetie adore country music and go square dancing every Saturday night, a Western-themed event may appeal to you. The best environment for your hoedown wedding may be a historic barn, farm, or dude ranch.

Incorporating the Place into the Planning

If you selected an outdoor wedding location without thinking much about a theme, that is perfectly fine. In fact, it may be best to allow this special place to serve as the inspiration for the entire day. The more you learn about your chosen spot, the more ways you may find to incorporate its history, nature, and character into other elements of your event.

Know the Place Inside and Out

Even if you and your partner fell head over heels at first sight, you probably wouldn't deny that getting to know each other well is what has allowed your fondness to deepen and your love to grow. You may have selected your wedding site based on an impulse that took into account only its outward appearance, its proximity, or its role in your lives. There is always, however, more to a place than meets the eye.

rain or shine

Be sure to take notes as you learn interesting things about your wedding site. You may want to use these tidbits to create a fact sheet to include in your program or even to develop a fun trivia quiz for guests to play at their tables.

In order to glean inspiration from your chosen location, it is important to delve beneath the surface. Start by reading any available brochures or other promotional materials about the site. Next, check to see if there are any books, articles, or films about the specific place or the area in which it is situated. Seek out those who are knowledgeable about the property, and ask them to share stories of events that have transpired there, information about local customs, and details about the plant and animal life. Even if your wedding takes you only as far as your own backyard, there may be interesting things you can learn about the history of your home or even the trees that will shade your guests.

Make a Theme Game Plan

Establishing a theme and carrying it throughout your event is not something that can be left to chance. While you are familiarizing yourselves with your wedding place, you should simultaneously begin developing a theme game plan. Deciding just how you will incorporate and communicate the theme is important, whether you intend to go all out with a specific theme, such as "Victorian Garden Party," or to simply embrace the place as the basis for choosing other elements that will complement the event's overall look and feel.

piece of cake

In your wedding notebook, folder, or other organizer, set up a section dedicated to your theme. Use it as a place to jot down ideas as they occur to you and to list potential vendors who can supply or create unique items that coordinate well with your vision for the event.

As a starting point, here is a list of common wedding components that can be selected or styled to match a theme:

- Invitations and other stationery
- Wedding party attire
- Decorations and flowers
- Transportation
- Ceremony readings
- Music
- Placecards and table settings
- Cocktails and beverages
- Food
- Favors

Be creative, and brainstorm ways in which each of these items might reflect your theme, even if it is only through something as simple as color. You may not be able to coordinate every item, so circle or highlight those you feel are key to setting your event apart.

Local Lore, Language, and Libations

Now that you are intimately familiar with the spot you have chosen for your celebration, it is time to integrate what you have learned with your overall plan for the day. This is easier than you might think. In fact, you may be grateful to have a theme in mind as you wade through the myriad choices that are available to brides and grooms today.

Inspired Ideas

Let's look at invitations as an example of how your wedding setting, or the place combined with a well-matched theme, might shape your decision-making. Not that long ago, ordering invitations was a simple matter of selecting from among a few sample verses and choosing between white and ecru card stock. Today, wedding invitations come in all shapes, sizes, and shades, and the choices for format, embellishments, fonts, and wordings are nearly limitless. Visit a local stationer, and you could easily spend hours leafing through the pages of giant binders stuffed with samples.

You are at a distinct advantage if you have already contemplated how your invitation might set the tone for the event it will announce. For a beach wedding, you might choose a subtle, layered design featuring shades of aqua and blue. Invitations featuring seashell, lighthouse, or sand dollar images might also be appropriate. If there is pirate lore associated with this swatch of seaside real estate, you might order custom invitations designed to resemble a treasure map. Though you may find a colorful pressed-flower invitation attractive, you will be able to easily eliminate this choice, since it fails to meet your theme criteria.

rain or shine

Be careful not to become so swept up in sticking to your theme that you regret some of your purchases. The greatest danger lies in the selection of a wedding gown. Though a dress may suit your theme, if it doesn't make you look and feel absolutely stunning, it's not the right dress.

The wording and font you select can also reflect the theme and the setting. Instead of requesting the honor of their presence, you might beseech guests to "joineth" you and your betrothed for your Renaissance-themed nuptials in the courtyard. Bilingual invitations have become popular with cross-cultural couples, but they can also be employed to establish a sense of place, whether your wedding will be held in a foreign land or simply embrace the allure of another world.

Use your theme and your knowledge of the unique space where you will host your event to guide your choices throughout the wedding planning process. It is important, however, to remain flexible. Some of your best ideas for executing the theme may turn out to be those you didn't originally consider.

A Taste of the Place

Great food and drink are the hallmarks of any memorable party. If you host a backyard luau, for example, guests will more likely still be talking days later about the tropical drinks and the succulent roast pig than about how attractive the tiki torches were or how fabulous you looked in a grass skirt. Luckily, finding recipes to suit a theme or place is fairly simple.

Because most wedding receptions begin with a cocktail hour, the liquid refreshments you choose to serve may be your first opportunity to blend place and taste. Here are some examples of perfect pairings:

- Fruit-infused vodka at an orchard wedding
- Guinness at an Irish-themed castle wedding
- The winery's own reds and whites at a vineyard wedding
- Frozen daiquiris and piña coladas at a beach wedding
- Blue martinis for a wedding on the water
- Mint juleps at a Southern-themed
- Margaritas for a casual island wec
- Cosmopolitans for an outdoor soi
  the backdrop of a city skyline
- Hot buttered rum for a
  fall-themed wedding

Wedding meals have evolved dramatically from the "beef or chicken?" days of yore. An outdoor setting can be the perfect place to take liberties in devising a unique and inspired menu. A creative caterer or on-site chef can be your best ally if you hope to incorporate dishes that meld well with the essence of your event.

newlywed know-how

It has become trendy to serve a signature cocktail at wedding events. Talk to whoever will be tending bar about creating a new twist on an old favorite, inspired, if possible, by the location and your theme. Give your marital libation a creative name that is evocative of the event's overall flavor.

Food can play a central and defining role in your celebration. Your wedding might feature a chicken barbecue in your backyard, a traditional lobster bake on a New England beach, an elegant high tea in a traditional English rose garden, a gourmet picnic in the park, or a jazz brunch at a historic plantation house. Alternatively, select just a few special hors d'oeuvres or side dishes that use fresh local products or that are tied closely to your motif—pumpkin soup served in hollowed-out gourds, for example, at an autumn-themed affair. Many restaurants, inns, and historic properties that host outdoor weddings also sell their own cookbooks, which may be excellent sources for period recipes or specialties that feature the region's seasonal bounty.

Adding Theme Elements

You need not limit your theme planning to big-ticket items, such as food, invitations, and attire. There are many small yet effective ways to carry a color scheme, symbol, or concept throughout your event. In fact, you may discover that there are so many possibilities that you get a bit carried away. Exercising a degree of control and embracing the notion of subtlety will help you to ensure that your theme is executed tastefully.

Nice Touches

A mint on your pillow. A fluffy bathrobe in the closet. A gas-burning fireplace that provides golden warmth at the flick of a switch. In the hospitality industry, it is the little things that create a memorable experience.

Hosting a wedding provides you with a similar opportunity to impress guests with your attention to detail. Often, the nicest touches are those that are carefully conceived yet appear very subtle or effortless. Incorporating your theme into small details is also a playful way for you to make your special day both memorable and unique.

piece of cake

The Internet is a tremendous resource for anyone planning a theme party. The Web site *www.askginka.com* is one of the best places to find theme wedding ideas. The Web site provides suggestions for more than 500 wedding themes and links you directly to vendors that offer products perfectly suited to the theme you select.

Let's say you've decided on a springtime wedding at a colorful garden known for its ability to attract butterflies. Taking your cue from this place, you've decided to wholeheartedly embrace the butterfly theme. Your invitations will feature a butterfly design. You have ordered live butterflies to release at the conclusion of your ceremony, and guests will dine on sumptuous stuffed butterfly shrimp. How else might you ingeniously incorporate this theme into your event? Here are some ideas:

- Wear a butterfly clip in your hair.
- Sew dainty butterfly appliqués to your garter.
- Fasten beaded butterflies to the tops of your shoes.
- Incorporate silk butterflies into bouquets and floral arrangements.
- Choose the song "Butterfly Kisses" for the bride's dance with Dad.

- Dress the flower girl in a butterfly costume.
- Buy a mold to create butter pats in the shape of butterflies.
- Accent your cake with sugary butterflies.
- Choose stained-glass butterfly sun-catchers as a favor for guests.

Don't Go Overboard

You will be astounded by the number of unique, theme-related products and ideas you will encounter once you begin your search. Make choices wisely, not only for the sake of your budget but in order to keep the theme from overshadowing the true purpose of the event—to unite you and your sweetheart in marriage. Adhering too strictly to a theme can inadvertently make your special day more tacky than extraordinary. Releasing live monarchs at your butterfly-themed wedding is one thing; dressing bridesmaids in orange and black is another.

Avoiding Thematic Conflicts

Overdoing it is not the sole risk of taking a theme approach to your wedding. Nor is choosing a theme that is inappropriate for the setting. A variety of thematic conflicts can arise that result in an event that simply doesn't work. When you select a thread to run throughout your event, you must be sure that you won't want to switch to something entirely different midstream.

One Is Enough

Any wedding begins with the decision to share your life and your dreams with one special someone. Along the road to "I do," you will have to make many other singular choices. What one gown will make you appear most ravishing? Which wedding ring will you wear for the rest of your life? What song will accompany your first dance as husband and wife?

When it comes to selecting a theme, you must also pick just one. Juggling multiple motifs is a surefire way to create an event that seems disjointed and leaves guests puzzled. If you adore animals, for example, and want to marry at the zoo, stick with wild creatures as your defining theme, and don't try to integrate your passion for cuddly stuffed teddy bears, too. Pulling off a party dedicated to one central focus is tricky enough, so choose a theme that excites and delights you. Once you've made a few key decisions and purchases, it may be expensive and complicated to change your mind.

ask the wedding planner ?

Can you incorporate your theme into the ceremony?

A civil service provides the greatest flexibility, but even religious ceremonies may include readings, music, or a sermon that is reflective of your theme. Discuss your ideas with your officiant well in advance to ensure that he is comfortable with your plans and that there are no potential conflicts.

Color Coordination

Do you have an eye for color? If not, you may want to seek help from a friend or consultant as you choose your wedding color palette. Color can either set a mood or, when left to chance, create unwanted dissonance. Though you may have favorite colors in mind, if they clash with your environment, you'll be disappointed in the results.

rain or shine

As you consider colors, think not only about the outdoor setting you have selected but about the indoor space that will serve as a backup in the event of bad weather. Most tents are white, and most interiors are fairly neutral. If that is not the case for you, you may wind up with some color conflicts if the party moves inside.

It is important at the outset to consider what colors will be naturally dominant in the landscape you have selected. Scarlet bridesmaids' gowns and a bouquet of red roses may stand out oddly against a backdrop of purple mountains. An ivory gown may appear dingy against a fresh-painted white garden arbor. When fall colors the hills in shades of orange and gold, the pale lavender and mint green table linens you selected may look sorely out of place.

Sneak Preview and Welcome Ideas for Guests

Half the fun of a wedding with a novel theme and setting is building guests' anticipation for what's in store. Though you may want to have a few surprises up your sleeves, don't hesitate to provide guests with a sneak preview of the event. In addition to creating added drama, you'll also help guests who feel uneasy about a nontraditional wedding become comfortable with the notion of something a bit out of the ordinary.

Coming Attractions

Many weddings are planned a year or more in advance. A fairly new custom is to mail a save-the-date card prior to extending a formal invitation to the event to ensure that family and friends don't make other plans. Providing advance notice is particularly important for destination weddings that will require many guests to budget for and make travel arrangements.

The save-the-date "card," which may take the form of something functional, like a magnet, can provide a first tease of the wedding you're planning. Color, graphics, and wording can be customized to set the stage. Even if you plan to select more formal invitations, the save-the-date card offers an opportunity to be innovative and bold. You'll really catch guests' attention, for example, if you send a message in a bottle alerting them to your upcoming beach nuptials.

Invitations, of course, are your primary vehicle for communicating wedding-day information to guests. For complex destination or multiday weddings, invitations have taken on the expanded role of providing such information as itinerary details, suggested accommodations, maps, and sightseeing and dining recommendations. If you expect guests to dress in accordance with a theme, such as a masquerade or a Hawaiian luau, the invitations should contain specific instructions. Each component of the invitation, starting with the envelope, can establish a sense of how your celebration will unfold.

newlywed know-how

If your event will bring many out-of-town guests to a destination, the area's visitors' bureau or chamber of commerce may be willing to send travel brochures to everyone on your mailing list. This allows you to provide an additional teaser without incurring the added costs of postage.

The number of households with Internet access has grown quickly. That means you can also take advantage of this technology to keep guests apprised of wedding developments. If your wedding location has a Web site, be sure to include the URL with your save-the-date cards or invitations. Create your own wedding Web site where you share regular updates and count down to the big day. You might also send periodic e-mail newsletters to entice guests with details about such things as the menu or the band.

First Impressions

With some foresight, your guests will feel welcome and involved from the moment they arrive for your bash. In fact, some couples are taking advantage of the ease and affordability of creating custom music CDs to provide guests with a travel soundtrack that will put them in the mood for a party from the moment they leave home. For a wedding at the shore, your beach mix might include reggae tunes, Beach Boys classics, or even a recording of the soothing sounds of crashing surf. There are many Web sites that provide affordably priced, legal music downloads you can use to create your own themed CDs.

For guests who are arriving from a distance and staying in area hotels, a wonderful welcoming gesture is to have custom gift baskets awaiting their arrival. Fill the baskets with sightseeing information, a small gift such as a travel alarm clock, water or other beverages, and snacks that are evocative of your theme or the local area. Include a personalized note thanking your loved ones for making the trip to share your wedding day.

While most guests know what to do when they attend a traditional wedding, your event may leave them a bit puzzled if they arrive and there is no obvious bride or groom's side. Your ushers should be called into action to welcome arrivals and to explain where everyone should sit or stand as they await your big entrance. A wedding program can also provide details of how the event will proceed, along with an explanation of why you selected this special place as the launch pad for your life together.

Dressing the Setting

While a bare hall may call for extensive accessorizing, an outdoor wedding setting may need no embellishment at all. Any decorations you do decide to introduce should enhance and not detract from the site's beauty, while providing the functionality you need to ensure the comfort of your guests. Carefully think through the logistics of how you will set up your event, keeping in mind that your collaborator is the artistic yet somewhat moody Mother Nature.

Outdoor Wedding Design

Do you need flowers in a garden wedding? This is a rhetorical question posed to jog your thinking about how you will dress up any outdoor wedding setting. Decorating an outdoor spot is a bit like moving into a furnished apartment. The basics are already in place, and any personal touches you add must coordinate well with the existing décor. Allowing nature to take the lead in furnishing the layout and design for your event has the potential advantage of saving you money. It's also a perfect solution if design is not your particular forte. However, if you have a strong sense of style, you may face a few challenges as you attempt to execute your own ideas within a setting that essentially needs no enhancement.

Don't Compete with Mother Nature

By deciding to wed outdoors, you have already given a nod to nature's ability to arrange an appealing backdrop. As you begin to consider the overall look, feel, and setup of your event, make a pact to respect nature's talents and to be a collaborator, not a competitor. Take cues from the environment as you select colors, textures, and styles. As you map out the location of everything from the buffet line and the dance floor to your sweetheart table for two, look for natural opportunities to fit these elements into the scene. Use trees, bushes, and other natural camouflage to hide such unsightly add-ons as portable toilets or amplification equipment.

rain or shine

It can sometimes be tough to visualize just how everything will look once it is in place. Photographs of other events at the site can aid tremendously as you design your own special day. Don't hesitate to borrow ideas and layouts that you find particularly striking.

Lessons in Design

Couples marry at all stages of life. Some brides and grooms have already had ample opportunity to develop a well-defined individual and joint sense of style. Others have only dorm-room, studio-apartment, or bachelor-pad decorating to their credit. If you have never really given much thought to your tastes and preferences, planning a wedding and setting up a new home together can be a prime opportunity for self-discovery. Though you may not become a decorating expert, you will learn to recognize what does and does not appeal to your own sense of aesthetics.

You have probably already started a clipping file of magazine and newspaper articles that depict cakes, bouquets, gowns, tuxedos, and other wedding ideas that have caught your eye. As you plan your wedding, you should also immerse yourself in publications and television programs that focus on home design and interior renovation. As you cut out images of rooms and spaces that appeal to you both, you will learn much about your style as individuals and as a team. Do your tastes run toward formal or casual? Classic or trendy? Bold or neutral? Busy or streamlined?

Honing in on your notion of a comfortable and inviting place can help immensely as you work with individual vendors or a wedding consultant to create a wedding event that is a reflection of you. You can apply many good principles of design to your arrangement of your outdoor celebration space, such as the following:

- Create one main focal point.
- Allow ample room and pathways for people to move about freely.
- Repeat patterns and colors to unify a space.
- Use lighting effectively to create a mood.
- Stay away from trends that are destined to be short-lived.

One intriguing design concept you may want to learn more about as you sketch out the plan for your wedding space is feng shui. Many modern books, articles, and practitioners now teach this ancient Chinese design philosophy as feng shui and other ancient teachings from the East have attracted new interest in the Western world. In brief, feng shui posits that the placement of objects within a space, such as a home or office, determines the flow of energy and the fortunes of its inhabitants. You may not create the perfect environment, with the power to keep estranged family members from squabbling and to ensure there won't be a moment of strife in your wedded lives. Still, feng shui may spark some interesting ideas that help you to create a balanced and pleasing configuration.

newlywed know-how

FYI International Locations and Events, with offices in Los Angeles, San Diego, Santa Barbara, Palm Springs, Las Vegas, New York, and Indiana, offers "Wedding Feng Shui" as one of its event-planning services. Learn more about this company's use of this ancient art at its Web site (at *www.fleureveryours.bigstep.com*).

Arches and Other Architectural Elements

An outdoor environment need not be entirely the product of nature's handiwork. In fact, architectural elements in the landscape can provide visual variety and serve as natural focal points for your ceremony and other wedding activities. Some architectural features are large and obvious, such as lighthouses, gazebos, covered bridges, or barns. Other more subtle structures, such as brick or stone walls, ornate gates, fences, doorways, columns, and footbridges can also lend visual interest and play a role as a backdrop for proceedings and photographs.

Many outdoor wedding sites already boast some architectural embellishments. If yours does, it will be up to you to determine how best to incorporate

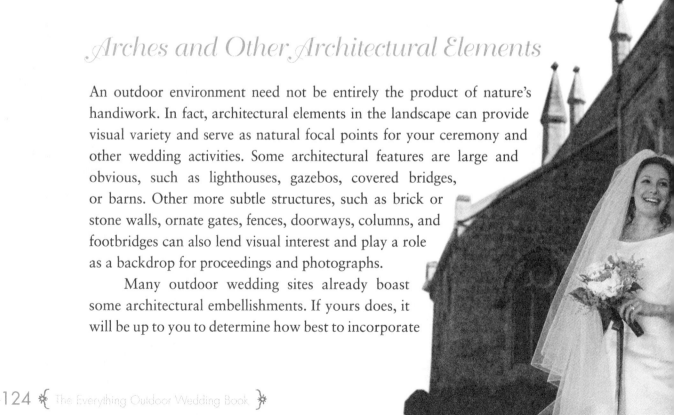

these decorative constructions. A high stone wall or trellised row of roses might provide the perfect curtain from behind which the bride makes a dramatic entrance. An arched wooden bridge over a fragrant lily pond may be the perfect pulpit, where your officiant will pronounce you husband and wife.

piece of cake

Make sure that if you rent an arch, it is not so heavy, so firmly anchored, or decorated so precariously that it cannot be relocated. That way, if you must move undercover in the event of inclement weather, your beautiful arch can go with you.

One key decision you will have to make is whether to decorate these structures. Many will be lovely unadorned. Some may become even more festive with the addition of silk or fresh flowers, greenery, tulle, ribbons, bows, white lights, or even leaves and corn stalks for an autumn affair. Your florist can be recruited to dress up arches, fences, lampposts, and other structures to your liking, or you can do it yourself. Try not to overdo, though, and to ensure that decorations are in keeping with your overall theme.

If your site is not blessed with any unique architectural elements, there is always the possibility of purchasing, borrowing, or renting decorative pieces. An arch is probably the most common structure imported for an outdoor celebration, as it can serve as an enchanting frame for your ceremony. Arches can be composed of wood, metal, or even balloons. Most rental companies offer a number of styles for your consideration.

Seating

You may view seating as more of a practical consideration than an opportunity to be creative. It is possible, however, to conceive of something different than rented folding chairs aligned in a row. In fact, an outdoor space provides unparalleled freedom when it comes to selecting and arranging resting places for guests.

Alternative Seating Arrangements

The tradition of seating friends and family members in rows, bride's side on the left, groom's side on the right, is frequently replicated at wedding ceremonies held in the great outdoors. Sticking with tradition is perfectly acceptable. However, you may find that an open-air setting is conducive to a different arrangement.

One alternative is to actually forego seating in favor of having guests stand. A standing-room only arrangement can raise the energy and involvement level of those who have assembled to witness your exchange of promises. However, if you decide to keep guests on their feet, you must also keep your ceremony short and sweet. It is also crucial to have a few chairs available for any guests who can't stand.

rain or shine

Though your ceremony and even a cocktail and hors d'oeuvre hour can be staged sans seating, if you will be sharing a meal with guests, you really should provide them not only with chairs or other seating but with tables. Plates balanced on laps are prone to mishaps.

A circular seating arrangement can be particularly effective in an outdoor environment. If you have ever attended a concert or theater performance "in the round," you know this setup can make an event feel more intimate and powerful. A distinct advantage of this layout is that it places all guests closer to the center of action. It also concentrates their attention on you, which can be particularly beneficial if the surroundings are potentially distracting. As your ceremony unfolds, you will be able to gaze in any direction and see the supportive smiles of those who surround you.

Chairs and Beyond

The white folding chairs that seem to be ubiquitous at outdoor weddings have some advantages. For starters, they are probably readily available from any rental company. They are lightweight and can easily be moved from the ceremony location to the dining area, meaning fewer chairs to rent. They can also be dressed up with drapes and bows to match just about any decorating scheme, if desired.

Before you sign on the dotted line to have dozens of folding chairs delivered, however, there are a few other options you might consider. For starters, does the venue have any chairs, benches, bleachers, or other seating available? You may save some money by using what's there, even if you must cover mismatched chairs or agree to return anything you borrow to its original location.

If you definitely must bring in seating, consider some possible alternatives to folding chairs that complement your wedding theme, including these:

- Hay bales at a country wedding
- Colorful beach chairs at an oceanfront wedding
- Lawn chairs for a wedding in the park or your backyard
- Director's chairs for a movie-themed wedding
- Wicker chairs for an elegant garden wedding

A few guests may have difficulty getting in and out of chairs or other seats that sit low to the ground. As a courtesy, you may want to make a few sturdy chairs with arms available.

The Aisle and Altar

When determining the exact spot where your ceremony will occur, you may want to take advantage of the property's existing natural or structural features. A garden path, pebbled walkway, wood-plank boardwalk, tree-lined driveway, or stone staircase, for example, might serve nicely as the aisle. For the altar, you might consider the backdrop of a gazebo, latticed arch, courtyard fountain, stone wall, floating dock, or curved hedge. If the site you have selected is an open expanse of beach, meadow, field, or mountainside, however, you may want to employ some creative touches to indicate the path of your processional and to set apart the space in which you will wed.

For your aisle, a plastic runner may not be the prettiest option, but it can certainly prove a godsend if the ground is damp or dusty. You can create an aisle simply via the placement of chairs, or you can mark your route to the altar with ribbons, potted plants, or floral garlands. For weddings planned for late in the day, illuminate the way with strings of lights or evenly spaced tea lights or luminaries.

piece of cake

Whether your aisle follows a natural path or one of your own creation, make sure it is wide enough so the bride's gown won't get snagged on a plant, chair, or worse—a candle.

If your aisle leads to a spectacular scenic overlook, your work may be done. Otherwise, you might consider renting an arch, chuppah, platform, podium, or table to position at the ceremony site. If you have marked your aisle with candles, potted plants, or garlands, the same items might be arranged in a ring to mark off the altar. Brainstorm other possibilities based on your location and theme, such as these examples:

- Position topiary trees on either side of the altar space for an elegant touch.
- Create bride and groom scarecrows to mark the ceremony site for a festive fall celebration.
- Ask guests to join hands and create an intimate circle within which to celebrate your union.
- Arrange seashells in the shape of a large heart for a wedding at the beach—but be careful to check the tide table.

Keep in mind that all of your ceremony photos will be taken against the backdrop you select or create, so you must be pleased with the appearance of the scene from a variety of angles. You may want to discuss your ideas for decorating the altar space with your photographer in advance.

Where's the Sun?

Worrying about whether the sun will shine at all is a common pastime for those who intend to marry outside. The absence of sun is not the only potential pitfall, however. Sunlight will be your primary source of illumination, and while natural light can be most flattering, your only real influence over the sun's position and intensity is timing.

Outdoor weddings are almost exclusively planned for daylight hours. While most couples choose the time of their wedding based on convenience, travel requirements, and site availability, those planning outdoor celebrations should also carefully consider the location of the sun. At high noon, for example, the sun's light can be harsh and shadows pronounced—not optimal conditions for photography. As the sun rises and sets, it can also cast its intense beams in such a way as to blind you and your guests.

The muted, warm glow of sunrise can provide lovely lighting, but an early morning celebration allows little time for preparation and can result in bleary-eyed, unenthused guests. Sunset, with its rosy purple skies, can provide equally striking illumination without the early wake-up call. Your location will influence your timing decision, too. Water can intensify the sun's glare. A mountain face may appear sharp and majestic when front-lit by morning's rays but hazy and less impressive as the sun falls below its peaks.

Daylight hours and the sun's trajectory vary based on the time of year. If you are planning your special day far enough in advance, your best bet is to visit the site at about the same time of year as your wedding date at the time of day you hope to schedule your event. Try to get a feel for the sun's position, shadow patterns, and intensity of glare under a variety of conditions—full sun, partly cloudy, and overcast. Consult your photographer, too, for tips on when to hold your event at this particular spot.

newlywed know-how

At *www.sunrisesunset.com*, you can determine the exact time of sunrise and sunset for any date at any location in the world, even if you are planning your wedding years in advance. Your free custom sunrise and sunset calendar can also include information on moon phases and twilight and moonrise times.

Seasons Change

There are a few places on Earth where the climate is temperate year-round and the foliage stays relatively static. Most locales, however, experience some degree of seasonal variation. The season you select for your outdoor wedding affects more than weather and temperature conditions. It can have a defining impact on the appearance of the setting and thus requires a bit of deference when it comes to selecting coordinating décor.

Mother Nature, the Ultimate Decorator

Home redecorating reality shows have become popular television fare, but one need only gaze out the window on successive days in most parts of the world to watch one of the best decorators of all time at work on a really big project. Mother Nature has a knack for making subtle yet constant and perceptible changes to the landscape. Of course, she is more ambitious about undertaking major remodeling projects in some regions than others. Any area that experiences four distinct seasons presents the greatest challenges for those arranging an outdoor affair.

Any wedding is best planned a year or more in advance. For an outdoor wedding, it can be critical to get an impression of the site at the exact time of year when you intend to marry there. Take a camera along so that you need not rely on your memory for details about what colors were predominant and which backdrops were most lush. While a beach setting may be mostly blue and beige year-round, it is important not to assume that the lovely rose garden you visited in June will be as abundantly colorful come the dog days of August; the clear, still pond you loved in summer might be choked with leaves and weeds in the fall. When it is impossible to visit the site a year before the wedding, try to see photos taken at close to the same time of year as your expected wedding date.

piece of cake

It's a good idea to visit your wedding site a year in advance to get a sense of seasonal coloration and conditions. You should also make a point of revisiting the venue a month or two before your event to ensure there have been no unexpected changes due to natural or human forces.

As with other elements of the setting that will shape your decorating decisions, the season should be allowed to inspire the colors and types of embellishments you choose. Gravitate toward pastel shades in the spring; feel free to embrace bolder colors when summer blazes; or shift toward a palette of warm, rich tones in the autumn. Be careful to picture decorative elements against the anticipated seasonal backdrop. An arch entwined with vibrant fuchsia flowers might look gorgeous at the florist's but sadly out of place against a landscape painted with the oranges, golds, and reds of fall.

Seasonal Hazards

Mother Nature doesn't always do a very good job of cleaning up after herself when she undertakes a remodeling project. In some places, there are spring days when the whole world seems coated in fine green pollen dust. Come fall, tree debris, including leaves, pinecones, and acorns, can be found scattered far and wide.

While you can't change nature's untidy ways, you can take a few precautions to ensure that guests aren't sitting on sappy seats, picking seed pods out of their hair, or making excuses about why they really don't want a piece of cake. Here are a few strategies to employ for combating seasonal hazards:

- Try to schedule site setup for as close to the time of the ceremony as possible. The longer tables, chairs, and decorations sit outside, the more likely they are to collect an unwanted layer of dirt, sand, or plant material.
- Use tarps or large sheets to protect decorations that must be set up in advance.
- Have the following equipment available, if possible: a rake, power blower, feather duster, long-handled broom, sponges, paper towels, and glass cleaner.
- Be cautious about anything you place under trees, particularly at certain times of the year and if conditions are windy.
- Be particularly careful not to allow your wedding cake and other edibles to sit outside unprotected for a long period of time.

If your chosen site has an on-site grounds manager, be sure to discuss site preparation responsibilities such as who will rake leaves or collect grass clippings. If you'll be left to your own devices to clean up your wedding scene, be sure to enlist the aid of a volunteer brigade that will scout and prepare the property a few hours before your event is slated to commence.

Embracing Natural Elements

From Web sites to catalogs to bridal boutiques, there are plenty of places to shop for favors, decorations, and other miscellaneous wedding supplies. If you want to give your day a one-of-a-kind look, however, nature offers some attractive—and less expensive—alternatives. Though the diversity of items offered by wedding suppliers is impressive these days, natural elements collected from your outdoor wedding site, combined with a bit of your own ingenuity, can help you create an event that is truly distinctive.

Gathering Decorations

What items can you gather from the outdoors to incorporate into your wedding decorating projects? Sand, seashells, starfish, herbs, flowers, petals, stones, leaves, ferns, palm fronds, vines, driftwood, corn stalks, acorns, pinecones, feathers, seeds, berries, and pumpkins are some of the many possibilities. Before you grab a pail and head for the beach or set out into the forest with a collection bag, try to accurately assess just how much natural material your projects and decorating schemes will require.

newlywed know-how

If you are planning your wedding far enough in advance, you can save money on decorations and craft supplies by shopping at post-season sales. Pick up strings of white lights when they are discounted after Christmas. Scoop up deals on faux foliage as fall fades.

Whether you hope to procure materials from your actual wedding site or another outdoor spot, it is important to obtain approval from the property's private owner or to inquire about any regulations against removing objects from a public place. While you're not likely to raise eyebrows if you collect shells at the beach or pick up brilliant autumn leaves that have drifted to the ground, it is another matter entirely to take your pruning shears into a public garden without permission. If you do receive an okay to gather live plant materials, be sure you know correct techniques for clipping and cutting so that you won't cause permanent damage to bushes, plants, and trees.

When creating keepsakes, you may prefer to incorporate artificial rather than natural elements. Craft and party stores stock a variety of outdoor-inspired items such as silk leaves and flowers, plastic fruits, dried herbs, and Styrofoam topiary trees. Whether you intend to search for your decorating and craft supplies indoors or out, remember that different seasons influence not only what nature produces but what stores have in stock. If you need pressed or silk fall leaves for your September wedding, for example, you should shop for them about a year in advance, as you will be hard-pressed to find them in January or even June.

Ten Crafty Ideas

If you have ample time and a bit of artistic talent, do-it-yourself projects are a perfect way to really make your wedding your own creation. There are entire magazines, books, and Web sites devoted to wedding crafts. Here is a sampling of creative ideas that incorporate natural elements to spark your imagination:

1. Use glitter-sprinkled pinecones as place-card holders, or fill bowls with cinnamon-scented pinecones to use as table accents.

2. Write guests' names and table numbers on clamshells with a paint marker.

3. Press leaves or flowers by placing them between sheets of white paper and tucking them into a book. Pile other heavy books on top and allow several days for flattening and drying. Pressed leaves and petals can be glued to placecards, arranged in the shape of a heart inside a glass frame, or laminated to create bookmark favors.

4. Use seasonal foliage and flowers to create garlands to drape along your head table, wrap around tent poles, or festoon your path to the altar.

5. Make colorful centerpieces by using hollowed-out pumpkins as vases. Your best bet is to insert a container inside the pumpkin to hold water or dampened floral foam.

6. For a beach wedding, fill Ball jars two-thirds full with sand tinted with food coloring, and then insert a votive candle in the center. These twinkling sand candles can illuminate walkways at dusk or provide romantic table lighting.

7   Place leaves, ferns, or starfish, textured side up, under paper and use a peeled crayon to create a rubbing. Use these hand-decorated papers as the pages of your guest book, or imprint or inscribe them with your program or menu. This simple technique can also be used to create unique thank-you notes.

8   For garden or floral-themed affairs, create custom seed packets so that guests will be able to cultivate a reminder of your special day. Type "seed packet template" into an online search engine, and you will find several packet designs that can be printed, personalized, folded, and assembled.

9   Create unique favors by purchasing a glycerin soap-making kit at a craft store. You can mold soaps into shapes that complement your theme, such as butterflies, sunflowers, fish, or apples. You can also dip silk rose petals in clear soap or embed seashells or other surprises within clear bars.

10 Dry flowers, herbs, and leaves you collect and make your own signature potpourri. Fill small, decorative boxes or silk bags with the fragrant mix to use as favors, or create centerpieces with potpourri-filled baskets or glass bowls.

If you prefer to work solo, that's fine. Otherwise, plan a fun and sociable afternoon of crafting with a few close friends or family members. Even younger relatives may enjoy helping with basic assembly tasks. This will help make your event a family affair, from start to finish.

The Ceremony

Outdoor spaces offer unparalleled flexibility when it comes to personalizing the ceremony that will unite you in marriage. The words, music, and activities you incorporate can make your service a unique expression of your love as you begin your journey as husband and wife. However, ceremonies conducted outdoors do involve a few logistical considerations. You want to minimize distractions, keep the ceremony focused and fitting for the environment, and ensure that, at the end of the day, you are legally married.

Selecting an Officiant

Do you want your ceremony to be solemn or lighthearted? Deeply personal or basic and simple? Traditional or avant-garde? Choosing the right individual to preside over your celebration can make a huge difference in whether you achieve the tone and spirit you desire.

newlywed know-how

In California, any person may apply for and be granted authorization to perform one civil marriage by being designated a deputy county clerk for a day. Similarly, in Massachusetts, a friend or family member may apply to the governor's office for the one-time authority to perform a marriage ceremony.

Lawfully Wedded

What makes a marriage legal? In the United States, each state and territory establishes its own marriage laws, so you must research the requirements of the specific place in which you plan to exchange vows. The office of the local town or county clerk is your best resource for information on local laws. Individual states' provisions for granting a marriage license differ in a number of key areas, including these:

- Minimum age to marry, with or without parental or judicial consent
- Waiting period between granting of license and formalization of marriage
- Necessity of a blood test or medical exam
- Rights of same-sex couples to wed
- Fees and filing deadlines

A legally recognized marriage requires both an executed license, which represents a legal contract between you and your spouse, and a ceremony. Though the prerequisites and procedures for obtaining a license are standardized at the state level, a ceremony can be just about anything you imagine. The only requirement is that the officiant be authorized to serve in this capacity, whether by state statutes or judicial decree, and that the ceremony is witnessed as dictated by law.

rain or shine

A number of organizations advertise the availability of instant and free online ordination. One of the most active is the Universal Life Church Monastery, found online at *www.ulc.org*. While some states do recognize the rights to perform wedding ceremonies of individuals ordained in this fashion, it is crucial to check local policies. There may be additional requirements; for instance, the celebrant may need to register with the clerk's office.

You must decide at the outset whether you prefer a religious or a civil ceremony. Most states recognize the power of clergy members of all faiths, including rabbis, priests, ministers, pastors, cantors, imams, and shamans, to perform marriage rites. Depending on the state, those permitted to conduct civil ceremonies may include judges, justices of the peace, and court clerks.

Questions to Ask

If you already have a potential officiant in mind, you are at a distinct advantage. It can be difficult to select the person who will perform the rather significant act of joining you in matrimony from a list of names provided by your wedding venue or the town clerk's office. Try to ask around for recommendations if you are starting your officiant search from scratch.

Questions to Ask

Whether you hope to engage the services of someone you have known for years or an individual who is a complete stranger, here are some key questions to ask during your initial interview:

- Are you available for the date and time we have selected? For a rehearsal, as well?

- Are you willing to travel to the outdoor site we have selected?

- What are your fees?

- How many marriages have you performed?

- Will you marry us if we are of different faiths? If one or both of us has been divorced?

- Will we be required to attend premarital classes or counseling?

- What components of the ceremony do you consider to be mandatory?

- Do you have sample ceremonies available for us to review?

- Can we write or select our own vows? What about readings, prayers, sermon, and music?

- Would you be willing to allow others to take part in leading the ceremony?

- Can we schedule a meeting to discuss our wishes with you?

piece of cake

Though only one authorized individual will legalize your marriage by pronouncing you husband and wife and signing your license, there is nothing to preclude you from inviting more than one person to conduct your celebration. Interfaith couples may wish to engage an officiant representing each religion; others might ask eloquent friends or family members to preside over key ceremony components.

A Service That Fits the Setting

As you consider the structure and content of your ceremony, be sure to take the setting into account. Try to match the formality of the proceedings with the overall character of the venue. Just as a simple civil service would seem out of place in a grand cathedral, a theme park is probably not the right atmosphere for a solemn religious service. Be alert, too, for opportunities to select readings and pen vows that reflect the space in which they will be uttered.

Timing Is Everything

Your love will go on and on, but in an outdoor setting, your ceremony shouldn't. Though you have immense latitude in the great outdoors to personalize your event, this does not mean it should feature a marathon recitation of every poem you have ever read to each other, concert-length musical performances, or long-winded speeches. A half hour from processional to recessional is a good goal for outdoor nuptials.

rain or shine

Remember that your guests will have assembled sometime before your grand entrance, so if your ceremony lasts a half hour, their actual time in the sun, wind, or drizzle may be quite a bit longer. As a courtesy to your loved ones, make sure you arrive and begin your outdoor ceremony on time.

There are several reasons that it is advisable to rein in the duration of your outdoor ceremony. For starters, you can't count on optimal weather conditions. Though you may proceed with your outdoor plans if conditions are a bit cool, damp, blustery, or even excessively sunny, asking your captive audience to endure the elements for much more than thirty minutes can lead to widespread discomfort. In addition, by keeping your service brief and focused, you will be able to move things along quickly should you find yourselves in a race against looming storm clouds. It may even be a wise idea to tell your officiant which readings or song selections can be skipped if you need to cut your ceremony short.

Readings and Rituals

As you consider the readings and traditions you will weave into your wedding, your location may provide inspiration. If the fields, shores, or mountains where you will marry were once the domain of native peoples, for example, you may want to incorporate Native American prayers, stories, or customs into your celebration. Consider the writings of any notable individuals associated with the property as you search for compelling thoughts to share with guests. Books or Web sites that index religious texts and secular quotations can be used to identify passages related to your setting or theme.

Your unique outdoor wedding location may also inspire you to invent a ritual of your own. Here are some suggestions to jump-start your brainstorming:

- Arrange to purchase and donate a tree or flowering perennial to be planted at your wedding site, and ask representatives from each of your families to participate in a planting ceremony.
- While guests await your arrival for a beach wedding, invite them to take turns scooping colored sand into a large fishbowl, creating a one-of-a-kind wedding day keepsake for your mantel or curio cabinet.
- For a fall wedding, furnish guests with bags of pressed fall leaves instead of rice or birdseed to toss in the air as you are pronounced husband and wife.

- If postcards depicting the site are available, provide each guest with a stamped card addressed to the two of you. As they anticipate your arrival, guests can jot down their advice or warm wishes for your married life. Ask them to mail the postcards when they return home, and your mailbox will be filled with a wonderful collection of souvenirs when you return from your honeymoon.

Writing Your Own Vows

More and more couples are pledging their love in words of their own. If you decide to write your own vows, your primary aim should be to express your deepest feelings and your love for your chosen partner. If you have selected your wedding site for private reasons, your personal vows may provide an opportunity to enlighten guests as to the special meaning this place holds.

piece of cake

Write your vows on paper. Do not rely on your memory, no matter how well you think you've memorized them. It'll boost your confidence to have those precious words on a slip of paper in your pocket, just in case. Practice reciting them before the big day, and be sure your officiant has the opportunity to review and okay your vows in advance.

You might begin your vows like this, for example: "Here, in this place where our eyes first met, I promise to always see and appreciate you in new ways." If the site did not play a role in the development of your romantic relationship, it might still inspire your expression of commitment, as you promise that your love is as deep as the ocean, as perennial as the grass, or as tender as a butterfly's wings. You might want to visit your wedding site with a notebook and pen and jot down thoughts and phrases about love and life that occur to you in this space. Arriving at just the right language to convey your emotions requires time and patience, but the result will be a moving and heartfelt pledge that your beloved will always cherish.

Keeping the Focus on You

Short of seating guests so that their back is to the view or situating your proceedings away from the most scenic vistas, how can you keep everyone's attention focused on you? The best defense against visual distractions is a good offense. A ceremony that is compelling, entertaining, and visually stunning in its own right will ensure an engaged audience.

There is no hard-and-fast rule that says a bride and groom must stand front and center with their backs turned to the assemblage for the entire ceremony. Build in opportunities to turn around, move about, and interact with guests. Don't be afraid to inject lighthearted, laughter-inducing moments or to choose lively, up-tempo tunes. This is, after all, a joyous occasion in a glorious location and a prelude to the merrymaking that will ensue once the formalities have concluded.

Remember, too, that guests aren't the only potentially guilty parties when it comes to being distracted by spectacular surroundings. Concentrate on the ceremony, and make a concerted effort not to look away every time a wave crashes or a bird swoops overhead.

Not every second of a wedding ceremony needs to be filled with words and music. Strategically schedule moments of silence during which you and your loved ones can simply soak up the sights and sounds. Rather than segueing directly into your ceremony after your processional, you may want to plan a hand-in-hand stroll to greet guests and appreciate the visual splendor. Then, when it is time to begin, you will feel less overwhelmed and better able to focus on the business at hand—marrying the person of your dreams.

Sound Issues

Even within houses of worship, where the acoustics are usually excellent, a bride or groom's vows can sometimes be inaudible to all but the guests seated in the first few rows. Outdoors, where your voice can be carried away by the wind or drowned out by the din of surf, birds, shouting children, or passing traffic, the risk of your ceremony being seen and not heard is even greater. As you consider whether to amplify your ceremony, take into account the size of your gathering, the potential for sound interference, and the vocal ability of anyone who will deliver key portions of your ceremony, including the two of you. Remember that even if you are able to project your voice with confidence in most situations, your wedding day may cause a few nerves and emotions to bubble up, leaving you less articulate than usual.

There are some definite benefits to using a sound system. When you have worked diligently to make your ceremony individual and meaningful, it is important that your words can be heard. However, there are also a few potential drawbacks to amplifying your event. Chief among them is that anyone who will speak will probably need to wear a clip-on microphone, and with some attire, particularly bridal gowns, there is often no ideal place to conceal a mike. Also, your every word will be audible from the moment your microphone and the sound system are switched on, so you will need to watch what you say, as even your private whispers may be broadcast loud and clear.

If you decide that amplification is for you, start by asking your host site about the availability of sound equipment. Some venues that cater to outdoor weddings have already outfitted gazebos with microphones or have a public address system available for use. If you have hired a professional videographer, he may already plan to wire you for sound. Check to see if his equipment can be connected to external speakers, as well. Your DJ may also be planning to employ sound equipment that can serve a dual role.

newlywed know-how

If you decide to hold your event without amplification equipment, you may want to print the full text of your ceremony, including vows, readings, and prayers, in your wedding program so that guests can follow along and understand the proceedings in case they can't hear every word.

Even if electrical power is readily available at your ceremony site, you may want to avoid the hazard and unsightly appearance of tangled electrical cords. A battery-powered, portable, wireless microphone system may be the optimum solution. Check with local rental centers or call a professional sound company for a price quote. Be sure to test equipment at a rehearsal prior to your wedding day if at all possible.

If roaring winds, booming thunder, speeding powerboats, or other noisemakers render it difficult for guests to hear your ceremony with or without amplification, try to mask your frustration with good humor. Even under optimal circumstances, few guests will recall the actual words that were spoken on your wedding day. What they *will* remember, however, is the love you exhibited and the feelings evoked by your laughter and your joyful smiles.

Music

Music has unparalleled power to move and to set a mood. Whether your ceremony is accompanied by light and airy woodwinds, bold brass, classic strings, lively fiddles, or even recorded selections, music can be one of the most uplifting and memorable aspects of your special day. Before you burn a CD or book an ensemble, though, there are a few things you should know about music played or performed in the outdoors. Selecting songs that blend well with the overall ambiance you are seeking to create is also key to making the most of your ceremony's musical interludes.

Live or Recorded?

Most wedding ceremonies incorporate music in some form, whether it is gentle background melodies played as guests arrive, an attention-grabbing processional march, a tear-producing romantic song, a rousing recessional, or all of the above. Once you have affirmed that you indeed want music to be part of your celebration, your first decision is whether to use live or recorded tunes. In an outdoor setting, each option offers both advantages and disadvantages.

rain or shine

If you plan to play ceremony music on a portable stereo or boom box, be sure you have extra batteries on hand. Even if electrical outlets are available near your ceremony site, it is wise to have a set of batteries as a backup.

Live music is usually perceived as a classy choice, but like any elegant touch, it comes at a price. As a rule, the larger the ensemble and the more professional the caliber of musicians, the more you will pay for their services. Still, if you can afford live musical accompaniment, you will be treating yourselves and your guests to a performance that is guaranteed to be one of a kind. Professional musicians know how to match a song's tempo, volume, and duration to your proceedings and can usually make adjustments on the fly; it can be rather awkward when your recorded version of "Here Comes the Bride" ends while you are still only halfway down the aisle.

What canned music lacks in adaptability, it makes up for in cost savings and in the sheer variety of musical selections from which you can choose. Certain instruments, such as an organ, are impractical in most outdoor settings, but you can have the booming rendition of the traditional "Wedding March" you've dreamed of by using a recording. In fact, you can feature quiet strings as a prelude, a jazz march as a processional, a gospel hymn as a musical interlude, and a trumpet fanfare as your recessional if you'd like, all for the cost of a few CDs. Keep in mind that you need to check with your host site about any restrictions on playing music and on volume levels.

Instrumentation

You may not have experience selecting and booking musicians, so if you do opt to splurge on live music for your outdoor affair, there are a few things you should know. For starters, in the outdoors, some instruments can be heard better than others, particularly when they will have to compete head-on with natural noises such as pounding surf. In general, higher-pitched instruments such as the flute, trumpet, or violin can rise above ambient sounds better than the lower tones of a bass clarinet, French horn, or cello. Some instruments, such as an electric keyboard, will require a power source. Others, such as a harp, may be lovely but simply too bulky to transport to your ceremony site if drive-up access is unavailable. Here are a few of the best music choices and combinations for a wedding outdoors:

- Bagpipes
- Classical guitar
- Flute and violin duo
- Recorder or wooden flute ensemble
- String quartet
- Violinist or fiddler
- Pair of trumpeters
- Single vocalist

Most musicians who regularly play at weddings can cover all the standards. Ask for a list of the soloist's or ensemble's repertoire from which you can make selections. If there is a special song you really want to include, you may need to pay an arranger to write the sheet music. Be sure to allow ample time following special requests for the group or individual to rehearse important numbers.

piece of cake

Even a slight breeze can send sheet music flying. While most experienced musicians who accept outdoor engagements are prepared to handle this potential problem, it wouldn't hurt to include a bag of clothespins in your wedding-day emergency kit (details on page 247).

Be sure to communicate with potential performers about the exact conditions under which they will be expected to play. Some instruments don't fare well in direct sunlight or misty rain. Some are difficult to play when cold air makes fingers numb, and some are tricky to keep in tune when the air is thick with humidity. Read the musicians' contract carefully so that you understand any conditions under which they might not play.

Song Selection

The musical compositions you choose to feature preceding, during, and immediately after your ceremony are primarily a matter of personal choice. Though some religious facilities have rules about the music that can be played at weddings, you aren't likely to encounter any such restrictions in an outdoor environment. Still, song selections should be made with a few things in mind.

Try to select songs that synchronize with the overall tone and theme of your event. Even if you think you know a song well, listen again, paying particular attention to all of the lyrics, before you decide to include it in your play list. Even though anything goes musically in an outdoor space, you still want your choices to be tasteful and to convey an appropriate message. As you evaluate possible song choices, think beyond the words, too, and assess the feelings each selection is likely to elicit.

Once you have narrowed the list of possibilities, there are a few other practical considerations. Time the music, and try to keep all selections to a reasonable length. Remember, you want your ceremony to be relatively brief, so you may need to cut a few verses or opt for abridged song versions. Also, if you have hired a live ensemble to perform, try to match selections to the available instrumentation. No matter how valiantly he tries, your bagpiper isn't going to pull off either Pachelbel's *Canon* or Aerosmith's "I Don't Want to Miss a Thing."

Involving Guests

The most memorable weddings are those at which guests feel like more than a placecard at table number eight. Though the reception is traditionally a time when guests can get up and take an active role in the celebration, there are also many ways in which they can bless a couple with more than their presence during the ceremony portion of the proceedings. As you plan your ceremony, look for opportunities for your loved ones to be participants, rather than merely spectators.

Evoke Emotions

Weddings are emotional events for the bride and groom and their immediate families. Whatever you are feeling, one of the most intimate ways to draw guests into your ceremony is to express your emotions openly. If you allow laughter, tears, smiles, and loving words to flow without reservation, those who surround you will be able to sense the unique vibe that surrounds your union. In addition to music, vows, and rings, your ceremony might incorporate elements of storytelling that convey the singular aspects of your romance. This is true whether the two of you have endured many hardships or whether you both knew you were destined for this day at the outset. Even guests who have followed your saga intently will enjoy hearing a retelling of your love story as you prepare to embark on this new phase of your lives together.

Though your predominant emotions are likely to be joy, love, and excitement, some weddings can be tinged with a hint of sorrow if a close loved one is absent. The care and affection of those who *are* in attendance can help to assuage your sadness if you do experience some mixed emotions. Invite guests to join you in a moment of silence, a prayer, a candle-lighting, or another symbolic remembrance of those who could not be with you.

Ways Guests Can Participate

In addition to sharing in the sentiments of the day, there are many other ways in which guests can become active ceremony participants. Some are rather traditional, such as singing, reciting prayers or poems in unison, or participating in responsive readings. If you would like guests to speak or sing, include the text or lyrics in your wedding program.

ask the wedding planner ?

How can you involve children?

If you have children, either together or from a previous relationship, your ceremony might include a special vow in which you both promise to love and support them. Some couples choose to present each child with a ring or other token symbolizing the new family that has been created and the promises made on this day.

In an outdoor setting, you also have the freedom to involve guests in creative ways. For example, rather than asking them to simply sit and watch, why not include everyone in a lively musical processional to your wedding site? During the ceremony, ask guests to join hands, share memories, ring bells, or play handheld instruments such as tambourines, triangles, and wood blocks to accompany your instrumental ensemble or recorded musical selections. At the conclusion of your ceremony, guests might release butterflies or simply applaud wildly. Rather than setting up a traditional receiving line or vanishing for a photo session, head off hand-in-hand to the reception location, inviting the crowd to follow you as your recessional plays and the party gets immediately underway.

11

Outdoor Receptions

Many outdoor weddings are actually hybrids. They begin with an outdoor ceremony, which is perhaps followed by a cocktail hour on the patio, by the pool, in the garden, or out on the lawn. At some point, however, everyone moves indoors to enjoy a meal, dancing, and other festivities. Any outdoor component of your celebration adds a layer of complexity. Those who face the greatest challenges of all choose to hold their entire event, including the reception, outdoors.

Shelter

Unless you are willing to move your entire event to an alternate, indoor location at the slightest hint of bad weather, outdoor receptions require the availability of some type of on-site shelter. While your ceremony might last only thirty minutes, your reception is likely to be going strong for four hours or more. That prolonged exposure to possible adverse environmental effects necessitates making provisions to protect people, equipment, gifts, and food.

Temporary Shelter

Weather forecasting is an imprecise science, and summer days can be especially unpredictable. Sometimes, they start out hot and hazy. Then, a sudden, violent thunderstorm rolls through without warning, and twenty minutes later, the air is fresh, skies are blue, and a rainbow appears.

The first vow couples who plan to marry outside must make is to be prepared for anything, and that includes a sudden but short-lived shower. If it's only your ceremony that will take place outside, you can always figure that folks will flee to their vehicles or huddle under umbrellas in the event of an unheralded downpour. However, there are many more concerns when you have set up your entire party in an outdoor venue. For example, you definitely do not want to leave your wedding cake out in the rain.

piece of cake

Buy a case of paper towels, and ask a responsible friend or family member to transport it to the site. You will be glad for this abundant supply if a passing shower leaves chairs and tables wet and your dance floor slick with precipitation.

Ideally, the site you have selected will offer some type of covered or enclosed space for waiting out a storm. Hopefully, that same space can provide temporary storage for sound, video, and other electrical equipment; musical instruments; gifts; prepared food items; linens; paper goods; and anything else that might be irreparably damaged when drenched. It must be located close enough to your ceremony site that items can be whisked indoors quickly in the event skies start to darken and winds begin to howl. Be sure that the facility will be unlocked and accessible and that all of your vendors and bad-weather helpers are aware of its availability and location.

If there is no built-in cover, it is critical to find out whether you can erect your own tent or other shelter. Even if you do not wish to make use of a large tent that can accommodate the entire gathering, a small tent, canopy, or gazebo should be positioned on site so that some protection is available for the most sensitive items. If pitching a tent is impossible, you may want to arrange to rent and park a moving truck or small RV nearby to serve as a temporary storage area if the need arises.

Under Cover in the Great Outdoors

If you really want to embrace the atmosphere of the outdoors from start to finish but are a bit apprehensive, there is a compromise solution that presents minimal risk. Find a location that offers a covered outdoor space. Possibilities include these options:

- An awning-protected patio
- An open-sided porch, deck, or verandah with a roof
- A pavilion
- A permanent tent with flaps that can be removed or a site that would accommodate such a tent
- A restaurant with a sheltered outdoor seating area
- A covered bridge that is closed to vehicular traffic
- A barn with large sliding doors

With a roof over your heads, you will have less fear of a washout, but without walls, nature's sensory delights will still color your celebration. As you make a determination about how many invitees a covered space can accommodate, keep in mind that you will want to maintain a buffer zone of at least three to five feet around the perimeter of the covered space. This will protect those seated around the outer edge in the event that wind accompanies any rain.

Restroom Facilities

If you will remain outdoors for your entire event, even the bride will need to heed the call of nature at some point. That means a port-a-potty or two just might not do. Few couples choose an outdoor wedding location based on the quality of its restrooms, but if your site does offer facilities of some sort, you are at a distinct advantage. Otherwise, you will need to consider your rental options. Either way, it is important to do some advance thinking about this very practical matter.

Comfort and Convenience

When it comes to comfort, if you happen to have selected an outdoor venue that has indoor, air-conditioned, handicapped-accessible restrooms with several stalls each for men and women, you've got it made. If you didn't visit the facilities at the time you booked your date or did but can't recall what they were like, make a point of scheduling a time when the two of you can make another site visit to inspect both the men's and women's rooms. Also ask the manager of the property how often restrooms are cleaned and whether someone will be on duty to touch up and restock the restrooms during your event.

Unfortunately, many outdoor locations have facilities that are somewhat more primitive, if they have them at all. If a reasonably nice restroom building is available but it is not climate-controlled, you may want to check for the availability of electricity and consider procuring several oscillating stand fans to help keep the air circulating. If the site's facilities are more along the lines of portable toilets, you will need to determine whether they can be cleaned just prior to your event and what their condition is likely to be if the weather has been rainy or extraordinarily warm.

rain or shine

If the property has restrooms, but they are not within walking distance of your reception location, you may want to evaluate the cost of renting a golf cart to shuttle guests against the cost of renting close-by portable toilets.

If available facilities are limited, nonexistent, unattractive, or very distant, you will likely need to rent portable units. At the top of the line are mobile restrooms housed in trailers. Though more expensive than traditional port-a-potties, this option will eliminate the sensation of roughing it. Most mobile restrooms can be powered by a generator and can carry their own water tanks if these utilities are not available on-site. If you opt for more traditional portable toilets, you may want to order a wheelchair-accessible version, not only to accommodate any physically handicapped guests but to provide more interior space for the bride if she is wearing a full skirt and will need some assistance.

When it comes to choosing a location for your rental restrooms, it is important to consider both convenience and aesthetics. Toilets should be positioned on level ground in a shaded area. While they should be close enough that guests can find and reach them easily, be careful that they are not too prominently visible, as you don't want them to show up in the background of all of your first-dance photos, for example. Also be sure not to locate port-a-potties anywhere near where food will be prepared or served.

Keep It Clean

While on-site and mobile restrooms are usually equipped with sinks and soap, if you are renting port-a-potties, you will need to offer guests some means of cleaning up after they use the facilities. Some rental companies also offer hand-wash stations equipped with water tanks and sinks, which may be worth the added cost. Compare this expense to the price of choosing upgraded toilet chambers that have sinks and even flushing capabilities. At bare minimum, set up a small card table near the restrooms and stock it with wet wipes, antibacterial hand soap, lotion, and other toiletries.

It is important to assign someone to monitor the cleanliness of your sanitary station throughout your event. If you will be using the property's restrooms, ask if there will be a maintenance person on duty to handle periodic inspections and any necessary cleanups. If not, perhaps you can sweet-talk a sibling or school buddy who owes you one into volunteering for this somewhat unsavory task. Be sure to stock an easy-to-carry bucket or basket with cleaning supplies that might be required. If you are uncomfortable with the notion of asking someone to do you this favor, consider calling a home cleaning service to see if you might hire someone to perform this job during your event.

An Intimate Atmosphere

While some outdoor spaces have been cultivated to be cozy, others are vast, open expanses. If you have chosen a wild and natural place, how will you create an atmosphere of intimacy for your celebration? The good news is that outdoor weddings are part of a larger trend. The popularity of outdoor living and entertaining has escalated in recent years, and the result is that creative ideas for shaping and utilizing outdoors spaces abound.

Defining the Space

Some outdoor spaces have defining boundaries. A hedge might enclose a garden. A fence might ring a farmyard. A stone patio runs the length of the home it backs, or a big deck overlooking the cliffs and sea.

newlywed know-how

Just as a fireplace can be the central focal point of an indoor room, a clay chiminea or fire pot made for use outside can serve this role, adding the warm glow of a hearth to your outdoor dining environment. Be sure to check with the site manager, though, to ensure that a fire is permitted.

If instead you have chosen a seemingly endless hilltop, field, beach, lawn, or parkland as your wedding site, your first challenge is to decide exactly how much space you will use. Measure it off, and make yourselves a makeshift blueprint. Then, begin to visualize how you will define the perimeter or at least the four corners of the territory you intend to utilize as your reception space. Here are some possibilities:

- Lighting, such as luminaries, torches, citronella candles, pathway lights, paper lanterns, tube lights, tea lights, colored floodlights, strings of themed patio lights, or even a curtain of lights
- Foliage, including potted plants, trees, shrubs, topiaries, or flowers, or natural garlands strung between posts
- Functional structures, such as the bar, the buffet table, or the bandstand.
- Decorative structures such as benches, fountains, pedestals topped with floral arrangements, an entranceway arch, a trellis, a folding screen, garden statuary, or even a gallery of photos or art displayed on easels
- Curtains made of sheer fabric, tulle, beads, or other materials and suspended from a clothesline draped between trees or posts
- Ground coverings, such as sisal rugs, canvas floor cloths, or synthetic grass

There are many books, magazine articles, Web sites, and television programs focused on outdoor entertaining and creation of an "outdoor room." Turn to them for inspiration as you brainstorm ways to give your setting the feel of a contained environment, in spite of the fact that it has no real ceiling or walls. Though the boundaries you create will be more illusionary than concrete, they will help to create a sense of unity and togetherness that would otherwise be lost in a large, open space.

A Shared Experience

While there are physical ways to define a space, there are also less concrete means of achieving a sense of intimacy. Any place can become memorable due to the people who gather and the events that transpire there. Particularly if your budget for outdoor decorating is limited, you may want to focus on creating a sense of togetherness through shared experience.

If you have written your own vows and created a unique marriage ceremony, you have already taken a first step toward drawing guests into a special world where your love is showcased and celebrated. That mood can continue as you segue into your reception. Words and music have the power to move people, and they can be wonderful tools for creating moments of shared joy, love, and laughter. In addition to the traditional best man's toast and newlyweds' first dance, think of ways that you can engage your loved ones through other speeches, toasts, songs, and dances that will touch funny bones, stir emotions, or get everyone up and on the dance floor.

During a wedding ceremony, the lighting of a unity candle by the bride and groom or by representatives of their families is sometimes employed as a symbol of two families coming together. Sadly, at many receptions, the families still sit on opposite sides of the dance floor and hardly intermingle. You can increase the intimacy quotient of your event substantially by providing guests with reasons and opportunities to bond.

At small gatherings, make a point of taking time to formally introduce each guest and to say a few words about their relation to you. At larger gatherings, purposefully dispense with the notion of bride's and groom's sides and consider scheduling a formal, five-minute portion of your reception program during which guests are encouraged to introduce themselves to those at neighboring tables. Consider square dancing, contra dancing, or country line dancing as part of your entertainment line-up, as these forms of dance are fun for all and encourage guests to branch out, rather than only dancing with their usual partner. Involve all guests in creating a memorable keepsake by decorating blank quilt squares with fabric markers and displaying their creations on a table or tarp so that everyone can view the diverse designs. Or create leaf, apple, or other paper cutouts with each guest's name inscribed, and ask them to hang them from a mural-size tree, indicating their position in your new family.

Music and Dancing

Opportunities to go out dancing are few and far between for most folks these days. For those who love to dance, a wedding invitation is often a welcome chance to kick up their heels. While music and dancing certainly aren't mandatory at wedding receptions, they add energy and fun to the occasion. That means it is definitely worthwhile to include dancing in your plans, even if you have to rent a floor and don't have a place to hang a disco ball.

Where Shall We Dance?

Deciding where the dancing will occur is a trickier proposition than you might initially expect. For starters, you will need a smooth, flat, supportive, unblemished surface. You will likely have to rule out most ground coverings that already exist on site. Any cracks between deck boards or patio stones are an invitation for someone to catch a heel and trip. Soft, uneven ground can lead to twisted ankles, and recent rain and poor drainage can combine to create a slick and unsafe surface.

ask the wedding planner ?

Should we plan to dance on the lawn?

Not unless you own the lawn and don't mind having to re-seed after your event. Lawn dancing is likely to do significant damage to grass and thus is not likely to be permitted by your outdoor venue.

The best option for most outdoor locations is to rent a portable dance floor. While someone handy might be able to construct a suitable surface using durable interlocking floor panels or old-fashioned plywood on a frame of 2' x 4's, you will then need to concern yourselves with transporting the floor and on-site assembly and tear-down, not to mention that you will also own a dance floor that you might not ever use again. Dance floors in a variety of sizes and configurations are available from most rental companies. As a frame of reference, an 18' x 16' dance floor would accommodate a party of about 100 guests. Keep in mind that musicians may want to set up on the dance floor, so you may need additional space.

When deciding on the location for your dance floor, there are a few other factors to consider. If you will be hiring a DJ or will be dancing into the evening and require lighting, you will need access to a power source. While dance floors are often centrally located at indoor weddings, you may want to situate the dance space so that it has a wonderful view. Keep in mind that acoustics are different in the outdoors, where sound tends to dissipate faster. That means sound may not carry far without amplification, which could impact your decision about where the dance floor should be placed in relation to seating.

Choosing Reception Music

From a DJ spinning hits of the '80s and '90s to the Big Band sound of classic swing dance numbers, to a small combo enthusiastically belting out the familiar strains of the Chicken Dance, the music you choose for your wedding reception can take many forms. The musical style you select should reflect your event's setting, its level of sophistication, the age range of guests, and your personal tastes and preferences. Keep in mind that the dance segment will be one of the guests' final impressions of your event, so decide up front if you want them waltzing off or brushing themselves off as they stumble out of the mosh pit.

newlywed know-how

Whether you opt for a band or a DJ, do your homework. Call references, and if possible, see them in action at another wedding or party. That way, in addition to having a sense of their sound, you'll see how they interact with an audience and keep a party flowing.

The first decision you will face is whether to go with a DJ or live band. Both can provide suitable musical accompaniment for an outdoor affair, and each has its pros and cons. A DJ has an incredible assortment of tunes at his fingertips that cross many musical genres, offering the possibility for infinite musical variety. Most also serve as your master of ceremonies for the evening and can coax reluctant onlookers onto the dance floor. Furthermore, a DJ is less expensive, takes up less space, offers musical consistency and predictability, can easily comply with requests to turn the volume up or down, and can play music throughout your reception without a break.

In contrast, a live band may have a limited repertoire, may struggle with requested numbers that don't fit the group's usual style, will take breaks, and will definitely cost you more money and a few additional meals. Still, nothing quite beats a band of talented musicians that performs together regularly and really knows how to entertain a crowd. Live music can make an occasion extraordinary, and it's often well worth the extra expense.

The songs that you select for the reception will be influenced somewhat by your choice of music providers. Most couples prefer that soft background music be played during the dining portion of the reception, with the volume and tempo increasing after the cake is cut. Keep in mind that your host site may have restrictions on how high the decibel level can go.

If your party is heavily themed, you may want to carry that thread through to the musical entertainment. A wedding at a ranch could feature a country-and-western band or a DJ with a large selection of country favorites, while a beach wedding might engage a steel drum or calypso band to lend a tropical island sound. If you aren't in theme mode, musical versatility is an admirable goal. The greater the variety of styles and tempos you offer, the more likely it is that everyone will get out on the dance floor before the evening is through.

In addition to selecting a first dance song, most couples also have other requests for special dances, such as the bride's dance with her father or a special slow dance for all married couples. Determining whether the ensemble or DJ you have selected can cater to your desire to hear particular songs played in the way you'd like to hear them performed should be a major part of your decision. Some couples take a carefree approach to the rest of the music that will fill their reception, trusting the band or DJ to keep the party going. Others feel strongly about scripting their wedding-day soundtrack from start to finish.

rain or shine

Some brides and grooms get so caught up in creating a playlist for their band or DJ that they forget something equally important—a don't-play list. If there are songs or artists that dredge up unpleasant memories of former loves, that you think are overplayed, or that simply annoy you, be sure to make your feelings known ahead of time.

Whatever your inclination, be sure that your DJ or band is clear about your wishes and familiar with the outdoor environment in which music will be played. If you plan to let go of the musical reins, you should still provide as much detail as possible about the event you are designing so that the performers can make appropriate selections. If you have distinct musical tastes, be sure you have hired a music provider who is happy to take your requests.

As the Party Heats Up

Dancing tends to be the final chapter in a wedding-day story, so by the time the band or DJ starts to play, the sun may have dropped in the sky and temperatures and humidity may have eased. That's not always the case, though. Even if conditions were tolerable during the ceremony and meal, once guests start to dance, they will really feel the effects of heat and mugginess.

Dancing is vigorous exercise, and as such, it is important to make sure that guests warm up gradually, stay well hydrated, and take breaks. Talk to your band or DJ about starting the dancing off slowly and reserving those up-tempo disco or salsa numbers for after everyone has limbered up. Alcohol is dehydrating, so be sure to have plenty of cold, nonalcoholic beverages readily available near the dance floor. While bands usually take breaks, a DJ may be in the habit of spinning tunes continuously. You may want to discuss incorporating a few intermissions that allow dancers to take a short breather, particularly when conditions are steamy.

When Darkness Falls

Unless you plan to marry in the morning and wrap up your reception by midafternoon, you should be ready for your party to continue after dark. While lovely, starlight and moonlight are neither powerful nor reliable enough to allow your party to go on once the sun has set. Essentially, there are two choices. You must either end your event with plenty of daylight still lingering to allow for site cleanup and everyone's safe departure, or you must ensure the site is adequately illuminated by artificial means.

Have an Ending Time in Mind

As you map out the timeline for your day, it is important to have not only a start time but an ending time in mind. You may determine the party's end based on several factors. Some venues have strict rules about either a curfew or a maximum duration for your event, which will make it easy for you to set an ending time. Others offer a standard five-hour package but will allow you to buy additional hours on request. Still others give you open-ended access to the site for the day.

If the length and lateness of your celebration are in your hands, first consider your budget. In addition to any extra site usage fees, you will have to provide some form of refreshments and entertainment throughout the event and may want your photographer to be present for the duration, as well. Next, take into account the crowd that will be attending. If there will be many young single people, your party has a better chance of staying lively late into the night than if the cast is composed mainly of aunts, uncles, and married folks with kids at home. Think, too, about your own schedule and whether an evening event is what you had envisioned. If you will be departing for your honeymoon on an early flight the next morning or seeing everyone one last time at a post-wedding brunch, you may be just as happy to wrap up your wedding early and allow yourselves time to unwind and share some private time.

newlywed know-how

Sunset is followed by a period known as civil twilight, during which there is still ample natural illumination to continue outdoor activities. In the continental United States, civil twilight goes on for thirty to sixty minutes after sunset, depending on the location and season, with summer offering the longest twilight window.

Light Up the Night

If you have decided that you do indeed want your party to last into the night, it is time to plot your lighting strategy. You need to keep two goals in mind. First, you must have ample illumination available so that the celebration can continue comfortably. Second, you must light the way back to the parking area so that your guests can return to their cars without mishap.

Start by asking the property manager at your reception site whether any outdoor lighting is available. If the venue regularly hosts evening events, you may receive an encouraging response. If the site does not own lighting equipment, you may at least obtain the names of rental or lighting specialty companies that have worked on site in the past.

For your party to continue past nightfall, you don't need stadium-quality towers of light. You do, however, need enough brightness so that conversations can continue across dinner tables, dancers can see their partners, and revelers can still find their way to the restrooms. A company that is experienced in lighting design can offer you the best menu of options, which may include battery-powered flood lights mounted in trees to light your dance floor and the path to the port-a-potties, or strings of clear lights that mark walkways and add a festive twinkle wherever they are strung. For tabletops, consider metal lanterns or hurricane lamps powered by long-burning candles or lamp oil. You may also want to consider fun lighting touches, such as suspended paper lanterns, a tabletop disco ball, strobe lights, police beacons spinning atop portable toilets, or glow necklaces.

piece of cake

For an outdoor wedding that will last into the evening, custom-imprinted flashlights make great party favors. You can order flashlights featuring your names and the location and date from a promotional products store. While keychain flashlights may be fun, you might want to choose something a bit more powerful and practical.

Because safety is at stake, lighting the path by which guests will exit is an even more important consideration. If your wedding site regularly hosts nighttime functions, chances are good that walkways and the parking lot are already adequately illuminated, but be sure to ask rather than assume. Better yet, visit the property on a very dark night to evaluate the lighting situation yourselves. If you will need to light the way, consider lining the path with luminaries or solar-powered garden lights, and keep in mind that the task of positioning them must be completed before sunlight fades. Marking the edge of the exit path still may not provide adequate light, so you may also need to provide all guests or a few volunteer escorts with heavy-duty flashlights or something fun, but functional, such as an illuminated umbrella.

Bringing the Outdoors In

An outdoor reception isn't for everyone. If you decide to play it safe and host the party portion of your event inside or under a tent, you needn't feel as though you have compromised on your dream of an outdoor wedding. To make the transition from outdoors to indoors less abrupt, you may want to consider using an interior decorating scheme that mimics the ambiance of the outdoors.

newlywed know-how

The more elaborate your ideas for décor, the more helpful it may be to engage the services of a professional bridal consultant or event planner. The Association of Bridal Consultants maintains a geographical directory of wedding professionals (on the Web at *www.bridalassn.com*). Be sure to check references and see samples of the consultant's work before signing a contract.

There are many creative ways to bring the outdoors in. Use copious quantities of fresh flowers indoors following a garden ceremony. Scatter hay on the floor and post scarecrow greeters at the door if you move to the barn after marrying in a field. Decorate with miniature palms, hibiscus, or other tropical flowers, seashells, and maybe even a sandbox that holds buried treasure when you move from the beach to a sheltered reception site. Use slide projectors to cast images of the outside onto the plain white walls of a tent or hall.

12

Catering Considerations

Food just seems to taste better when consumed in the great outdoors. However, cooking under open skies can present some culinary challenges, particularly if you envision a meal more elaborate than burgers and dogs. Finding a talented and experienced caterer and selecting a suitable menu are two undertakings that deserve your serious attention. Food, after all, is the one component of your celebration that will be enjoyed by all. Nothing makes an occasion universally memorable and festive quite like bountiful, delicious cuisine.

Dining Al Fresco

Open air dining can be lovely, but it can also be fraught with potential perils. As you make a decision about whether to host all or part of your reception outdoors, consider both the benefits and drawbacks of dining al fresco. Planning and foresight are essential to ensuring that guests will enjoy their hors d'oeuvres or meal with a view.

Outdoor Dining Delights

When you have selected a beautiful location for your wedding ceremony, you may feel compelled to take advantage of its scenic majesty for more of your celebration than just the ceremony. Of course, the moment you are pronounced husband and wife, the majority of guests will have one thing on their minds— food. Serving cocktails and appetizers outside allows you to get the party off to an immediate start. If you also choose to hold your entire reception in the same open space, you will truly establish your event as distinctive. A picnic in the park, a luncheon in the garden, a clambake at the beach, or a pig roast in the backyard will seem a treat to guests accustomed to the typical fare served at most wedding receptions.

Fresh air has a way of boosting the appetite, and dining outdoors on a warm, sunny day is an enjoyable, relaxing, and social experience. You will find that guests seated at outdoor tables feel less chained to their assigned spots and will mingle more freely. If you are hoping to create an atmosphere of casual fun,

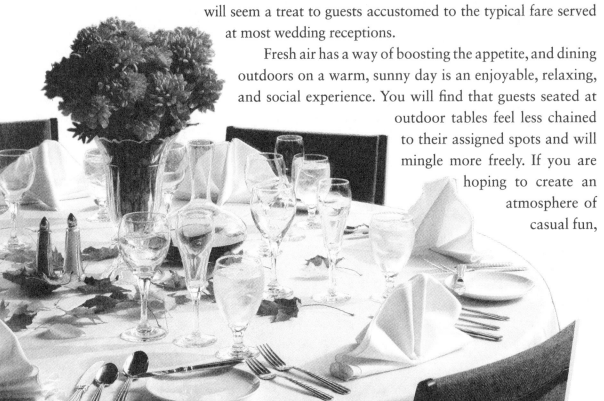

remaining outdoors for your meal can foster this sense of lightheartedness. Though some upscale indoor receptions feature theatrical lighting effects, you can't achieve a prettier look than that provided free of charge by the sun as it sparkles off vases, china, and crystal.

Outdoor Dining Disasters

What's not to love about the prospect of celebrating your union with an outdoor feast? For starters, the success of your event becomes even more weather dependent. It is not nearly as much fun to dine outside when it is cool or rainy. Your next big worry is whether you'll be sharing your meal with unwelcome guests like ants, flies, and seagulls. It is important to assess the likelihood that hungry and aggressive outdoor pests will intrude on your meal.

rain or shine

Don't be tempted to cut costs by opting for paper plates. Even disposable plates made of sturdier Styrofoam or plastic are prone to leaks, breakage, and spills. Rent china, use plates that you own or can borrow, or acquire a lovely if eclectic mix of pieces at flea markets and yard sales.

Protecting your spread from the elements will be a key concern, as you won't want to discover seed pods in the punch bowl or a layer of sand coating the paté. Wind not only can kick up dust and sand clouds, it may even topple tables if it really gets gusty. Heat and cold can both make it challenging for your caterer to maintain foods at the temperature at which they should be served.

Many of these outdoor dining hazards can be avoided with some careful planning. Securely anchor any items that might be blown by the wind. Choose menu items that will hold up well under any conditions. Devise a means of keeping food sheltered, even if you intend to eat outdoors. Most of all, find a caterer who has extensive experience with outdoor affairs. Be sure to thoroughly discuss any concerns you have; your caterer will likely offer solutions to ensure that all food served is safe and tasty.

Interviewing Caterers

Your search for a caterer will require quite a bit of talking and maybe even some tasting. First, check with the manager of the venue you have selected to see if a list of recommended caterers is available. Ask friends and family members for referrals, too. Bridal expos and food festivals in your area may also provide opportunities not only to learn about caterers but to sample their cuisine.

newlywed know-how

In some instances, you may find that you don't have a choice if your preferred venue has an on-site chef or an exclusive relationship with a single caterer. If this is the case, be sure to determine whether your food requests can be fulfilled within the budget you have allotted before you book the site.

Service and Special Requests

A full-service caterer can often provide much more than food. As you meet with culinary professionals, it is important to take careful notes about what services they include in their pricing and what helpful options may also be available for a fee. For example, some caterers will acquire all rental equipment, such as tables, chairs, glasses, plates, silverware, serving dishes, and coffee urns, on your behalf, eliminating much legwork on your part but possibly exceeding the cost of a do-it-yourself approach. Most will provide linens in colors of your choosing. The majority will also handle all setup and cleanup chores, but there may be an additional charge for trash disposal.

piece of cake

If you intend to serve alcohol at your reception, be sure to discuss options with your caterer. Some will provide a bartender and all beverages. Others will suggest that you order liquor, beer, and wine on your own but may still assess a corkage fee and an hourly wage and gratuity for the bartender.

Questions to Ask

You should be able to pare down your list of possible caterers through an initial round of phone calls. Ask each prospect to mail, fax, or e-mail to you a catering menu and price list. Also determine whether each caterer on your list has experience in cooking and serving outdoors. Ask if they would accept a job at the site where you intend to wed.

Once you have narrowed the field to a handful of potential candidates, schedule meetings to discuss your event in more detail. Visit caterers armed with a list of questions, including these:

- How many weddings and other events do you cater each year? On a typical weekend? What percentage are outdoor functions?

- What do you consider to be your specialties? What standard menus and pricing plans do you offer? Are you willing to consider special recipe requests and menu modifications to fit our budget?

- Would you recommend we hold a sit-down dinner or serve guests buffet-style?

- What type of cooking and refrigeration equipment do you use for outdoor events?

- What type of insurance, permits, and licenses do you hold?

- Will you be able to adapt our menu if our event is forced indoors? How much notice of a change of venue would you require? What is your cancellation policy?

- What do you usually do with leftovers? What options are available to us?

- What's the payment schedule? How do you handle gratuities? Are there additional charges?

- Is a minimum number of guests required? When will you need a final guest count?

- Can you provide us with a per-person price quote, a contract, and a list of references?

In general, caterers also provide their own service staff. You will want to know how many waiters, bartenders, and other helpers will be present for your event. As a rule, more servers are required for a sit-down dinner than for a buffet. Be sure to ask how the catering staff will be attired.

Finding a qualified caterer is one thing, but identifying one that is able and willing to actually cater to your wishes can sometimes be another. Be sure to discuss the site you have chosen for your event. Be forthcoming about any difficulties the location may present due to such things as distance from access roads or lack of electricity and running water.

rain or shine

Some caterers will provide your wedding cake and other dessert selections. However, if your caterer does not have an experienced pastry chef on staff, it is better to order your cake from a bakery instead. Be sure to ask, however, if you will be charged a cake cutting and plating fee.

It is also important to let your caterer know from the start if you will have special menu requests and requirements. Some caterers will try to steer you toward their set packages. While they may acquiesce to small menu alterations, they may be reluctant to try new recipes just for your event. Ethnic menus may, in particular, present a challenge for some caterers. If you will need to meet the dietary requirements of some or all guests by providing dishes that are kosher, vegetarian, organic, lactose-free, or suitable for diabetics, for example, you will need to determine any potential caterer's ability to prepare acceptable fare.

The Proof Is in the Tasting

Many caterers are happy to invite prospective clients to a tasting, particularly if they compete for business with many other area catering services. You should not request a tasting unless you are quite serious about engaging a caterer's services, though. Being engaged is not a license to enjoy free meals all over town. However, if you are struggling to choose among two or three food providers, putting them to a head-to-head taste test can be the easiest and most informed way to make a final selection.

If a catering firm you are strongly considering is not willing to provide you with a complimentary sample of items from your desired menu, you may want to hire them to cater a small supper party or even dinner for two in order to be sure that you are making the right decision. Alternatively, if a chef you are evaluating operates a restaurant, be sure to have a meal there if you haven't already. Consider the expense a worthwhile investment that provides peace of mind that you've made a good choice.

Menu Do's and Don'ts

If the menu you have in mind for your mountaintop wedding consists of puffed pastry filled with seafood in cream sauce, broccoli cheese soufflé, and banana flambé, it is likely that your caterer will try to steer you in another direction. In fact, as you begin to consult with caterers, it is best to have few preconceived menu selections in mind. Food-service professionals experienced in outdoor affairs will be able to provide expert guidance on dishes that will work well in your chosen environment, where space and equipment to prepare, cook, and store food may be limited. The good news is that food does not need to be elaborate to taste fabulous.

Foods to Include

As you begin to build a menu with your caterer's input, strive to make selections that not only will be easy to prepare ahead or to cook outdoors but that fit your event's theme and level of formality. Typical picnic and barbecue foods always work well outdoors and are suitable for a casual celebration. In fact, anything that can be cooked on a grill, even gourmet choices such as lobster or sirloin kebabs, are some of the best choices if your caterer will be cooking on location.

While a buffet makes for simple serving, it is often a challenge to keep foods in chafing dishes piping hot, even indoors. A better strategy may be to take a "tapas" or small plate approach and to serve many small courses in rapid succession. Your guests will appreciate lighter fare on a hot day in the outdoors. Food items that can be served at room temperature or just slightly chilled make good menu selections. Finger foods are best if guests will be required to stand during the cocktail hour.

Your catering company will offer its own list of specialties. However, here are a few ideas for dishes that work well in outdoor settings:

- **Hors d'oeuvres:** Smoked salmon, filled pastry pockets, stuffed clams, crab cakes, ceviche, bruschetta, cold teriyaki beef skewers, spring rolls, tea sandwiches
- **Starters and sides:** Chilled fruit soup, chowder, green salad with a vinaigrette dressing, tea breads, corn bread, baked beans, steamed potatoes, couscous, grilled marinated vegetables
- **Main dishes:** Barbecued chicken, sausage on rolls, steamed whole lobster, chilled split lobster, smoked beef tenderloin, roast whole pig, grilled tuna, seafood or beef kebabs, grilled filet mignon
- **Desserts:** Fresh fruit, sorbet, pies, cookies, wedding cake

newlywed know-how

Your catering contract should include a specific list of all menu items that you have selected. Be sure to carefully read any contract language that pertains to the caterer's ability to make reasonable menu substitutions. When you confirm a final guest count with your caterer, it is also a good idea to review the menu one last time.

Foods to Avoid

Food safety is a serious matter. All perishables should be kept cold or hot until just before serving time. Your catering crew should be diligent about monitoring the freshness of any dishes presented buffet-style. If something looks unappealing, there is usually a good reason. Don't hesitate to call upon your catering staff to remove anything that seems to be past its prime. If you have taken a do-it-yourself approach to the food for your affair, it is a good idea to appoint a helper to periodically inspect and restock the spread.

Just because you will be dining outdoors does not necessarily mean that you will not have access to a full kitchen and ample refrigeration. If the site you have selected is well equipped for large gatherings, your food worries will be few. However, if you will be relying on coolers filled with ice and carting cooking equipment and food a distance, it is more critical to streamline your menu and to avoid certain items. Foods that are most prone to spoilage include melon, mayonnaise, eggs, raw meats, raw fish, cold cuts, custards, cheeses, and other dairy products.

piece of cake

Two hours is the maximum time that perishable foods should be allowed to sit out. When temperatures exceed 90 degrees, that time is cut to just one hour. Ice, concealed ice packs, and frozen plates and serving containers can help to keep chilled foods fresh in the outdoors.

Liquid Refreshment

If alcohol is permitted at your wedding site, you may want to partake of a traditional champagne toast. Your caterer should be able to keep champagne on ice until the appointed time arrives. A full bar is costly and, in the outdoors, sometimes difficult to stock. Most guests will be quite content if you opt instead for just beer and wine.

In addition to alcohol, be sure to discuss with your caterer your desire to have plenty of nonalcoholic beverages available. Punch, lemonade, sparkling water, fruit juices, and sodas are good options for children and those who do not drink. On a hot day, all guests should be encouraged to consume plenty of nonalcoholic fluids. For parties that will last into the evening in particular, it is a nice gesture to make hot beverages, such as coffee and tea, available. Be sure your caterer will supply a thermal carafe to keep cream, milk, or half-and-half cold.

Seating Arrangements

Outdoor settings often provide great flexibility when it comes to devising a seating arrangement. Since you will probably be renting tables, you won't be locked into the round tables for eight available at most banquet halls. In many cases, you will also have boundless space in which to create a pleasing arrangement of tables that need not adhere to the convention of dividing the bride's and groom's sides of the family by a central dance floor. You might, for example, put rectangular tables in a U shape so that all diners can enjoy dinner with a view. Or, if you will be hosting a small affair attended mostly by couples, seating them at candlelit, café-style tables for two might make for romantic dining for all.

Before you begin to sketch out your table layout, consult your catering manager. If you have decided to serve your meal buffet-style, you will need to know how much room to allow for the spread and think about the traffic pattern guests will follow to reach the feast. If table service is your choice, your caterer may have a strong preference for a seating arrangement that allows servers to work efficiently. If your meal will feature many courses, try to position tables as closely as possible to where food items will be stored, prepped, or cooked.

Wind Concerns

High winds may force you to move your meal indoors, and even intermittent gusts can prove a nuisance. At any other outdoor dining event, you might be tempted to rely on the old trick of using rocks found lying around to hold down tablecloths and paper goods that might be picked up by the wind. However, your wedding calls for solutions that are a bit more elegant.

Rely on your caterer for sage advice on how prepared foods and table settings can best be protected from the breeze. Chances are good that your caterer owns or can rent such items as tablecloth clips, napkin dispensers, mesh food tents, and entrée domes. While a punch bowl may be pretty, a beverage dispenser may be safer. Also ask for suggestions on taking advantage of features of your site, such as fences, embankments, or a dense row of trees, to serve as a natural windbreak.

rain or shine

Winds and exposed flames are a potentially dangerous mix. If your caterer will be cooking over an open fire, be sure to discuss strategies for sheltering grills in the event that the day is breezy. Ask your catering company to provide a fire extinguisher if one is not readily available at your venue.

Carting in the Cake

As weddings have become more individual, cakes, too, have undergone a transformation. No longer limited to the standard three-tiered white buttercream-frosted tower with a plastic bride and groom on top, couples are choosing cakes in new flavors, colors, designs, shapes, and sizes. Still, wedding cakes tend to be grand confections that are difficult to bake, assemble, and transport. In the outdoors, the cake can be the one menu item that causes the greatest concern. Before you commit to a cake, consider dessert alternatives.

piece of cake

If you really want cake, why settle for just one? Rather than fret about transporting and safely displaying a single large, lavish cake, opt for an assortment of beautifully decorated, table-size cakes or even mini cakes for every guest.

Sweet Selections

A wedding deserves a sweet ending, but it is nowhere written in stone that you must serve cake. Conclude your casual wedding picnic or barbecue with a watermelon cutting ceremony instead. Hire an ice cream truck to deliver guests' choice of cold, sweet treats. Other nontraditional dessert possibilities include the following:

- Cookies iced with your new married monogram
- Fruit sorbet
- Strawberry shortcake
- Red gelatin hearts
- Apple, blueberry, cherry, or key lime pie
- Lemon squares
- Grilled bananas

Confection Protection

If you are a traditionalist at heart, go ahead and have your cake. However, there are a few precautions you should take. First, be sure that you will have some form of cover—at minimum a fabric canopy—to protect your cake from the sun and the elements. Position the cake in a shaded place away from high-traffic areas.

newlywed know-how

Rolled fondant is an increasingly popular wedding cake icing that is rolled like dough, then draped over layers of cake and trimmed. It is strong and hardens to a smooth, porcelain-like finish. It is frequently more expensive than traditional buttercream, but it has the advantage of not requiring refrigeration. In fact, refrigeration is a no-no, as a chilled fondant will sweat as it warms.

Next, speak to your baker about the possibility of performing as much of the cake's assembly work on site as possible. This will eliminate anxiety about a mishap occurring in transit. The cake need not be displayed from the moment that guests arrive but might best be kept protected until the meal is underway.

Fondant icing is a good choice, not only because it holds up well in the heat but because it dries hard and sleek. Thus, unlike buttercream, it is unlikely to melt or ensnare any curious winged intruders that fly too close. Be sure to avoid any cake fillings that are perishable, such as those containing cream, custard, fresh fruit, or eggs. Be careful with your selection of decorations, as well. While fresh flowers are a popular choice, when used as a cake embellishment, they have no source of water and may quickly brown and wilt in the heat of the day. Ask your baker if a similar look can be achieved with silk, marzipan, or candied flowers.

13

Photography

Your vision of captivating images of the two of you declaring your devotion in a glorious setting may have been one of your primary motivators to marry outdoors. What you need to know is that behind every striking wedding image you've ever seen is a brilliant photographer. Finding the right photographers for your event can be time-consuming, and their work can be costly. But if you choose wisely, you will wind up with photos and maybe even a video to cherish anniversaries hence.

Selecting a Photographer

Photography is part art, part science, and part sport. The best photographers know how to compose interesting candid shots and pose formal portraits. They understand, both technically and intuitively, the results achieved through the combination of shutter speed, aperture, film, lenses, filters, and lighting. They possess a knack for being in the right place at the right time and have the reflexes to capture for posterity scenes that last but a moment in time. As you search for the right photographer, you will need to consider each individual's style, skill level, and eye for catching a wedding's most dramatic images.

Style and Substance

Most couples begin their search for a wedding photographer by focusing on a particular style of photography that appeals to them. Just as no two watercolor artists paint in precisely the same way, no two photographers have exactly the same approach. However, wedding photography generally falls into three basic styles:

- **Traditional:** Focused on portraiture, family groupings, classic scenes, and posed images.
- **Photojournalistic:** Designed to be unobtrusive, natural, and documentary in approach.
- **Artistic:** Aimed at capturing one-of-a-kind images in a less traditional manner by zooming in on singular elements, such as the bride's shoes, by utilizing unique angles, and by experimenting with softer focus, off-center framing, and other creative techniques.

Within these basic categories, you will still find that photographers differ greatly in many ways, such as use of light and shadows, propensity to zoom in or to use a wide angle, use of soft versus sharp focus, emphasis on scenic as well as people elements, and reliance on or avoidance of props. Because many outdoor celebrations tend to be more casual in nature, a photojournalistic approach is often preferred. In the course of their search, however, most couples discover that they would prefer a photographer who can blend several styles. Be sure to see a variety of work by each photographer you are considering as you make a decision about whose style best aligns with your wishes.

Beyond style, it is important to consider each potential photographer's substance, as well. Seek out a photographer who has extensive experience, not only with weddings but specifically with outdoor weddings. You also want the photographer you select to be reliable, so evaluate how quickly candidates respond to your phone calls or e-mails and how thoroughly they answer your questions. In addition to technical and artistic prowess with a camera, good wedding photographers also have strong interpersonal skills and genuine passion for the work they do.

Costs and Conditions

Sticker shock often accompanies couples' first meetings with professional photographers. Not only will it cost thousands of dollars to hire a pro to shoot your wedding, the initial fee you are quoted usually covers only the photographer's time plus film and development costs. Additional charges will apply to all prints and albums you order after receiving your proofs. It is not uncommon for photography to eat up 10 percent or more of a couple's wedding budget.

Before you contemplate asking your cousin to take on the job of photographing your wedding with her point-and-shoot camera, consider the importance of having a quality visual record of your special day as it unfolds. Your wedding will be over in a flash, but images will remind you and your loved ones of the promise and hope of that day for many years to come. While photography prices may seem exorbitant, take into account the fact that a wedding photographer's job is not an easy one. In addition to working weekends, lugging equipment, and catering to demanding clients, wedding photographers are under enormous pressure to produce stunning images at every wedding, even though conditions may not always be optimal, and brides and grooms may not always resemble movie stars.

In spite of the cost, hiring a professional is the best way to maximize your chances of getting great photos of your wedding. You will find as you begin to prospect for a photographer that those who specialize in weddings vary widely in their level of experience, their price, and the quality and freshness of their work. Because photography is a demanding profession, many photographers dabble in it part-time or pursue it only for a little while. You will need to manage your expectations a bit. Remember that the photographers who shoot magazine spreads charge even higher commercial rates, working with professional models, jetting off to exotic locations, and not likely spending their weekends trying to get just anyone's grandma to smile for the camera.

rain or shine

Few couples realize that their photographer will own the rights to all of their wedding images. Federal law dictates that copyright is established the moment a photograph is taken. Unless you arrange in advance to retain rights or to purchase negatives, you will need to obtain any prints and reprints through your photographer according to his pricing and terms.

Once you have found a photographer whose style you admire and whose price you can afford, you must still review the contract and understand exactly what you are purchasing. Your agreement should spell out who specifically will photograph your event, the number of hours and rolls of film included, the specific shooting locations, the format via which proofs will be delivered, ownership of the proofs, pricing including any charges for travel expenses, and payment schedule. Carefully read any clauses pertaining to cancellation or postponement of the event and the photographer's liability for not fulfilling contractual obligations. Be sure to obtain a current price list for albums and prints with a guaranteed date through which these prices will be honored.

Questions to Ask

Before you schedule meetings with photographers, narrow the field. You can hone in on a few likely candidates by perusing friends' and family members' wedding albums, clicking through photographers' online portfolios, attending a bridal fair, or browsing through ads placed by photographers in local bridal magazines. Once you have decided that a photographer deserves your consideration, pay a visit and ask questions, such as:

- How many years have you been in business, and how many weddings have you photographed?

- What experience do you have with shooting outdoor weddings and outdoor scenes in general?

- Are you familiar with the site(s) we have selected for our wedding?

- Will you be the individual photographing our wedding, or will there be another photographer in addition to or instead of you? If so, can we meet this individual and see samples of his work?

- Do you have a backup plan in case illness or emergency prevents you from covering our wedding?

- What specific equipment and films do you use, and what do you see as the advantage of these formats? Do you use a flash or other ancillary lighting?

- What packages do you offer, and what is included, both in coverage time and in the number of rolls of film that will be exposed? What schedule of payment do you require?

- Will you take direction as to what photos we would like to see taken on our wedding day?

- Can we have a copy of your standard contract and price list to review? Can we see samples of the albums you make available to customers?

- Will we be able to purchase proofs? Negatives?

- Who develops the film you shoot, and what is the production timeline for proofs and prints?

As with any wedding vendor, checking a photographer's references is a prudent step. Be sure to ask not only whether the newlyweds are satisfied with the images they received but how well the photographer fulfilled special requests and interacted with them and with guests. You may also want to ask about the turnaround time they experienced on proofs and their final album.

The Proof Is in the Proofs

Couples are often surprised to learn that it may be many weeks after their event before they see proofs of their wedding photos. When the proofs arrive, they are sometimes equally astonished by the great number of unacceptable images. What happened?

piece of cake

The wedding photographers you interview will all be eager to show you their best work. In addition to reviewing each photographer's portfolio, either online or in person, be sure to ask to see a proof book from a recently photographed wedding so that you can get a sense of the overall body of work each candidate is likely to produce.

The answer is that even skilled, experienced photographers must take many shots in order to come up with a few winners. This is even more evident when a photojournalistic style is employed and few, if any, images are posed. Keep in mind that you will only select thirty to forty enlargements for your wedding album. The key is to realize that within the hundreds of proof images that you receive, those few dozen gems usually do exist.

Before or After?

For those who choose to include formal portraits on their photography wish list, deciding where a posed photo session will fit into an outdoor wedding schedule can present a bit of a dilemma. There is, of course, a commonly held but somewhat antiquated notion that on the day of a wedding, it is bad luck for a groom to see his bride before the ceremony. However, there are some distinct advantages to getting the formal portraits out of the way before guests arrive and the proceedings get underway.

rain or shine

When camera-wielding amateurs try to horn in on the formal portrait taking, it often creates two problems. First, it makes the whole process take longer, and second, it creates a situation in which subjects may be looking in the wrong direction at another shutter, rather than at the hired photographer. Completing formal photography before guests arrive minimizes this potential disruption.

One primary benefit of posing for photos early is that it eliminates the concern that participants' appearances won't be at their best later on in the day. Even if your ceremony is brief, thirty minutes in the beating sun or raging wind can leave hair disheveled, makeup marred, and attire moist. If your formal portrait list is long and requires participation from a large number of

family and wedding party members, after-ceremony photos will also delay many people's enjoyment of the festivities. That includes the two of you, and the time you will have with your loved ones will seem far too short when all is said and done.

Your photographer may also have concerns about the time of day when photos will be taken, particularly if your ceremony is scheduled for late afternoon and the daylight hours remaining afterward may be limited. Be sure to discuss the benefits and drawbacks of various chronologies and to weigh any preferences your photographer expresses. The final decision will be a matter of your own beliefs and desires and the photographer's availability, but if images are one of your top priorities, you may want to dispense with tradition.

Out of the Shadows

Though you may be disappointed with a day that is overcast, your photographer may be delighted. Not only do colors appear more vibrant in soft light, the absence of harsh sun also helps to eliminate one potential problem associated with outdoor photography—shadows. Of course, shadows in and of themselves are not necessarily a bad thing. In fact, the long shadows of early morning or late day can add depth and a three-dimensional illusion to outdoor photos. A shadow that makes the bride look as though she's grown a beard is, however, definitely a problem.

piece of cake

In addition to shadows, you should also be mindful of any background elements that could create strange optical illusions, such as trees that appear to grow out of people's heads. A cluttered backdrop can present particular problems if you have opted for black-and-white photography.

When a scene is masked in shadows, most skilled photographers know how to effectively use a fill flash to brighten dark areas. However, your images still may not be optimal if heavy shadows obscure vivid colors. Friends and family members who want to take snapshots may have a particularly difficult time getting good images in a shadowy environment. Unless he is intimately familiar with the property, your photographer should visit your wedding site with you in advance in order to scout out angles, assess what equipment will be required, and provide guidance on how best to use the natural environment you have selected as a backdrop for your wedding images. Together, discuss any potential problems presented by such things as overhead trees, rocky cliffs, tall structures, or latticed arches, which may cast shadowy patterns on your ceremony scene.

Makeup Touchups

If you've ever watched a television taping, been on a film set, or viewed a behind-the-scenes clip about movie production, you probably know that makeup artists play an active role in keeping stars' appearances polished. On your wedding day, when the cameras will be following your every move, it may make sense to have a person assigned to keep your makeup fresh. Even if you intend to do your own makeup at home before arriving at your ceremony site, you may find it difficult to sneak away for the frequent touchups that may be necessary on a sweltering, sticky day in the outdoors. On top of all this, your restroom facilities may be cramped and poorly lit, providing a far-from-ideal place for primping.

ask the wedding planner?

Will dark under-eye circles show up in photographs?

If weather worries have kept you from getting adequate beauty rest, use a yellow concealer under your foundation to camouflage dark circles. The yellow counteracts the blue hue of under-eye blood vessels, particularly as it is seen by the camera's lens.

If the cost of hiring a professional makeup artist to tail you throughout your event is a bit rich for your budget, there are a few alternatives. Ask the salesperson at the cosmetic counter where you shop whether she freelances. Contact a local cosmetology school to see if a student might be available at reasonable rates. If you have a friend or family member who always looks put together and who doesn't have other wedding-day duties, perhaps she would lend a hand, particularly keeping a watchful eye out for makeup disintegration during your formal portrait session.

Creative Effects

No other art form has been as substantially impacted by technological advancements as photography. Both at the instant a photo is captured and later, during the development and editing processes, a skilled photographer can manipulate images in unique and inventive ways. Improvements since its inception have made digital photography a legitimate option for weddings, opening new avenues for creative enhancement thanks to the ease with which digital images can be altered. Still, there is timeless appeal to black-and-white film photography, and while neat effects might be fun, many couples who marry outdoors prefer photographs that are more natural and true-to-life.

The Negatives and Positives of Black and White

It may seem contradictory, but black-and-white photography is both classic and contemporary. Now, as always, the documentary quality of black-and-white images allows viewers to feel as though they are witnessing a moment as it occurred. There has been an upsurge in interest in black-and-white photography for weddings, and a talented photographer can effectively capture many moods, expressions, and details in shades of black, white, and gray. Many outdoor wedding locations, particularly those with historic significance, lend themselves well to a wedding shot in black and white.

rain or shine

The good news is that you really don't have to choose between opposite ends of the color spectrum. Most wedding photographers have experience working in both color and black and white and will gladly provide you with a mix. If you choose a photographer who works with an assistant, you may be able to request that one concentrate on black and white while the other handles color work.

Beyond its look, black and white offers certain advantages. It gives the photographer superb control in both the image-making and developing processes. Black-and-white prints also have better archival qualities and tend not to fade as easily as color. The best black-and-white images come from black-and-white film, so your photographer should plan on shooting several rolls if black-and-white images are important to you.

Even if you do not specifically request black-and-white photography, it is a simple matter to render color originals in black and white. Color negatives can be printed in black and white, and vibrant digital images can be converted to shades of gray with the click of a mouse. It is very important to realize that the opposite is not true; black-and-white images cannot easily be transformed to color. Hand-coloring of black-and-white images is an available service, but it is expensive. While the technique may yield lovely images, they will not be an accurate representation of your event in all its colorful splendor.

Special Effects

Special photography effects, such as those created with a fisheye lens, a star filter, infrared film, Polaroid transfer, or multiple exposure techniques, have been around for years. The advent of scanning and digital photography has made it possible to achieve even more unique effects, from altering the color of the sky to supplanting your officiant with Elvis. As you visit photographers and review their work, pay attention to whether and how well they use these types of techniques in their finished work. While some effects are subtle and artistic, others are a bit unnatural, such as those that use multiple exposure to create an image of the bride and groom looking at themselves. You may be intrigued by the tricks that photographers can employ. Still, keep in mind that having chosen a natural environment for your wedding celebration, you may be happier in the long run with a photographer who concentrates on documenting the event as it truly appeared.

Digital Photography

When it was first introduced, digital imaging could not rival the quality and richness of film photography. Like computers, cellular phones, and other gadgets, however, digital cameras have evolved and improved at a remarkable rate. The result is that the differences between images captured digitally and those committed to film have become nearly imperceptible. Some professional photographers have even made the decision to embrace digital exclusively.

Digital photography is becoming an increasingly popular option with brides and grooms, particularly those who are tech savvy. A chief reason is that digital proofs are often available much faster than print proofs. If the photographer offers online previewing, images can easily be shared far and wide with loved ones, who can usually order prints directly from the photographer, saving the newlyweds the effort of showing proofs to interested relatives and friends and coordinating order-taking. Digital photography also offers couples enhanced peace of mind that they will have plenty of wonderful images from which to choose. That's because a photographer can monitor the quality of the images he is taking throughout. He can easily adjust settings on the fly without having to change lenses or films. Also, it's possible to shoot hundreds of images much more affordably than with film. This lets the photographer experiment freely, taking advantage of the tremendous capacity and flexibility that digital imaging offers.

If you want to consider digital photography for your wedding, seek out a professional photographer who has been working with digital for quite some time and is completely comfortable with the format. Ask to see samples of all-digital weddings, and also compare the photographer's digital work to images he has taken using traditional film cameras. Above all, do not select a photographer simply because he offers digital imaging. You still must be impressed with the individual's talent and style and find him personable and eager to fulfill your photography wishes.

A Shot List for the Photographer

You won't need to give your photographer implicit instructions to take photos of your best man delivering a toast or of the two of you cutting the cake. Experienced wedding photographers are accustomed to anticipating these wedding rituals. However, you should prepare a shot list for the photographer that includes anything that might be unexpected; anticipated highlights of the day; specific locations that you particularly want to use as backdrops; and a detailed outline of formal family and wedding party portraits that you would like to arrange.

piece of cake

When it comes to specifying family groupings for formal portraits, some couples struggle with whether to include potentially impermanent family members, such as the bride's brother's girlfriend. To avoid hurt feelings while still allowing for future changes in your family, have your photographer pose a variety of groups, some just family and some with dates and significant others included.

Type or neatly print your list of important images so that the photographer can easily scan it and check off items as they are completed. While you should try to introduce your photographer to the people he will be photographing, it doesn't hurt to also provide a quick cheat sheet with the names of parents, grandparents, and bridal party members to which the photographer can refer. Keep your must-take photograph list manageable, allowing your photographer to spend most of his time moving about freely and operating on instinct. The images brides and grooms treasure most are often those that were spontaneous.

Videography

When consumer-grade video cameras were first introduced, they were hulking machines, perched atop monster tripods. Often, they were equipped with lights that shone like high-beam headlamps upon the head table, causing the entire wedding party to squint throughout the celebratory meal and to seek cover as soon as the cake was served. Still, many brides and grooms were thrilled to have video cameras on hand to diligently record every mouthful and utterance. Why? There is simply something incomparably powerful about reliving events through video.

Memories in Motion

Videography has come a long way. Now, weddings can be filmed unobtrusively, images are stable and crisply focused, and desktop computers can be used to edit raw footage so that the finished product is cinematic in quality. All of these improvements have fueled rapid growth in the number of couples who choose to have their weddings captured in full motion. An outdoor setting often provides an ideal arena in which to shoot video, as locations for concealing cameras are many and ambient light is almost always sufficient.

If you are on the fence about whether to have your wedding recorded, consider this. While photography can immortalize a wedding's visual splendor, the day is about much more than still, unmoving images. From the music that is played, to the words of love that are proclaimed, to the loving glances that are exchanged, a wedding ceremony and reception are filled with dramatic action and palpable emotions. You may believe that you can rely on your recollections and that photographs will adequately jog your memory of the events that transpired, but the unfortunate reality is that much of the detail will begin to seep out of your brain within a few months after the big day.

newlywed know-how

If you are interested in locating a professional wedding videographer in your area, a good place to start is the Web site of the Wedding & Event Videographers Association International (at *www.weva.com*), where you can browse an online directory listing videographers by state.

Video has a way of bringing past events back to life. The sounds of laughter. The tinkling of glasses. The blush and shy grin of the young man who caught the garter to thunderous applause. With the touch of a play button, faded memories can be refreshed each time your wedding anniversary rolls around.

Many couples shy away from video, only to regret that decision as time passes or sometimes even immediately following the event when they realize how quickly it all flew by. While budgetary restrictions may be a factor, video cameras are so widely owned these days that you probably can find a willing volunteer to videotape your day. The only solid reason for forgoing video entirely is if you are prone to stage fright and know that awareness of the camera will make you too nervous to confidently recite your vows and too uncomfortable to enjoy the day.

Selecting a Videographer

Technological advances have made it possible for amateurs to do an admirable job of shooting video. If there is a video buff on your guest list, that person may even be eager to donate his services as your appointed cameraman. While this is certainly a budget-friendly way to go, there are a few things to consider before choosing this route. One is that while the resulting tape may be something you cherish, it may not approach a professional level of quality. Another is that while your friend may be happy to keep the camera rolling during your ceremony, he may want to actually enjoy the party that follows, so the coverage following your pronouncement as husband and wife may be spotty at best.

piece of cake

If possible, your videographer should attend your rehearsal in order to get a sense of where and in what order events will transpire. Be sure that your videographer is aware of your plans to relocate your event in the case of rain and will be equipped to adapt if a sudden shift to an indoor environment is warranted.

Finding the right professional videographer is very much like selecting a photographer. In fact, it is a good idea to hire your photographer first and then to seek a videographer whose style and personality are complementary. A photographer charged with capturing classic black-and-white images may wind up at odds with a videographer who operates as if he is shooting a rock video. Your wedding photographer may even have recommendations on video professionals you should consider. As with a photographer, it is important to review many samples of a videographer's work and to be satisfied with the visual quality and style of his productions. You should evaluate the packages and options that are offered, learn about the advantages and disadvantages of various recording formats and equipment, and feel confident that the videographer will be dependable.

Questions to Ask

Before you meet with videographers, try to familiarize yourselves with video technology by reading magazines or visiting Web sites targeted to video enthusiasts. Decide in advance how much you want to spend, and have an idea of what features are most important to you so that you can remain focused if the videographer offers a tempting menu of add-ons. Be prepared with a list of questions like these:

- How many years have you been in business, and how many weddings have you filmed?

- Are you accustomed to shooting outdoor weddings, and how do you usually operate in an outdoor environment?

- Are you familiar with the site(s) that we have selected for our wedding?

- Will you be the individual filming our wedding, or will there be another videographer in addition to or instead of you? If so, can we meet this individual and see samples of weddings he has filmed? Will remotely operated cameras be employed?

- What specific equipment and formats do you use? In what final formats can we purchase copies of the video?

- What system do you use for capturing audio? Will we need to wear microphones?

- What weather conditions, such as high winds or light mist, would affect your ability to videotape our event?

- Do you do your own editing? How long will it be before we receive a completed video?

- What packages do you offer, and what is included in coverage time, final video duration, and editing services? What schedule of payment do you require?

- Can we have a copy of your standard contract and a list of references to review? Can we see full samples of videos that you have produced, not just clips?

Many videographers will attempt to dazzle you by screening their most elaborate and expensive video productions when you visit. You may see montages of baby and family photos, a full-blown recounting of the couple's love story, interviews with wedding guests, and even some honeymoon footage. While these bells and whistles may be nice if you can afford them, keep in mind that they will not only cost more money, they will require added time on your part in rounding up photos and sitting for interviews. If your budget for video is limited, your main priority should be to obtain quality raw footage of the event as it unfolded. You can always spring for enhanced editing and added features in honor of a future anniversary when you aren't as taxed by other wedding expenditures.

14

The Invitations

Invitations and save-the-date cards provide guests with their first glimpse of the event you are working so hard to plan. For an outdoor affair, invitations establish your theme, reveal the location, and communicate critical information to those who will attend. Whether you opt for traditional invitations or something more inventive, you will want to think carefully about what this communiqué should include and what information you will need to receive from guests with their responses. From the essential information to fun extras, invitations are an important part of your outdoor wedding.

Save the Date

Save-the-date cards are a relatively new addition to the line-up of wedding stationery. Though they are far from mandatory, these first alerts that a wedding is in the works can help ensure that guests reserve your special day. Unlike wedding invitations, which traditionally are not sent until six to eight weeks before the event, save-the-date notices can be mailed six months to a year in advance. Wedding stationery companies have embraced this trend, so if you decide to send save-the-date cards, you'll find a diverse selection of designs to consider.

Early Warning

Once you announce your engagement, you will be asked repeatedly, "Have you set a date?" The beauty of save-the-date cards is that they answer this question for all of your curious friends and family members. At the same time, they also provide people with hectic schedules plenty of advance notice of your impending nuptials. Of course, save-the-date cards also represent an additional expense for printing and postage and the added labor of addressing cards and taking them to the post office.

rain or shine

Before you order save-the-date cards, be sure to formally reserve your wedding venue or venues for the date you have selected and to finalize your guest list. Once you've asked guests to hold the date, you don't want to change your mind about when the event will occur or who will be invited to attend.

Don't send save-the-date cards just because they are available. Decide first if they are truly necessary and if they will help you to set the tone and build anticipation for your event. Save-the-date cards are most helpful in conjunction with weddings that will take place over a holiday weekend or that will require many guests to make travel arrangements. They also make sense if yours will be a small and intimate affair—one that you won't want any of the people on your short guest list to miss.

Selecting a Save-the-Date Card

There are two basic approaches to selecting a save-the-date card. One is to match these mailers to your other wedding stationery. Invitation suppliers are increasingly showcasing coordinating save-the-date cards with the wedding ensembles they offer. You can also use pieces designed to serve as invitations or response cards as your save-the-date by customizing the wording.

newlywed know-how

If you are trying to save some money on postage, choose save-the-date cards that can be mailed as postcards rather than cards that require envelopes. Call or visit your local post office or visit *www.usps.com* to check current regulations regarding pieces that qualify for the discounted postcard postage rate.

One drawback to taking a coordinated approach is that it requires you to select all of your wedding stationery at the time you intend to send out save-the-date cards, which may be far in advance. Because invitation styles change frequently, there is a danger that your design may be discontinued. However, ordering invitations and other stationery items many months ahead requires you to have all of your details in place and to incur this expense earlier than you may have projected. It also means you will need to find a safe place to store invitations until it is time for them to be addressed.

Many couples are choosing to take a different approach to the save-the-date card, opting for something light-hearted and eye-catching, even if the invitations that will follow will be more traditional and elegant. Outdoor weddings especially call for a splashy introduction, and the possibilities for whimsical and unique mailings are nearly limitless. Many wedding stationers offer fun designs that incorporate such graphics as a calendar with your wedding date circled in red. Some cards even incorporate peel-off stickers to be placed on guests' calendars or scratch-off sections that keep recipients in suspense until they reveal the bride's and groom's names and their selected date. Others offer options that incorporate images such as a couple's engagement photo, baby pictures of the bride and groom, or even custom caricatures.

piece of cake

If you really want to ensure that your wedding stays on guests' minds, you can opt to announce the date via something tangible that guests are likely to keep around, such as custom-imprinted refrigerator magnets, puzzles, bookmarks, candy tins, or coasters.

As with other aspects of your wedding, try to select a save-the-date card that is in keeping with your personalities and the overall theme of your event. If the perfect announcement card is elusive, feel free to create your own using scenic postcards, hand-written notes tucked inside confetti-filled envelopes, colorful printer-friendly papers from the office supply store, or plain cards that you embellish with rubber-stamped ink designs or glued-on pressed flowers, glitter, or colored sand. For a truly frugal approach, take advantage of Web sites that offer free e-mail cards or invitations to alert your connected friends, or include a small note about the date with holiday cards you were already intending to mail.

Themed Invitations

As weddings have become more individualized, invitations, too, have evolved into personalized expressions of the couple and their upcoming event. Much has changed since the days when most couples stuck with a standard verse in a standard font centered down the middle of a crisp, white card. Today's invitations feature layered papers, bold colors, romantic images, clever sayings, unusual shapes and sizes, and decorative typefaces and add-ons. This variety makes it possible to select or create an invitation that is the ideal introduction to your outdoor wedding's unique theme and flavor.

A Formal Introduction

Whether or not you opt to send a save-the-date announcement, your wedding invitations serve as the formal request for loved ones to join you on your special day. As such, it is your primary vehicle for enticing guests, revealing your plans, and setting a tone for the celebration. Whether your invitation is classic, cute, bold, sophisticated, or a one-of-a-kind work of art created as a keepsake, it is also a functional document that must adhere to the basic rules of invitation etiquette.

newlywed know-how

Even if you are planning an informal affair, etiquette dictates that all wedding invitations be addressed by hand. If your own penmanship is not attractive, you may want to enlist the aid of a friend with an elegant hand or a professional calligrapher.

Every outdoor wedding invitation should communicate vital information, including the following:

- Who is getting married
- The date and time of the event
- The event's hosts (usually whoever is paying for the wedding)
- The exact location of the ceremony and reception, including specific mention that all or a portion of the proceedings will take place outdoors
- Expected dress
- Specific instructions in the event of inclement weather

Selecting Invitations

There are several ways to shop for wedding invitations. Visiting a print shop, stationer, or wedding boutique gives you the advantage of seeing many designs. It also lets you view and touch actual samples in order to get a feel for the weight and texture of papers, exact colors, and the appearance of raised lettering or embossed elements. Mail-order catalogs and Web sites, however, can't be beat for the sheer variety of options they offer, their convenience, and, quite often, their pricing. Many will mail actual samples of invitations you are considering, so if you have ample time, ask if this is a possibility.

piece of cake

Order more invitations than you think you will need, plus an extra supply of envelopes. You will want to reserve several copies of your invitation as keepsakes, and a few slipups are inevitable when you hand-address envelopes.

As outdoor weddings have become commonplace, the number of invitation designs available to complement such themes as a beach wedding or garden party has grown exponentially. If you are inclined to communicate the theme of your event in a more subtle fashion than selecting an invitation featuring seashells or flowers, color is an excellent alternative; today, white and ecru aren't the only shades in vogue for wedding stationery. Choose a sepia tone or classic black and white for a wedding at a historic location, vibrant blues and aquas for a seaside gathering, or rusty reds and turquoise for a desert union.

Think carefully, as well, about how the wording you select might reflect your theme. While much of your

invitation's language will be informational, there is often room for a short personal expression. Avoid clichéd sayings, such as "Today I will marry my best friend." Instead, strive for something creative and unique to your event, such as, "Against the backdrop of autumn's hue, join us as we say, 'I do.'"

Thematic Accents

Originality in invitations extends beyond the looks that can be achieved purely with paper and ink. Increasingly, invitation designers are incorporating eclectic accents or offering optional add-ons. The possibilities include bows, beads, feathers, gold seals, felt flowers, pearls, and charms.

The invitation industry is also devising new methods for holding together all of the components of wedding invitations. Since outdoor weddings tend to be some of the most involved, requiring that invitations include such additional enclosures as maps, hotel suggestions, and inclement weather instructions, you may want to look into some of these options. They range from simple ribbons, cords, and coils, to transparent overwraps, built-in pockets, lace-up eyelets, and colorful brads, clips, grommets, and safety pins.

rain or shine

Always have your complete invitation with all inserts weighed at the post office before you purchase and affix postage stamps. Invitations marked "insufficient postage" and returned to you will result in very unwelcome expenses and delays.

Even the stamps you select can help to convey your theme. While it has become de rigueur to use "Love" stamps on invitation and response-card envelopes, the post office often has floral, scenic, historic, and other unique designs available that might make appropriate accents. If there is nothing fitting among the postal service's current line-up, consider visiting a collectible stamp dealer or searching online auction sites for stamps from prior years that match your theme or color scheme. As long as they have not been cancelled, old stamps always hold their face value, though you may have to acquire them at a premium.

Designing Your Own Invitations

With the number of designs readily available, there are really only two reasons to take on invitations as a do-it-yourself project. One is to save money. The other is to create something truly personal and extraordinary.

If cutting costs is your motivation and you are computer savvy, your best bet is to purchase invitation papers and envelopes at an office- or art-supply store. Try to keep your invitations simple. The text can be laid out in any word processing or desktop publishing application. Watch out for graphic design no-nos that will make your finished results appear amateurish, such as use of bold type, mixed fonts, or all capital letters. Be sure to print and proofread a test copy on plain paper before you begin printing the actual invitations. Don't be tempted to run envelopes through the printer while you're at it; they should still be addressed by hand.

If you are tempted to design your own invitations as a method of achieving the exact look you envision, first realistically evaluate your artistic and creative talents. If you are a professional photographer, artist, designer, or craftsperson, this may be completely feasible, but producing your original design in the quantity you require may still require an inordinate amount of time or money. If your design experience or time is limited, you may be better off enlisting the assistance of an artist in your community or a company that specializes in custom invitations. Keep in mind that while one-of-a-kind invitations are the ultimate in personalization, they are also quite costly. Unless money is no object, be sure you have conducted an exhaustive search of commercially available designs before you head down this road.

Instructions for Guests

Whatever lovely design you select, it will serve as a clever disguise for your invitation's true mission—to serve as an instruction manual for guests. Outdoor wedding invitees need to know a bit more than when to show up and where. You will help to put guests at ease if you provide them with thorough, up-front information about your event. Though incorporating all of the necessary details can lead to an overstuffed envelope, your day will run more smoothly if guests receive clear and precise directions in advance.

Details, Details, Details

You have already discovered that attention to detail is one of the most critical aspects of successful outdoor-wedding planning. While you may be inclined to keep some details under wraps so that your loved ones will be enchanted when they arrive upon your wedding scene, as a general rule, it is better to err on the side of revealing more detail rather than less. You certainly don't want guests to be surprised to find that your wedding is outside, nor do you want them to learn too late that they will be required to hike up hill to your wedding site, pay an admission or parking fee, stand for a prolonged period of time, or catch a boat at its appointed departure time.

piece of cake

If guests are invited to participate in additional activities, such as a rehearsal dinner or a post-wedding brunch, this is a detail that should also be communicated specifically. Use additional enclosures to extend an invitation to these events.

It is best not to assume that guests have heard wedding details through the grapevine. Neither should you conclude that just because a place is well known, all those attending will know what to expect. Even for weddings held at home, you should specifically indicate that festivities will transpire outside. Depending upon the invitation wording you choose, you can incorporate language such as, "Your presence is requested at the outdoor marriage of," or "You're invited to the outdoor wedding of," or simply, "Join us outdoors." Alternatively, mention the location as "in the outdoor courtyard," "in the rose garden," "on the sandy shore," or "under the open skies" at the site you have selected.

Rain or Shine

The most important detail you will need to communicate is your backup plan in the event of foul weather. Details of an alternate date or site are best included on the main invitation, though a separate card with inclement weather instructions is another option, particularly if you want to provide guests with extended details, such as a phone number to call or a Web site to visit for up-to-date location information. If your event will move inside a tent or other facility if storms roll through, this should also be clearly stated.

Incorporating Enclosures

Invitations, response cards, response-card envelopes, reception cards, at-home cards, "rain" cards, hotel information, maps, ancillary event invitations and details, registry cards, inner envelopes—the contents of your invitation can easily become rather bulky, particularly if you are hosting a multiday affair or a destination wedding. While some invitation designs specifically strive to address the emerging need to organize and assemble all of these components, many couples still find that they must contend with a plethora of loose inserts as they prepare their invitations for mailing. As long as your outer envelopes seal neatly and completely, you may want to simply stuff away. However, if you are hoping to reduce your postage expense or present a more streamlined appearance, there are several strategies you might employ.

newlywed know-how

Tissue paper inserts, traditionally positioned over the printed face of an invitation, are a throwback to the days when oil-based invitation inks might not be completely dry and could potentially smudge. They are really unnecessary thanks to modern printing advances.

First, evaluate whether all of the enclosures are absolutely necessary. Might you, for example, send at-home cards with your new address along with thank-you notes after the wedding? Though they are convenient, the bridal registry inserts provided by department and specialty stores are actually an etiquette no-no, as they are akin to asking for a gift; rely instead on word of mouth to spread the news of where you have registered. For more casual weddings, some couples are choosing to do away with the traditional inner envelope, and this, too, can reduce your invitations' heft. Posting information such as hotel recommendations or nearby attractions on a wedding Web site is another possible way to cut down on the number of enclosures.

In order to ensure that all critical enclosures find their way into each outbound envelope, set up all materials assembly-line–style on a table that is free of other clutter. For invitations that have wording on the outside, enclosures should be placed on top, type-side up; for invitations whose details are printed inside, enclosures are tucked under the first folded flap. From bottom up, the invitations should be followed by the reception card, other inserts in size order

from largest to smallest, then response cards tucked under the flap of stamped, self-addressed response envelopes. If you are using an inner envelope, insert materials so that the fold of the invitation is "in" and the printed side of all materials faces the back or flap side of the inner envelope. The inner envelope, upon which tradition dictates you should handwrite the names of invited guests, should be inserted within the outer envelope so that this hand-inscribed wording faces the back or flap side of the outer envelope and is immediately visible when the envelope is opened.

Directions to Hard-to-Find Places

Some outdoor spots can't be pinpointed with a street number. For a large complex with many landmarks, such as Walt Disney World, directing guests to the proper location within the site probably won't prove terribly difficult. If you will be marrying at Cocoa Beach, though, how exactly will guests find you along that six-mile stretch of sand?

rain or shine

You may need to have volunteer escorts lead guests from the parking area to your ceremony site if there isn't a clearly marked path. If this is your plan, alert guests to look for these guides when they arrive on site so they won't panic and attempt to proceed on their own if an escort is not immediately visible.

Enclosing a detailed map with your invitations is one answer. Many locations that commonly host weddings or other functions have reproducible maps available for your use. It is always a wise idea to augment a map with some written directions, as well. Spell out the specifics of how the location is best approached based on your own experience of accessing the site. While online mapping and directions programs can be a helpful starting place, their accuracy is not perfect. Be sure to field test any directions before providing them to guests.

RSVP with Contact Information

For most weddings, selecting the wording for response cards is a very simple task. Usually, guests need only indicate whether they "will" or "will not" attend. In some cases, they may be asked to check off their preference for chicken, beef, fish, or vegetarian entrees.

For an outdoor wedding, it is a good idea to make use of the response card to obtain a bit more information about those who do plan to join you. Work with your invitation printer to incorporate additional blank lines where guests can jot down their contact information, including home and cellular phone numbers, e-mail address, and the hotel or other location where they will be staying while in town for your wedding. If there is simply no room on the response card, you may need to include an additional small index card or printed form for guests to complete and return. In the event you need to make a last-minute alteration to your plans, you will be glad to have these contact details at your fingertips.

Something Fun

For all of the fancy papers, inks, formats, and decorative add-ons available, most wedding invitations are still, at their essence, printed, two-dimensional paper products inserted within envelopes. Want your invitation to be something completely different that really stands out in a mailbox filled with catalogs and sweepstakes notices? Innovative invitation possibilities do exist for those who want guests to know from the outset that they have been invited to attend a somewhat novel event. Even seemingly traditional invitations can incorporate interactive elements that offer a unique twist.

Thinking Outside the Envelope

Many couples who choose an outdoor setting are seeking to differentiate their celebration from other weddings, perhaps even a previous one of their own. If that is your situation, you may feel compelled to do everything just a bit differently. Why not start with your invitations? Here are a few creative alternatives that will definitely set your event apart from the start:

- For a wedding at a vineyard, send guests a bottle of wine with a custom-printed invitation label affixed. Just be sure to check your local alcohol mailing regulations, as some states do not accept alcohol shipments from other states.
- For a beach wedding, order and mail custom-imprinted beach balls, available from promotional products vendors, or order a supply of plastic message-in-a-bottle mailers from a specialty retailer. Insert your invitations, and be prepared to receive a slew of phone calls from delighted recipients.
- Turn your invitation into a keepsake by printing it on a ceramic plate.
- Mail guests CDs featuring a handpicked soundtrack of themed songs that they can enjoy on their drive to your wedding, and print your wedding invitation details on the CD sleeve.
- For a garden ceremony, tuck your invitation inside a clay flowerpot filled with green tissue paper, raffia, or Easter grass. Tuck a packet of seeds or some flower bulbs inside, too, for guests to plant at their homes as a reminder of your special day.

Interactive Invitations

Another way to make your invitations more than just words on a page is to incorporate an interactive element. Since you will be asking guests to supply additional contact information with their RSVPs, you might also request that they take a moment to write down their tips for wedded bliss, draw a picture of what they think the two of you will look like on your wedding day, or answer a question, such as, "How did you meet the bride and groom?" or "What is your funniest memory of either the bride or groom?" The responses or sketches can be collected in a scrapbook that is displayed at your wedding or perhaps even used as a guest book for contributors to sign on your wedding day.

Some socially conscious couples also use their invitations as a call to action. If you support a specific charitable organization or endeavor, you may see your wedding as an opportunity to do something meaningful by asking guests to contribute to a special collection. For example, you might request that guests bring canned goods for donation to a soup kitchen, teddy bears for delivery to a police department or children's hospital, or phone cards for shipment to service men and women stationed overseas. Guests' participation should, of course, be optional.

15

Outdoor Attire

From the bride's glamorous gown to the guests' get-up, an outdoor wedding calls for a bit of forethought when it comes to choosing appropriate apparel. Just as you would consider the elements when choosing an outfit for any outdoor party, you must take unpredictable environmental conditions into account when selecting your attire and advising guests on appropriate dress. Whether you are planning a formal affair or a more casual celebration, applying a bit of common sense to decisions about dress can ensure that you look and feel your best.

Bridal Gown Selection Tips

No matter how dashing the groom, at a wedding, all eyes are on the bride. The bridal gown is the single most important item of wedding day attire, and as such, it should be selected with utmost care. Luckily for the bride, trying on gorgeous gowns can be one of the most enchanting and fun-filled wedding preparation tasks. When you have chosen an outdoor setting for your celebration, it is important to keep a few extra details in mind as you zero in on the dress that is "the one."

rain or shine

Start your search for the perfect gown about nine months before your wedding day to allow ample time for ordering and alterations, but do not make a final selection until you have confirmed the location where your event will be held. If you change your mind about marrying outside, your ideas about the gown you would like to wear may also change.

Best Dressed

The bride is traditionally the belle of the ball, the most lavishly attired person on a day designed to allow her to shine. All others, including the groom, the wedding party, and guests, take their wardrobe cues from the level of formality established by the bride's choice of a dress. If you are the bride, that can put you in the position of having to choose between your childhood fantasy of wearing an elaborate, shimmering ball gown and your adult sensibility, which tells you that in an outdoor setting, everyone else will be happier if they can dress more comfortably and casually. There is also the important matter of your own comfort.

As you start to consider dress designs, it is important to step back for a moment and think of bridal wear along a continuum from most to least elegant. At the top of the scale are one-of-a-kind couture gowns that cost thousands of dollars. You might feel apprehensive just trying on one of these masterpieces and certainly wouldn't want to sully it at an outdoor fete. For a glimpse at the opposite end of the spectrum, open your closet and decide what you would wear if you had to get married tomorrow. For some brides who decide to elope on a whim or to marry hurriedly before their honeys are deployed or undergo urgent surgery, the choice can be that simple.

Chances are good that your own wedding dress selection won't fall into either of these categories. You will shop for a dress that is far lovelier than anything you currently own, but you will also shy away from the most elaborate and expensive designs. In the vast territory between these extremes, you will find plenty of gown designs that will be comfortable and appropriate in the outdoors.

Colors, Fabrics, and Styles That Work Outdoors

Browsing in a bridal boutique is no longer like fishing in a sea of white where dresses differ only in the design of their neckline, the fullness of their skirt, or the length of their train. It is an exciting time to be a bride. The sheer abundance of choices means you may need to try on many dresses, but the chances are excellent that your efforts will be rewarded when you find the gown that is a perfect fit both for you and for the event you have envisioned.

Each bride is individual, so generic advice on choosing the best dress is difficult to dispense. The best overall strategy for those marrying outside is to keep the setting you have selected foremost in your mind. Even as you twirl in front of the three-way mirror on the carpeted floor of an air-conditioned shop, heed the opinions of your trusted shopping companions. Be open to

trying on dresses that do not match any preconceived notions you might have about the gown you will wear.

Color is one aspect that outdoor brides may want to totally reconsider. Yes, white and off-white are traditional and most popular. However, you can now find bridal attire in shades of rum pink, peach blush, champagne, softly brushed metallics such as gold, silver, platinum, and copper, and even hazy blue and brilliant red. Colored embroidery, ribbons, and sashes on white and ivory gowns are also more prevalent. The prime disadvantage of wearing white or off-white in the outdoors is that these are the colors most likely to show any dirt and other stains that may be difficult to avoid when you will be walking along dusty pathways and through grassy or sandy areas. If your skin tone is fair, the combination of a white gown and harsh sunlight can also leave you looking washed out.

newlywed know-how

A bridal consignment store can be a perfect place for the outdoor bride to shop—and save. In addition to once-worn gowns and vintage styles, many consignment boutiques also carry never-worn dresses from designer closeouts at a fraction of the original cost.

Fabric is another factor that outdoor brides should consider carefully. While it can be more costly, silk is the crème de la crème of wedding gown fabrics. That is because, like cotton or wool, it is a natural fiber that is strong, breathes well, is colorfast when dyed, and drapes beautifully. Synthetic fibers, such as polyester, rayon, and nylon, emulate the look of silk but can't match its comfort and elegance.

Whether made of synthetic or natural fibers, fabrics have many names based on their weave, which affects their texture, appearance, and most important, weight. Outdoor brides should look for lighter-weight fabrics, such as chiffon, charmeuse, georgette, organza, shantung, and Dupion, as opposed to the heavier satins, crepes, taffetas, failles, brocades, and velvets. Netting and lace can create a layered and full effect without adding substantial weight. For brides in search of a more casual dress or suit, cool and absorbent linen is a good choice, though you will want to be sure not to dress until you arrive at your ceremony site, as linen has a tendency to wrinkle.

While bare styles are all the rage and well-suited for less formal environs, think carefully before selecting a strapless gown. If you are fair, you will need to slather your shoulders and chest with sunscreen in order to prevent a serious sunburn. Bare styles can also be chilly if temperatures are below average, and while beautiful shawls, stoles, wraps, and capes are available, they are most often sold separately at an added cost. You also must feel confident in a strapless gown, so evaluate the chances of tripping or catching your hem on an obstacle on the way to the altar or during the course of your celebration. There are several alternatives that offer added security while still showing some skin, such as a sleeveless halter, portrait, or bateau neckline or a spaghetti-strap style.

Think Twice About a Train

While a train is majestic and photogenic, you should accept that going without one is a small sacrifice to make in exchange for the stunning panorama you have chosen for your backdrop. Wearing a train in the outdoors is a bit like taking the quilt your great-grandmother made to an outdoor concert following days of rain. A train will get dirty—perhaps even so filthy or damaged that it is beyond cleaning and repair. Even a short sweep train, which extends less than a foot behind a bridal gown, is likely to act as a debris collector.

You will rationalize that there are ways to make a train work in the outdoor world, particularly if you fall in love with a dress that has one. Sure, most trains can be bustled, but if you have already picked up some mud and grass stains before bustling time arrives, buttoning up your train will make things worse by exposing its dirty underside to everyone at your wedding except you. You might reason, as well, that an aisle runner is a potential solution. However, you will likely still have to traipse quite a distance over open ground to get to the aisle, and being trapped on the runner eliminates the possibility for spontaneity during and immediately after your ceremony.

In addition to floor-length options, you might also want to consider dresses that are already designed to be ballet length—just above the ankles—or tea length—about 8 to 10 inches above the floor. A flamenco or high-low hemline, which is longer in the back and shorter in the front, can also work well outdoors. While you are thinking about hemlines, keep in mind that the length of some styles is altered not by hemming but by hoisting up the skirt at the waistline seam in order to preserve any decorative edging at the base of the skirt. Ask your seamstress specifically how she intends to modify your dress, and be sure she is aware that you will be marrying outside. You may want to discuss the possibility of hiking or hemming your skirt up a bit higher than would usually be recommended in order to minimize the possibility that the hem will tear or get dirty.

With a shorter hemline, your shoes will be more visible. Unfortunately, the white or ivory satin pumps that are commonly matched with bridal gowns are very prone to picking up dirt and other environmental blemishes. You may want to either invest in a backup pair to reserve for photos after the ceremony or break with tradition. Possibilities include going barefoot; wearing gold or silver sandals at a beach wedding; making your shoes your very dramatic something blue; choosing colorful, floral-print pumps for a garden party; or trading fragile heels for durable white leather boots at a country barnyard fiesta.

How to Wear Your Hair

Once you have found your dream gown, it is time to focus on completing your look with just the right shoes, handbag, jewelry, undergarments, hose, garter, and other accessories. The most important finishing touch is the style and adornments you select for your hair. The right hairdo and headpiece will draw attention to your radiant smile and sparkling eyes. For outdoor brides, whose tresses may be mussed by wind, drizzle, or humidity, there are some added practicalities involved in deciding how to wear your hair.

Up or Down?

Unless your current hairstyle is short, your first major decision is whether to wear your hair up or down. Updos, which are popular with many brides, actually take a variety of forms including buns, French twists, braids, pinned-up ringlets, crowns, ponytails, chignons, and knotted styles. Some updos appear sleek and sculpted, while others are more loose and free.

In the outdoors, updos offer several advantages. For starters, if secured firmly via clips, elastics, bobby pins, gel, and hairspray, they are likely to stay in place, even if the day is breezy or damp. Many updos look fabulous with just a tiara, headband, or decorative clips, which can eliminate worries about how a veil might be affected by windy conditions. One disadvantage of an updo is that it will likely need to be styled by a professional, which means there is a cost involved. Also, should the style come undone in a gust of wind or fall flat in a sudden shower, you may be hard-pressed to make repairs on the spot. Another drawback of opting for an updo is that for most women, the style can be quite a contrast to their everyday look. While you might relish the idea of altering your image for this special day, some brides may prefer a more natural appearance, particularly if they are marrying in a natural setting.

newlywed know-how

If electricity is not available at your ceremony site, you may want to consider purchasing a butane-powered curling iron for last-minute fixes. Invest in a backup butane cartridge, and practice with the device in advance to be sure you are happy with the curls it creates.

If you choose to wear your hair down, you may want to at least be prepared to clip it back in the event of high winds. While long hair and a veil moving gently in a soft breeze is a romantic look, you don't want to contend with long locks blowing in your face as you try to speak your vows. It is also important to keep in mind that humidity and drizzle can cause hair to frizz and curl, and breeze-tossed tresses can look dry and matted. You may want to have a spritzer bottle, curling iron, and brush available for periodic touchups.

Veils

The custom of veiling the bride is an ancient one, and while its origins are uncertain, most of the plausible explanations are not likely to inspire modern brides to embrace the tradition. For example, many believe that the custom dates to an era when marriages were arranged for economic reasons, and shrouding the bride until after the ceremony was insurance against a groom taking flight the moment he laid eyes on his betrothed. While veils are still common bridal accessories, increasing numbers of brides are opting to forego this traditional accent. While wearing a veil is a matter of personal choice, for those marrying under open skies, the decision to remain unveiled may be a good one due to the problems that may arise if a veil is caught in a gusty wind.

There are many lovely alternatives to a veil, and some of them are quite apropos for a wedding in an outdoor environment. For example, several designers offer tiaras made of pearls or seashells that are perfect for beach brides. A halo of flowers tied with colorful ribbons may suit you if you are celebrating a garden or Renaissance-themed wedding. For a tropical occasion, a single exotic blossom tucked behind your ear may make a dramatic statement. A wedding at a historic property may send you off to antique shops in search of vintage hats, barrettes, or other hair accessories. For something unusual, twine long tresses with wired ribbons or spray your mane with sparkly hair glitter.

If you do decide to wear a veil, stick with one of the shorter styles. You may want to investigate the availability of headpieces equipped with a snap-off veil, which would allow you to make a last-minute change if winds pick up. Veils need not be boring—many styles feature lacy, embroidered, beaded, or beribboned edges, and some are scattered with pearls or rhinestones. Shimmer veils are particularly popular with outdoor brides because of the way they sparkle in the sunlight.

A Trial Run

Whether you will be doing your own hair, relying on a friend, or hiring a professional, it is important to schedule a trial run a few weeks before your wedding day. A practice session is particularly critical if you are getting married out of town and will be enlisting the services of a stylist who is not familiar with your hair.

rain or shine

With your wedding day looming, it is not the time to experiment with a radically different hairstyle or color. Be sure to schedule an appointment with your regular stylist for a fresh trim about two weeks before your wedding day. Grooms should also book a haircut appointment for about a week in advance.

You want to ensure that the person who creates your wedding look understands your wishes clearly and that you actually like how the style you've chosen frames your face. It must also work with the headpiece and veil or other hair adornments you have selected. You might admire dresses you've seen in photos, but you would never buy your bridal gown off the rack without trying it on. Similarly, you can't know how a hairstyle you've selected from a book or magazine will look on you until you give it a try.

Bridesmaids' Attire

They are the women who have listened to you, laughed with you, and dragged you out for ice cream sundaes when your hopes were dashed or your heart was broken. They encourage you, support you, share their wisdom with you, and allow you to always be yourself. Now that it is time for them to line up by your side as you make a momentous leap into the realm of matrimony, you want them to feel beautiful and comfortable.

newlywed know-how

The number of bridesmaids you choose to include is a matter of personal choice. The average number is four to six. For small weddings, there is a trend for couples to forego attendants altogether. Invite only those close friends and family members whose participation you will cherish, and keep in mind that an even number of maids and groomsmen is not absolutely necessary.

Comfort Is Key

The bride sets the model for the attire worn by other wedding party members, and she ultimately gets to make the final decision about bridemaids' outfits. The key, though, to wedding-party harmony is seeking input from those who have agreed to take on the role of bridesmaid and making their comfort a primary consideration. Accepting an invitation to serve as a bridesmaid can require a hefty investment of money and time. It should not also come with the risk of shivering in a spaghetti-strap mini dress on a cool fall day, twisting an ankle in stilettos, or trying to look sophisticated in a long black satin number in ninety-degree weather.

The good news for outdoor bridesmaids is that designers are increasingly offering styles that are sleek, short, and sophisticated, made of lightweight fabrics that breathe and move, and available in flattering, subtle shades. Many of these designs are simple yet elegant enough to complement even the most formally attired bride. When the leading lady has decided to dress a bit more casually herself, the choices for bridesmaids become even more open-ended, and colorful sundresses, crinkly skirts, or crisp shorts with silk tees or weskits, and even halter tops, sarongs, and sandals might be appropriate.

As you consider how to outfit your bridesmaids, keep the following comfort factors in mind:

- Dark colors hold heat.
- Hats may provide some shade, but on a hot and humid day, they can also leave hair-dos beyond salvation if bridesmaids intend to remove them at some point. Wind can also wreak havoc on hats.
- A dress with a matching jacket, shawl, or wrap is a good choice for open-air weddings in the spring and fall, in the evening, or near the seashore.
- Short, flowing skirts can be hazardous on windy days.
- Neutral shades and prints are least likely to show dirt and other accidental stains that a bridesmaid might pick up during the course of an outdoor event.
- On a hot day, bridesmaids may be thankful for a dress style that looks great without pantyhose.

Getting Everyone to Agree

If you've ever been a bridesmaid, you already know that it can be quite a challenge to find a single style and color that pleases the bride and all of her women attendants. The larger the wedding party, the more difficult it is to achieve unanimity. Most brides want their friends and relations to be happy with the final choice, and many spend hours listening to input from various factions and agonizing over the ultimate selection.

An outdoor wedding provides an opportunity to minimize some of this angst. You've already decided to take a somewhat novel approach to your wedding day. Why not also adopt a less traditional and more flexible stance when it comes to choosing bridesmaids' attire?

For example, if you have your heart set on a pale lilac color for your spring garden wedding, why not allow your attendants to select the style of their choice in that hue? Many bridal-wear designers offer collections that feature a variety of dress styles in a single shade or a color family; some have even created two-piece options that allow for ultimate mix-and-match flexibility. By controlling only the color, you allow each bridesmaid to find a dress silhouette that flatters her figure, while still achieving a coordinated look for your wedding party.

Alternatively, if you have a dress style in mind because it matches your wedding's theme or your own gown, allow bridesmaids some flexibility in selecting the color they would like to wear from a palette that blends nicely with the rest of your event. For example, for a fall wedding, instead of inviting disgruntled whines by asking everyone to wear orange, allow bridesmaids to choose from a spectrum of autumn-inspired hues. This works especially well if you will have a large wedding party.

ask the wedding planner ?

What should the flower girl wear?

The outdoors is a child's play place, so expecting a little miss to remain prim and proper in her miniature, bridal-inspired gown may be a bit of a stretch. Consider dressing down the flower girl in a pretty sundress, a white eyelet tank and capris, or a fun and vibrant outfit that coordinates with your theme.

If you really feel compelled to dress all bridesmaids exactly alike, try to aim for a look that is classic, particularly if your attendants range in age, height, body shape, and skin color. You may still want to introduce some flexibility by allowing each bridesmaid to choose her own hairstyle and accessories. If disagreements do crop up, try to be as diplomatic as possible, and remember that true friends will accept your decisions gracefully. If they don't, a pre-wedding girls' day at the spa is a good way to alleviate any lingering tensions.

The Groom's Garb

While a bride's search for the right gown might require her to visit several boutiques, try on dozens of styles, and report for a series of fittings, the groom can be in and out of one tuxedo rental shop and have his wedding day attire arranged in about an hour. For most altar-bound men, this ease and speed is welcome, even if they don't particularly relish the prospect of wearing formal attire. This raises the very legitimate question many grooms may ask once plans for an outdoor wedding have been set: "Do I really need to wear a tux?"

The easy answer is "Maybe not," although finding a suitable alternative may require considerably more effort.

A Look That Suits

Grooms-to-be usually don't shop for wedding attire until about three months before the big day. The reason is simple. Through her selection of a gown, a bride gets to set the style and the level of formality for all members of the wedding party, including the groom. That means if she has chosen an intricately beaded and embroidered white ball gown with a chapel-length train, chances are good that his favorite khakis and a white golf shirt are not going to fly.

Though stiff, tight collars and hot, pinching rental shoes may not offer optimal comfort in the outdoors, most men acquiesce to the desires of their brides. A sweaty neck and blistered feet are, after all, a small price to pay for fulfilling her wedding-day wishes. It is tough to deny, too, that a tuxedo is a good look for just about every man.

For grooms who have a strong aversion to formalwear, the time to discuss attire is before your fiancée begins tearing out pictures of elegant ensembles from wedding magazines and dragging her mother to bridal boutiques. Before you broach the subject, be sure you can clearly articulate your concerns and desires. Be prepared to compromise, particularly if you begin on opposite sides of the casual-versus-formal-apparel debate.

Colors and Styles That Work Outdoors

Black is classic. Black coordinates well with everything. But when the afternoon sun reigns in a cloudless summer sky, black is, in a word, hot. Men who do plan to wear a suit or tuxedo for their outdoor nuptials may want to discuss with their partners the possibility of opting for a lighter color, such as a gray, platinum, or ivory. In addition to absorbing less heat, neutral colors also have the advantage of not showing dust, sand, pollen, or other outdoor lint as distinctly as black might. Don't be tempted, however, to stray far from a classic color palette of masculine shades. Unless you are the groom at a seventies-themed wedding, that vintage sherbet-pink tux you discovered at a thrift shop should stay in your closet until Halloween rolls around.

rain or shine

In the tuxedo selection process, shirts are usually an afterthought. It is important to ask your fiancée whether you should wear a white or an ivory shirt. It is also critical to try on your shirt before you leave the tux shop after picking up your rental to ensure that it fits properly.

Because you are marrying outside, the good news is that even if your wedding is dressy, it is not likely to be ultra formal. That means a cummerbund may suffice in place of a vest, eliminating one layer of material that would add to the bulk of your ensemble. Tails are heavier than a tuxedo jacket, and weight will be your enemy on a day when the mercury is high, so this is a factor to keep in mind. Be sure to tell tuxedo shop employees that you are planning to wed outdoors, as they will be able to steer you toward higher thread-count, lighter-weight fabrics that may well be worth a bit of added expense. Since a bow tie can't really be loosened without drooping, you may want to consider a necktie or even a mandarin collar that requires no tie.

If you and your fiancée have agreed to a casual approach, dark or khaki pants or even Bermuda shorts paired with a white button-down shirt may fill the bill. A linen or silk suit may be a good choice if you are looking for something a notch above informal. Shopping for the ideal relaxed wedding-day outfit can actually require a bit of legwork. Look for natural fibers and wrinkle-resistant fabrics, cleanly tailored styles, and quality that surpasses that of your everyday casual wear. If you plan to wear a boutonnière, keep in mind that the fabric you select must be sturdy enough to support the pinned-on floral piece.

As a rule, groomsmen and other male members of the wedding party, such as the bride's and groom's fathers, all wear attire that is identical to or closely matched to the groom's. When all tuxedos are ordered from a single rental shop or chain, you needn't give coordination a second thought. However, when the men's uniform will be a bit more laidback, it can actually be tricky to locate matching slacks or shorts and shirts to fit all of the guys, as even basic navy blue can come in a wide variety of subtly different hues. Aside from organizing a men's day at the mall, which may prove more frustrating and exhausting than productive, your best bet may be to order all of the men's coordinates from a mail-order retailer, which is more likely to have a wide variety of sizes in stock. Gather sizing information, and have all clothing shipped to one address first so that you can verify that pieces match before they are distributed. Order errors can occur, and even this approach can sometimes result in unacceptable color variation if dye lots are not closely matched.

piece of cake

If you are ordering casual attire for the men in your wedding party, be sure to understand the mail-order company's return policy and to allow sufficient time for exchanges. Don't forget that in addition to coordinating tops and bottoms, men may require matching belts and shoes.

Don't Sweat It

For some men, it isn't only the prospect of being less than comfortable that makes the notion of wearing formal attire in the outdoors unsavory. It is the fear that they won't look their best if that layered, long-sleeve get-up makes them hot and sweaty.

Every man is different, so it is important to evaluate your own personal proclivity toward perspiring profusely. Keep in mind that in addition to heat, nerves may add to your dampness level. While you will certainly employ a good antiperspirant and deodorant, and maybe even a dusting of baby powder, it may be impossible to keep sweat completely at bay. If sweat is a concern, you are actually better off sticking to black or other very dark colors; even though dark shades absorb more heat, they are less likely to show perspiration stains.

If you are known to sweat a bit, you may also have a strong stance when it comes to negotiating with your sweetheart, who may agree that you'll be a more handsome new husband in an outfit that is cool and comfortable.

If she is unconvinced, strategize ahead of time about how you will keep your cool—at least until the first strains of the wedding processional sound. Arrange to dress at the ceremony location if possible. If a climate-controlled building is not available, be sure an air-conditioned vehicle will provide you with a place to chill out in the minutes leading up to the bride's arrival. Wear an undershirt, and don't put on your dress shirt and jacket until the last possible moment. If you feel a tinge of nervousness, take deep breaths, and think about how lucky you are to have found a woman who adores you, even when you're glistening.

Communicating Correct Dress to Guests

As peculiar as it may seem, it is actually more difficult to communicate with guests about appropriate informal dress than it is about formal attire. That's because etiquette guides provide standardized definitions for formal dress requests. A white-tie affair, the dressiest designation, requires floor-length, elegant dresses for women and full dress for men, which means black pants and tailcoat and a white shirt, tie, and vest. A black-tie event means black tuxedos for men and nice dresses of any length or dressy suits or pants outfits for women. If an invitation states, "Black tie optional," men may opt for a dark suit instead of a tuxedo.

rain or shine

Be sure that any service providers who will be visible at your wedding, such as your bartender, photographer, DJ, and musicians, all get the message about appropriate attire, too. Everyone at the wedding will affect the total theme or atmosphere you've created.

As weddings go, outdoor celebrations tend to be on the more casual side, even when they are held in the evening. You may find, therefore, that none of these designations is appropriate for your event. Unfortunately, terms used to specify less formal dress, such as "semiformal," "neat casual," "festive casual," or "garden party attire," are less clearly defined and open to very broad interpretation by guests. If you use one of these phrases, be prepared to answer questions about what is expected from many uncertain guests. Alternatively, you may want to spell out exactly what you have in mind, like so:

- Casual dress, but no jeans, T-shirts, or sneakers, please.
- Colorful dresses for women and jackets for men requested.
- Please come dressed comfortably for a backyard barbecue.
- Feel free to wear shorts, sandals, and sundresses to our wedding at the beach, but no bathing attire, please.

If you are hoping that guests will dress in accordance with a theme, this should also be stated clearly in your invitations. In order to avoid intimidating guests who are uncomfortable in costume or period garb, your request should make it clear that participation is optional. For example, you might specify: "Though not required, we hope you will consider wearing a costume to our masquerade ball." You may want to provide guests with a list of local and online vendors if you are encouraging Renaissance or other period attire.

Changing Attire Midstream

So, you two really want to wear an elaborate white gown and a black tuxedo with tails on your wedding day. You're worried, though, about how your fancy duds will hold up when subjected to hours in the outdoors. It's a legitimate concern, particularly for those whose ceremony and reception are both slated to take place outside.

One solution is to pack a change of clothes. In fact, many brides and grooms already plan to have another outfit along, particularly if they are leaving directly for their honeymoon. Rather than waiting until your departure, after the ceremony and formal photo taking have concluded, duck into a restroom or behind a screen, and slip into something cooler, comfortable, and more casual.

piece of cake

If nothing else, the bride may want to trade her high heels for flats or slippers when it comes time for dining and dancing. Be sure your seamstress knows of your plan, and bring both pairs of shoes along to your dress fittings.

If you do plan in midstream to change attire, think carefully about how you can go on looking like bride and groom. For her, options include a flowing white or off-white sundress, a white or cream crocheted halter top with matching shorts, or a sequined white or pastel pantsuit. You may want to leave your tiara, jeweled hair clip, or floral headpiece in place, as well. For him, possibilities include pairing tux pants with a Hawaiian shirt or even a white T-shirt and a colorful cummerbund. If shorts are in order, choose a dark color, and match them up with a silk button-down shirt, a crisp golf shirt, or a gauzy poet shirt in white or another pale shade that coordinates with the new bride's outfit.

When packing his change of clothes, the groom should include matching shoes, socks, belt, and other accessories. The bride may need to think about a change of undergarments from what she wore under her gown, as well. Be sure you both bring along hangers and dry cleaning or garment bags to protect your gown and tux after you change.

16

The Final Countdown

It hardly seems possible: Your wedding day is just one week away. Even if you have remained relatively calm up until now, you may be surprised by the intensity of your emotions and the stress you feel as the hours until showtime slip away. If you weren't intimidated at all about getting married outside, that may change the first moment you hear a forecast for rain. Now, more than ever, it is important to stay focused, to confirm all details, and to rest easy knowing you are prepared for anything.

What Can Go Wrong

It's not news you want to hear, but it's true. There is a good chance that something will go wrong during the course of your wedding. Like anything complex, the more moving parts a wedding has, the higher the probability of a malfunction. On the bright side, any mishap is likely to be small and inconspicuous to all but the two of you. With a bit of mental preparation, you will be able to take any minor problems in stride.

The Big Stuff

The beach where you planned to marry is closed due to an oil spill. A hailstorm lays waste to the garden where you are scheduled to wed. Your reception pavilion burns to the ground a week before your wedding. A national security threat closes the nearest airport. A hurricane threatens not only to foil your plans for an outdoor ceremony but to force a mass evacuation from the area.

Yes, something calamitous might impact your plans. Chances are slim, and it is important not to succumb to irrational fears, but you may feel more in control if you develop a crisis plan in advance. The plan should include these elements:

- A list of possible backup sites likely to be available at the last minute, such as the residence of a friend or family member, along with contact phone numbers.
- Telephone numbers for alternate modes of transportation, including airlines, rail services, bus lines, limousine companies, and rental car outlets.
- A list of occurrences that would and would not lead you to call off the event (to be developed with your partner while you are both thinking rationally).
- A strategy for contacting all guests efficiently to communicate a change of plans.
- A contact list of all vendors who would also need to be kept abreast of any last-minute changes, along with copies of all contracts with cancellation policies highlighted.
- A wedding emergency fund or line of credit that could be tapped in the event that something unforeseen taxes your budget.
- A copy of your wedding insurance policy, if you have purchased one.

While it is a worthwhile exercise to think about how to cope with a serious incident that may require you to postpone your event, you should make your plan and then put it away. No amount of fretting can prevent a natural disaster, a human loss, a railway strike, or a whale beaching. The legal profession gives the name "acts of God" to things that are out of human control. Short of a change of heart, that would describe anything that would affect your ability to hold your wedding as planned, no matter how carefully you have prepared.

The Small Stuff

Aside from factors that would force cancellation of your wedding, anything else that could go wrong is really small stuff. Granted, it may not seem that way at the moment the groom can't button his shirt collar, the bride tears a three-inch hole in her gown, the limousine has a blowout, the photographer calls in sick, the band gets lost and arrives two hours late, the cake begins to lean, or the best man bails due to a family emergency. You will recall these minor mishaps with laughter years from now, but they can send you into a frenzy when they catch you by surprise with your emotions already running high.

In spite of all of your preparations, you cannot possibly anticipate every little thing that might go wrong. Making a list and checking it twice will keep the number of possible surprises to a minimum, but there is still a chance that accidents will happen. When a mishap occurs, you will get through it with grace by thinking on your feet, brainstorming creative workarounds, and, most of all, remaining levelheaded.

Keeping Your Cool

Remaining dignified and tear-free when something goes awry on your special day is easier said than done. When a problem arises, take a deep breath. Next, call in some reinforcements to help you calmly assess the situation and to brainstorm quick and creative remedies. Your maid of honor may help you quickly realize, for example, that though the bouquet that was delivered from the florist is not the one you ordered, it is actually quite lovely and will do just fine. An aunt who is talented with a needle and thread might stitch a torn sleeve or a separated bodice in no time flat. Arriving by taxi may not be what you had in mind, but your photographer may be thrilled by the colorful substitute of a yellow cab for a drab black limo.

piece of cake

The vast majority of people at your wedding will be oblivious to most things that don't go quite according to plan. It can be disappointing when something you've worked hard to plan doesn't materialize in quite the way you'd hoped. But if you can distance yourself a bit and view any mishaps from the perspective of guests, you will realize that everything appears to be fine.

While keeping your cool largely applies to managing emotions of disappointment and sadness, you may also find frustration and anger creeping up if you feel that a vendor has not delivered on a commitment. If you believe you have been overcharged or underserved, it is important to resolve to take matters up with the individual vendor at a later date. Your outdoor wedding under clear blue skies will be substantially marred if you engage in a red-faced shouting match. When you are in a calmer frame of mind, make notes about what happened, review your signed contracts, and, if necessary, retain an attorney to help you seek restitution.

Things to Do One Week Before

The week before your wedding day will be a whirlwind. Even though everything has essentially been arranged, there are many calls to make, details to double-check, and last-minute preparations to handle. Hopefully, you will be able to take time away from work or other obligations in these last few days so that you can focus on wrapping up final tasks, greeting guests as they arrive, and getting plenty of rest before the big day.

Calls to Make

You'll be spending some time on the telephone during the seven days preceding your wedding day. While you may feel confident that your vendors are all set to go, it never hurts to touch base and reconfirm plans. Here are some calls you should make as your event draws near:

☐ Contact any invitee who has not yet responded so that you can firm up your guest count.

☐ Call your caterer or site manager to provide a final guest count and review menu and setup details. If your cake was ordered separately, check that your baker knows when and where to deliver it.

☐ Provide a final count to the restaurant or other facility that is hosting your rehearsal dinner.

☐ Confirm the rehearsal and wedding-day schedule with your officiant.

☐ Call your photographer to confirm the date, time, and shooting locations and to review the list of images that are most important to you. If you are using a videographer, confirm those details as well.

☐ Connect with your DJ or band to ensure that directions to the site are clear and that you agree on an arrival and start time.

☐ Call your florist to go over the details of when and where all bouquets, corsages, boutonnières, table arrangements, and other decorations are to be delivered.

☐ Confirm any hair, makeup, manicure, and other appointments that you have scheduled.

☐ Call your limousine company, horse-and-carriage service, or other transportation providers to confirm pickup places and times.

☐ Touch base with all wedding party members to be sure they know times and places to meet for the rehearsal, rehearsal dinner, wedding, and any post-wedding events.

☐ Call your airline, car rental company, hotels, and any other travel providers to confirm your wedding night and honeymoon arrangements.

Site Preparation

In an ideal scenario, you could entrust every detail related to preparing your site to your wedding coordinator, the property manager, rental company employees, or your florist. Depending on the team you have assembled and the location you have selected, you may or may not need to take a hands-on role in readying the site for your event. At minimum, you may want to be present when setup begins to be sure that your ideas have been communicated clearly and that all will be arranged according to your plan.

If you will be taking a do-it-yourself approach to site design, it is important to assemble a reliable team of people to assist you. The shorter your time for setup, and the more elaborate your affair, the more helpers you will need. Keep in mind that it is likely to take longer than you anticipated to put everything in place, so allow extra time in order to ensure that you won't face a race to dress, primp, and make it to the altar on time. Having a written plan and sketches of where everything should be positioned will help to coordinate efforts and speed preparations.

rain or shine

It is important to determine exactly when you will have access to your wedding site for the purposes of setting up and decorating. Know who is scheduled to meet you to unlock any doors or gates, and be sure to confirm your meeting time and location, whether it is the day before or the morning of your event.

Once everything is in place, it is important to assess whether security is an issue. If you are marrying at a private property, the chances that anything will be disturbed are substantially smaller than if your ceremony is scheduled for a public place. Either way, it is a good idea to find out whether someone will be around to keep an eye on things until your scheduled start time. If not, ask a dependable family friend, neighbor, or other available person to watch your site during the interval between setup and ceremony.

Final Details

As the days until "I do" wind down, there are a few other chores to complete.
Attention to these final details will help to ensure that your event goes smoothly.

☐ The groom should pick up and try on his tuxedo and shoes, and the bride should also try on her gown and shoes one last time.

☐ Be sure you have obtained a marriage license and stored it in a safe place. Decide who will take the license to the ceremony, and devise a reminder system so that you will not forget this all-important document.

☐ Pick up wedding rings from the jeweler, try them on, and store them in a secure place until they are entrusted to the best man and maid of honor.

☐ Wrap attendants' gifts, assemble and deliver welcome baskets to hotels, and create a schedule of plane and train arrivals if you will be providing transportation for guests arriving from out of town.

☐ Gather all accessories, such as the bride's stockings, garter, headpiece or hair clips, and jewelry and the groom's cuff links, socks, and undershirt.

☐ Practice reciting your vows aloud.

☐ Create a seating arrangement, make placecards, and gather other items that must be delivered to the reception site, such as favors, programs, or the guest book and pen.

☐ Make final payments to vendors, or have checks ready for presentation on your wedding day. Purchase travelers' checks or withdraw cash for your honeymoon.

☐ Pack clothes you intend to change into during or after your reception and also pack for your honeymoon if you will be departing shortly after the wedding.

☐ Type up your honeymoon details, including any flight itineraries and phone numbers for where you will be staying, and provide copies to your parents in case of an emergency.

☐ Record the details of any wedding gifts that have already been received.

☐ If you have not already done so, select a wedding gift for your spouse-to-be and set aside a special time to exchange tokens of affection.

Looking Your Best

The stress of planning an outdoor wedding can take a toll on your appearance. While the week before your wedding is not the time for a crash diet, a new fitness regimen, or a comprehensive makeover, here are a few things both the bride and groom can do in these final days to improve their chances of looking and feeling their best when the appointed day arrives:

- Establish an early bedtime and stick to it, even if friends try to coax you to go out "one last time."
- Drink plenty of water and avoid consuming large quantities of either alcohol or caffeine.
- Eat sensibly, avoiding sweets and fried foods if possible.
- Pay close attention to your skin-care cleansing and moisturizing routine.
- Apply lip balm regularly to ensure you'll have kissable lips on your big day.
- Since the camera will focus on your hands during your exchange of rings, wear gloves when washing dishes or working in the garden. Apply hand cream at night, and have your nails trimmed, shaped, and polished by a professional.
- Get in the habit of wearing sunscreen, as you'll need it for your big day in the outdoors.
- Whenever you feel overwhelmed, close your eyes, take deep breaths, and imagine that you are already on your honeymoon.
- Spend an hour each day engaged in focused relaxation, whether you choose to take a yoga class, visit a spa for a pampering facial or massage, meditate, walk the dog, watch a romantic movie, throw a Frisbee, or sip afternoon tea with friends.

Though it may seem silly, practice your smile in the days leading up to your celebration. Smile at yourself in the mirror. Smile at strangers you pass on the street. Smile when you are happy, when you are stressed out, and for no reason at all. More than anything else, it is your smile that will give you the perfect wedding day look.

The Everything Outdoor Wedding

Album

The Ceremony

The Bride and Groom

The Reception

...and they all lived

happily ever after.

The End

Watching the Weather

Even if you are not usually prone to obsessive behavior, you may find it impossible to control the urge to check the weather forecast, even if you just checked it five minutes ago. You will wake up restless in the night and turn on the Weather Channel. You will subscribe to weather alert e-mail notifications from five different online sources. You will skip over the sports section, the headlines, and the funnies in your haste to see what the newspaper's forecasters have to say, while simultaneously keeping one ear tuned to an AM radio station for the next live weather update.

piece of cake

Unless a severe weather emergency is forecast, make a pact with your partner that weather talk is off limits until the day before your wedding. Distract yourselves by planning a special date, perhaps his-and-hers pedicures or a rendezvous at the place where you first kissed, during the week before the big day.

It is going to be difficult, but for your own sanity, you really should quit your weather habit cold turkey. The truth is, forecasts can change many times, from the early ten-day predictions right up until the morning of your event. Even then, forecasts for the day ahead are not always accurate. Checking the weather constantly can only lead to unhealthy, yo-yo emotions. Allow yourself to check the weather forecast from your favorite source once each morning. Then turn it off. Remove those weather Web sites from your bookmark bar, and go back to reading the comics.

Rehearsals

A rehearsal and rehearsal dinner are traditionally scheduled prior to the wedding, usually the evening before. Since traditional indoor weddings are fairly straightforward, this is often more of a social occasion than anything else—a chance for family and wedding party members who may not have met each other to mingle and enjoy a relaxed evening together. When your wedding will take place outside, however, a bit more emphasis should be placed on the rehearsal portion of this event. Chances are good that the role of your attendants will be much more involved than walking from point A to point B, standing for a bit, and then exiting two by two. You will also need to be sure that everyone is prepared for both outdoor and indoor scenarios.

newlywed know-how

Whether you incorporate it into your rehearsal or schedule a session at an earlier time, it is important to meet with your officiant to review your ceremony and to discuss the order of proceedings and any exact language you might want to use.

A Written Plan

One way to ensure that both your rehearsal and your wedding go smoothly is to create a detailed written plan for the day. Copies of the plan should be distributed to parents, wedding party members, your officiant, vendors, and anyone who has volunteered to help with setting up, cleaning up, escorting guests, or any other important task. Make sure the plan clearly indicates who has been assigned to handle each to-do list item. You may want to use a highlighter pen or boldface type to mark the items that pertain to each individual on his or her copy of the document. If possible, the plan should be in key participants' hands a few days prior to the rehearsal so they can prepare any questions or raise concerns they may have.

What should be in your plan? Though it will vary based on the size and complexity of your event and on the availability of an on-site or contracted wedding consultant, here are some of the basics that you might include:

- Meeting times and transportation arrangements.
- Directions to all primary and backup venues.
- A map or sketch showing the layout of the site and the location of all items that must be set up.
- A schedule for the day from start to finish.
- A list of setup, ceremony, reception, and cleanup tasks, along with a designation of individuals responsible for each job.
- Specific instructions or diagrams that will help those assisting you to arrange things as you envision.
- A supply checklist and description of where to find all supplies.
- A list of important contacts and their phone numbers.
- Plans for disposal or removal of all items that cannot be left behind, such as gifts and cards, floral arrangements, decorations, your guest book, leftovers, and the top layer of the wedding cake.

rain or shine

Bring extra copies of your wedding plan to your rehearsal. Even if you have distributed the plan in advance, inevitably, someone will forget to bring a copy along. Keep these in a folder where you can keep them free of spills and tears, and distribute them as needed.

Practice Makes Perfect

The old adage "practice makes perfect" certainly applies to weddings. At your rehearsal, you will have an opportunity to walk the property once again, review setup details, provide participants with a tour of the facility, go over everyone's positions and responsibilities, and run through the program for your ceremony step by step. Regardless of how carefully you have imagined and planned, doing a dry run normally turns up a few details that you hadn't anticipated and allows you to make final decisions and adjustments. Approach your rehearsal with an open mind. If you find something that doesn't quite work, you still have time to make changes.

piece of cake

The little people in your wedding—flower girls and ring bearers—can be either adorable or horrible. A key to achieving the former, particularly in a distracting outdoor setting, is to dedicate a portion of your rehearsal to coaching them, discussing your expectations, practicing their entrance, and impressing upon them how important it is to stay focused on their job until the ceremony is complete.

Ideally, you will be able to book rehearsal time on the same evening at both your outdoor site and any indoor backup location you have reserved. If one or the other is not available, you should still rehearse both scenarios. If it isn't possible to physically walk through the proceedings, gather key players around a table with copies of your written plan in hand. Like actors in a television show or play, verbally rehearse your entrances and lines. Provide as much description as possible so that participants will know what to expect. If a wedding party member misses the rehearsal, ask another bridesmaid or usher to provide a brief.

Assembling an Emergency Kit

From umbrellas to duct tape, there are a number of items you will want to have on hand for any unexpected situations. Your emergency kit should help you cope with the elements, make last-minute repairs, and treat minor injuries. Hopefully, you have already acquired many of the items that will allow you to feel equipped to handle any emergency. Now is the time to review your checklist and to devise a plan for transporting emergency supplies to your wedding site and storing them so that they are easily accessible should any problems arise.

What You Need

First and foremost, your emergency kit should enable you to ensure people's safety and comfort. While a first-aid kit will probably be available if your location is open to the public, you should verify this. If you need to assemble your own first-aid kit, consider outfitting it with adhesive bandages and tape, alcohol wipes, antibiotic ointment, antihistamines, baking soda, a basic first-aid book, calamine lotion, chemically activated ice packs, cotton balls and swabs, elastic bandages, diarrhea medicine, eye drops, gauze pads and rolls, hydrocortisone cream, hydrogen peroxide, latex gloves, matches, needles, ibuprofen, safety pins, scissors, soap, a thermometer, and tweezers. You must also have a way to call for emergency help. If cell phone reception is unavailable or unreliable, consider renting a two-way radio or other communications device to summon assistance in the event of a serious accident.

rain or shine

A sudden downpour could turn your list of important contacts into an illegible, soggy sheet. You may want to have one copy of your contact list laminated in order to protect it from the elements.

To help guests feel comfortable in an outdoor environment, be sure to pack sunscreen, insect repellent, bottled water, and items to provide extra warmth or relief from the heat. Have plenty of umbrellas and flashlights on hand in case a storm rolls through and darkens the sky. If you will be stocking restroom facilities, don't forget to purchase plenty of toilet paper, paper towels, soap, lotions, feminine products, and air fresheners.

Wind and weather can disturb your carefully arranged decorations, so it is important to bring along a basic toolbox in case repairs are required. Stock your toolbox with a hammer, flat- and Phillips-head screwdrivers, adjustable wrench, utility knife, pliers, loaded staple gun, work gloves, duct tape, electrical tape, tape measure, bungee cords, twine, rope, nails, screws, fast-bonding glue, and a small handsaw. There are many other equipment items that may come in handy, including waterproof tarps and matches, a plunger, bucket, mop, broom, dustpan, utility light, fire extinguisher, towing chain, jumper cables, flares, orange safety vests for those directing parking, sponges, and a case of paper towels.

piece of cake

Choose a bag with many clear compartments for all of your beauty supplies, rather than allowing them to float around loosely in a duffle or tote bag. This will allow you to find what you need quickly so that you can expedite primping and return to the party.

It is also important to be able to respond to beauty emergencies. Most brides select petite and dainty purses to carry, and they are lucky if they can squeeze a tube of lipstick and a powder compact inside. In a separate, larger bag, you will want to pack a complete set of the makeup you intend to wear, including foundation, blusher, powder, eye shadow, eye liner, mascara, lipstick, and all brushes, sponges, or other applicators, along with moisturizer, sunscreen, a mirror, and a supply of makeup wipes for starting from scratch if necessary. Hair-care supplies, such as a comb, brush, curling iron, hairdryer, bobby pins, gel, mousse, and hairspray, are also a must. Also consider including tissues or a handkerchief, face-blotting paper, mints, toothpaste, a toothbrush, dental floss, deodorant, perfume, a sewing kit, safety pins, a lint brush, a backup pair of pantyhose, Band-Aids, antacids, pain-relief medication, prescription medications including birth control pills, feminine products, nail clippers, a nail file or emery board, and bottles of clear and coordinating nail polish.

Everything in Its Place

Having all of the right supplies on hand is important. It is equally crucial to be able to locate them quickly if and when an emergency develops. Organize like items together and clearly label the contents of each container. Be sure that more than one person knows the location of important supplies. You may even want to spell out in your written plan where you intend to store such things as the first-aid kit and the toolbox. Be sure that anyone who uses emergency supplies and tools returns them to their original spot.

Keeping Guests in the Loop

Your contact database has been compiled. Your communications strategy is in place. What remains in the final days leading up to your wedding celebration is the all-important job of remembering to put your plan into action.

A proactive communications strategy can head off the time-consuming phone calls from well-meaning friends and family members that are likely to begin the moment a less-than-fair weather forecast is announced for your date. Now is the time to post an update on your wedding Web site wishing any travelers a safe journey and welcoming everyone to your special wedding spot. If you were able to obtain e-mail addresses for the majority of invited guests, it may be a good idea to send a message a week before the big day reminding everyone of your inclement weather backup plans and expressing your optimism that you will be able to proceed as planned.

newlywed know-how

If you are sending an e-mail message to a large number of recipients, etiquette dictates that you should address the e-mail to yourself and use the blind carbon copy (abbreviated "bcc") option to send copies to those on your contact list. This protects the privacy of recipients' e-mail addresses and eliminates the possibility that someone will inadvertently send a reply intended for you to the entire list.

You'll be busy with myriad last-minute preparations, so make use of your answering machine. Each morning, record an updated message about the status of your plans that also instructs callers only to leave urgent messages. The week before your wedding is also a good time to enlist a volunteer, perhaps a younger sibling, to field phone calls and respond to messages on your behalf. Keep in mind, though, that there are some calls you should take, including those from wedding party members, vendors, your sweetie, and your mother.

17

The Day Dawns

The day you have planned for, labored over, and dreamed of is finally here. It's your wedding day. Hopefully, you will awake from peaceful slumber to greet a bright and beautiful dawn. Some soon-to-be brides and grooms, however, will lose sleep listening to the patter of rain on the roof and will face a few unwelcome decisions at daybreak. Whatever the day brings, endeavor to remain calm, collected, and happy. Come hail, wind, or pouring rain, at day's end, you will be married to the one you love.

Last-Minute Decision-Making

The further in advance you can make a final decision about your wedding location, the easier it will be to notify everyone and make final preparations. However, the weather may keep you guessing right up until the day of your event. As you drift off to sleep on your wedding's eve, you may not truly know what you will face in the morning, particularly if forecasters, in their typically imprecise fashion, are calling for a "chance" of precipitation. Since a last-minute call may be required, it is important to have a game plan for making that final decision.

When to Make the Call

There are many factors that figure into the cutoff time you will need to establish for making a decision, including these:

- Proximity of your indoor backup location to your outdoor wedding site
- Vendors' delivery schedule and setup time requirements
- Number of guests and the distance that some are traveling to attend your event
- Your indoor location's notification deadline
- Elaborateness of your affair, the number of items that need to be relocated, and the availability of helpers to make the move
- Flexibility in the start and end times for your reception

If your outdoor decorations consist solely of two large floral arrangements positioned on pedestals, and your indoor backup location is a banquet hall or tent located 50 yards away, you can literally make your decision at the final bell. If your assemblage will consist of only a dozen guests who will witness your mountaintop vows then join you for coffee and cake at home, it might be feasible for you all to camp out in your cars for an hour until a damp fog lifts and you can proceed as planned. However, if 300 guests are coming from all directions and must know whether to meet you at the beach or head for a hotel ballroom a half-hour across town, and your event planner requires at least six hours to transform that space into a tropical indoor oasis, waiting until a half-hour before ceremony time just won't do.

newlywed know-how

Sometimes, days of torrential rain leading up to the appointed day can force an early decision to move indoors. If you are faced with these circumstances, try not to feel too disheartened if the sun reappears just in time for your wedding but too late to dry up the muck. If possible, find a paved or other dry surface and at least head outdoors for a few photographs.

There is no easy formula for setting a deadline. You should speak to all vendors and location managers and carefully review your timeline. Take into account the complexity of your celebration, and then realistically establish the hour at which a decision absolutely must be made.

Don't Waver

Once you have decided that proceeding outdoors is either impossible or too risky, it is critical not to go back and forth. If you change your mind several times prior to the appointed hour, there are bound to be guests or vendors who get the incorrect message. While it may be difficult to watch the clouds break as you head inside to say "I do," be thankful that your decisiveness has eliminated much confusion and many potential headaches.

If your outdoor and indoor facilities are both in the same place, you have the luxury of delaying your decision-making until just before show time. Still, once a call has been made to move indoors, don't let a break in the weather tempt you to move back outdoors again. If the drumming of rain on your tent ends as your processional music fades, be glad that you will be able to enjoy the outdoors after the ceremony has concluded. Don't disrupt the flow of your marriage celebration by asking guests to pick up their chairs and head outside.

Sudden Upsets

The day arrives with blue skies and warm sunshine. Guests are seated, and the string quartet begins to play. The weather still looks fine, despite increasing clouds and forecasters' mention of a chance of showers. Then, just as the groom emerges and the flower girl begins her sprightly walk down the aisle, the sky abruptly darkens and large drops of rain begin to ping on metal folding chairs. What will you do?

For starters, don't panic. If you are well prepared, you have stashed a supply of umbrellas nearby just in case, and you have an action plan in place. Someone, perhaps your officiant or best man, should be prepared to immediately make an announcement so that guests know what is in store before they make a mad dash for cover. You have several choices:

- Instruct guests to proceed immediately to your indoor backup location.
- Instruct guests to remain in their cars for twenty minutes and, if the weather does not clear, to then proceed to your indoor backup location.
- Instruct guests to join you inside or under an on-site shelter, where you will wait for a period to see if the storm passes.

If rain begins after vows and rings have been exchanged, it may be wise to simply wrap up quickly. This is a potentiality that should be discussed with your officiant in advance. If there are musical numbers, readings, prayers, blessings, or other proceedings that must be omitted in the race for the groom to kiss the bride so that everyone can head inside, you may be able to incorporate some or all of them into your reception. Bear in mind, however, that you may not be able to immediately regain everyone's attention the moment you get inside.

Your Communications Plan

Long before your invitations were mailed, you devised a scheme for communicating with guests about any changes to your outdoor wedding plans—that is, if you move to a backup location. If you do decide you must move the celebration indoors, it is important to immediately activate your communications strategy.

Putting the Plan into Action

Hopefully, the plan you have in place allows you to delegate the majority of effort to others or to rely heavily on automated means of communication, such as e-mail or an answering machine recording. If that is the case, a few phone calls or a touch of a button may be all that is necessary to initiate the process of notifying guests of your change of plans. One task that must be completed as quickly and diligently as possible is contacting vendors, so be sure to either handle this responsibility yourselves or to involve a family or wedding party member who will make this job priority one until it is done.

piece of cake

Try not to tie up a phone line that is likely to be ringing with incoming calls from vendors, friends, and family members seeking information. If, for example, most inquiries are likely to come in on the bride's cell phone or her parents' home phone line, use a wedding party member's cell phone or a business or fax line to make outbound calls if possible.

When You Can't Connect

Inevitably, there will be a few folks whom you can't reach by any means. If one of them is your officiant, you may have reason to be concerned.

Otherwise, resolve to do your best to contact everyone on your list, but don't fret inordinately if you miss a few guests.

If the weather is obviously unsuitable for an outdoor event, most guests will have read your invitation carefully enough to know that there is an alternate location. For the rare few who do go astray, your communications plan should also include a method for redirecting them from your outdoor site, such as posting a sign or having a person available to meet them. If there were many guests who could not be contacted, you may want to consider delaying your start by ten or fifteen minutes to allow extra time for everyone to arrive at the right site. You may also want to ask a friend or family member to stay near the door to greet any latecomers once your ceremony has begun.

Getting Ready

For most brides and grooms, there are only two things left to do when their wedding day arrives: get ready, and get to the ceremony on time. Those marrying outdoors, however, may be much busier in the hours leading up to their wedding, particularly if the weather has not cooperated. Even brides and grooms blessed with a sunny day may find themselves with a hectic schedule that includes overseeing site setup and coordinating the efforts of volunteers. In these potentially chaotic final hours, it is important, nevertheless, to carve out space and time not only to dress for the big occasion but to relish these last moments of build-up and anticipation.

Keeping Appointments

If you have made wedding-day beauty appointments, it is important to keep them. This may seem an unnecessary reminder, but in the fray of checking forecasts, making decisions, and juggling phone calls, you may feel so overwhelmed that you think your nails look just fine as is.

Not only is it a good idea to keep your scheduled appointments, you should make every effort to arrive on time. Your hairstylist, makeup artist, manicurist, or other service provider may have a busy schedule, and the last thing you want on your wedding day is a rush job. Sitting in a chair being fussed over is not only a prerequisite to looking and feeling your best on this special day, it is an opportunity to decompress a bit. You can go back to making calls and worrying about the weather the moment the final tendril is sprayed in place, but until then, take time out to focus on inner peace and outer beauty.

Savor the Preparations

As you develop a schedule for the hours preceding your marriage celebration, try to allow plenty of time both for items that you know you must accomplish, such as putting on your dress or tux, and for those you might need to handle, such as notifying vendors of a location switch. While you may be able to do everything in a rush and still make it to your ceremony on time and looking fabulous, you will miss important moments that you can't ever reclaim. In fact, both the groom and bride should plan to spend this preparation time celebrating and having fun with their groomsmen and bridesmaids.

rain or shine

One key thing to remember to do while you are getting ready is to eat something. Many brides and grooms lament en route to their wedding night destination that they barely got a chance to eat a morsel of their meals or a bite of cake. Fortify yourselves for the long day ahead by eating a hearty lunch or snack.

Play music, set out a buffet of favorite decadent foods, tell stories, snap candid photographs. Take time to thank each person who is standing up for you for their presence in your life. Though marriage does not spell an end for relationships with girlfriends, guy friends, siblings, or parents, it does represent a change. Don't miss the opportunity to tell your mother you love her as she fusses with your veil or straightens your bowtie. The rest of the day will zoom by with a speed that you can't yet conceive, so make getting ready a time to do things deliberately and to cherish the final moments at the close of this chapter of your life.

Nerves, Tears, and Final Touches

One benefit of being a tad frantic in the hours prior to your wedding ceremony is that it leaves little opportunity for succumbing to a last-minute case of the jitters or weepies. On the other hand, if you allotted extra time to handle contingencies but the weather turned out to be spectacular, you may find yourselves with some extra time to pace and wait. If idleness is causing you angst, here are a few last-minute tasks to fill your waiting time:

- When her bouquet arrives, the bride should practice holding it in a mirror to see where it looks most flattering and to get used to its weight.
- If he has not already done so, the groom might make arrangements for champagne and roses to be waiting when he and his new wife arrive at their accommodations for the night.
- Either of you can reconfirm your honeymoon plans one last time.
- Take a moment to write a thank-you note to your parents, and ask one of your attendants to mail it for you after you have departed on your trip. You may also want to write a note to your new spouse's parents, thanking them for welcoming you into their family.
- Call any relatives who were unable to join you due to ill health and tell them they are on your mind.

While staying active may help to alleviate some stress, don't try too hard to suppress feelings that rise to the surface. Cry a little. Talk to your bridesmaids or groomsmen about your anxieties. This is a big day, and it will be filled with emotional highs, from your first glimpse in the mirror to the instant your eyes meet those of your mate-to-be. If you allow your feelings to flow freely, you won't risk the possibility that pent-up nerves and emotion will erupt at an inopportune moment.

Smile for the Camera

Most brides and grooms are not trained actors. That means they may have trouble putting on a happy face when they really feel terribly let down that their day did not turn out quite as planned. With videotape rolling and a photographer snapping away, however, it is important to try to shake off any bad-weather blues. Gray skies and drizzle won't ruin your wedding pictures, but a despondent expression or phony smile certainly could.

piece of cake

Many people find that positive affirmations repeated either internally or aloud help them to cope with difficult times. You may want to write a few on an index card that you keep tucked in your purse or a pocket. Refer to them if you start to feel overwhelmed by disappointment.

There are several ways to restore good cheer in the face of less-than-perfect circumstances. As you are getting ready, play lively music and encourage your attendants to share funny jokes and stories. Try to see wicked weather as merely the first of many obstacles that you will have the strength to conquer together. Once your eyes meet, shut out the world entirely and concentrate only on your beloved and the warmth and support that surrounds you. If a smile still remains elusive, ask your photographer to take a break while you retreat for a few private moments to breathe deeply and regain your composure.

Schedule Private Moments

There is nothing more intimate than the love between two people, but on your wedding day, you will present a very public display of your affection. If you have chosen to marry in a public place, you may even be surrounded by curious strangers. Standing at the altar, you will be together but far from alone. The moment the recessional concludes, you will be pulled in many different—and sometimes opposite—directions.

When a couple marries inside a house of worship and then travels to a separate reception destination, the ride in a limousine, carriage, or other vehicle often provides the opportunity for the newlyweds to share some time alone. However, in an outdoor environment, it is not uncommon for the reception to be held in the same location immediately after the ceremony. Unlike a hotel or banquet hall that may have a secluded bridal suite, an open expanse offers few places to hide.

newlywed know-how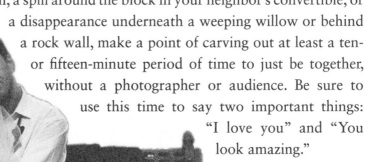

If you have opted to meet for photographs before the ceremony, this may be an apt time to also reserve some private minutes for just the two of you, either before the photo session begins or just after it has concluded. Other opportune times to sneak off include while guests are being seated for dinner, after your first dance, or while cake is being served.

Since opportunities for alone time may not present themselves naturally, it is important to schedule them. Whether it is a walk alone on the beach or down a wooded path, a spin around the block in your neighbor's convertible, or a disappearance underneath a weeping willow or behind a rock wall, make a point of carving out at least a ten- or fifteen-minute period of time to just be together, without a photographer or audience. Be sure to use this time to say two important things: "I love you" and "You look amazing."

When It's Not What You Hoped For

You knew from the start that choosing an outdoor wedding involved a degree of risk. Many of the greatest things in life, though, are only achieved through a willingness to gamble a bit on the outcome. Love is chief among them. Whether your wedding is held outdoors as you hoped or indoors due to foul weather or other unexpected obstacles, it is possible that it won't all go just as you'd envisioned. Rather than dwell on the negative, try to focus not on what you missed but what you gained—a loving partner to share life's wins and losses.

The Big Picture

As you planned your wedding, particularly a complex event in the great outdoors, you were likely hyper-focused on details. As the day unfolds, it is therefore quite understandable that you might perceive any detail that is out of place as a blemish. If you feel disappointed in how your wedding played out, it is important to step back and look at the big picture. Very few weddings are utter disasters. Years from now, even you will forget that the caterer had trouble keeping buffet dishes warm due to the cool weather or that all of your programs blew into the lake.

rain or shine

It bears repeating that you need a marriage license in order to be legally married. Of all the things that might go wrong, not remembering to bring along your license, or forgetting to obtain one altogether, is the one thing that can spoil your plans for accomplishing the most important intention of your wedding day.

Of course, everyone dreams of the perfect wedding day, but it is a bit unrealistic to expect that your celebration will be completely flawless. The object of a wedding is to unite two people in marriage. If, at the end of the day, you are legally husband and wife, everything else, truly, was just details.

Enjoying Each Moment, Indoors or Out

In addition to concentrating on details, the months leading up to your wedding day have been filled with anticipation for what was to come. When the big day arrives, it is important to switch gears. Instead of thinking ahead to the next item on the wedding itinerary, strive to stay present and to savor each moment. Don't mentally rehearse your vows as you walk down the aisle. Don't think about the cake as you eat your soup. Don't worry about your first dance during the best man's toast.

piece of cake

As you unwind on your wedding night or settle into your seats for a long flight to your honeymoon destination, make a point of writing down the most wonderful memories of your day. You might each make a list of your top five moments and then share them. Tuck your lists into a scrapbook or album to read in the future.

Focusing on the here-and-now is an excellent antidote to feeling glum if your outdoor wedding has been forced indoors. Inside or outside, you will share this short time with the people who matter most in your world. The chances that this same group will ever gather again in one place are slim, so cherish these moments together.

18

A Grand Entrance

Those who choose an outdoor wedding setting must give extra thought to transportation, not only for the bride, groom, and bridal party but possibly for guests. While an outdoor venue may present some added logistical challenges, it can also inspire creative ideas for arriving in style. Whereas the bride and groom tend to remain sequestered or to arrive after guests are already seated for an indoor affair, outdoors, your approach may be very visible. Think carefully about the visual impact of your grand entrance.

Transporting Guests

Guests are usually on their own when it comes to making their way to a wedding. If you have selected a venue that is easy to reach and that offers ample parking, it is perfectly fine to expect guests to make their own transportation plans. However, if your site is difficult to access, charges an entrance fee, must be reached via a toll bridge or boat, or in some other way presents an unexpected obstacle to those who will be sharing your celebration, you will need to be more involved in facilitating guests' travel arrangements. If many guests have traveled a distance to your destination wedding, you may also want to provide a shuttle to collect them from their accommodations and transport them to wedding events.

Carpools and Shuttles

Encouraging guests to carpool is always a smart idea. Besides being environmentally friendly, it is also a means of reducing traffic at your wedding site. This can ease parking hassles and also cut down on the amount of dust stirred up if access roads are unpaved. A fringe benefit is that fewer partygoers will need to assume the role of designated driver. If the site you have selected imposes tight limits on the number of vehicles that can enter and park, you may need to do more than simply recommend that guests share a ride. The bride or groom or a member of the wedding party may need to assume the job of carpool manager in order to organize rides for all while respecting the site's access and parking restrictions.

rain or shine

Actively discourage guests from drinking and driving. Reward those who agree to serve as designated drivers with a small token of your appreciation. Offer plenty of nonalcoholic beverage choices. Serve food for the whole time alcohol is available, and close the bar an hour before your event is scheduled to end.

If the number of guests will be large and the task of organizing a carpool seems overwhelming, or if there is no on-site parking available at all, you may need to spring for a shuttle van or bus. A shuttle is also a nice gesture if many guests are traveling by plane and without their own cars. Many limousine companies offer larger transport vehicles, and you might also get quotes from motor-coach operators, hotel and airport shuttle services, and even school bus companies. Keep in mind, however, that guests will obtain their first impression of your event from the vehicle they board. While a yellow school bus might be appropriate for a casual wedding, you may want to choose a plushier, air-conditioned ride if guests will be formally attired for a more elegant affair.

Paying Their Passage

If the site you have selected regularly charges for parking or admission, or if reaching the site requires purchasing a ferry ticket or paying a substantial bridge or road toll, it is important to determine in advance how to alleviate the potential for hassles for guests and, if feasible, to pay any fees ahead of time. In some cases, admission and parking fees will be included in the amount you are paying to rent the site. If this is the case, be sure guests know how to enter the property and what to say to ensure they won't be charged on the way in, or mail admission tickets and passes in advance to those who will attend. If you will be providing a guest list for gatekeepers' reference, be sure it is 100-percent accurate.

If your site refuses to waive admission or parking fees as part of your wedding event package, try to arrange to cover these costs if at all possible. If boat transportation is required to access your wedding location, make prior arrangements to ensure that guests' passage is not only paid but that ample spaces are reserved for your party. If there are tolls, admission fees, or parking charges that you expect guests to pick up, be sure to provide complete details with your invitation. The worst scenario is one in which a guest is surprised by a charge and is not prepared to pay.

Timing Is Everything

When it comes to timing, it can be equally bad for guests to arrive too early as too late. It can be uncomfortable for guests to wait for an extended period outside if there is no shade or shelter. When some guests arrive late, it not only prolongs the wait for the punctual, it can interfere with plans for your own dramatic arrival on the scene.

newlywed know-how

If you want to ensure that guests are in place before you make your grand entrance, arrange for your wedding coordinator or an usher to be in communication with both of you via cell phone or wireless radio. Provide this person with a final guest count so that they know how many people you are expecting and can judge when to proceed.

As you develop a timeline for the day, factor in a window of twenty to thirty minutes for guests to arrive. You may want to indicate on your invitations that the ceremony will start promptly at the appointed time. Be forthright with guests about how long it will take them to reach the ceremony site from parking areas. If guests will need to connect with a ferry, catch a train, cross a drawbridge, or enter the site before gates close to the public, be sure this crucial timing information is communicated effectively so that everyone allows ample travel time.

Your Transportation

While it is important to consider how guests will get to your wedding, your own transportation needs are paramount. No fairy godmother is going to turn a pumpkin into a coach for you, so you must arrange reliable transport well in advance. The operative word is "reliable." A mishap along the way will not only add to your anxiety and delay your big moment, it will try the patience of guests forced to wait, particularly if weather conditions are less than ideal. Calculating a transportation schedule is almost as critical as sticking to it.

The Importance of Being Punctual

While it may be fine to arrive fashionably late for some things, make it a priority to be on time for your outdoor wedding. There are several reasons that punctuality is a virtue for outdoor grooms and brides. If weather conditions are hot or chilly, your tardiness might leave guests melting under the sun or shivering in the cold. If your entire event must conclude by sundown or another prescribed time, starting late will diminish the time left to celebrate. If you selected the time of day for your ceremony based on such things as the tide table or the sun's position, a delay may cause you to miss out on optimal conditions.

Much of the responsibility for being on time rests firmly on your shoulders and depends upon your ability to awake on schedule, complete final tasks efficiently, and dress and primp quickly. But your transportation provider also plays a part in whether you will be at your wedding location at the appointed hour. Develop a timeline for pickups and drop-offs, and be sure to confirm all arrangements with those who will be

doing the driving. Ask all drivers to arrive at appointed meeting places at least fifteen minutes before you are scheduled to depart. Having a backup plan is old hat to you by now, so it wouldn't hurt to think through what you would do in the event the limousine gets hopelessly snarled in traffic, your horse and carriage does not materialize, or a car breaks down.

Your Transportation Timeline

Developing an accurate transportation timeline requires working backward from the time your wedding is slated to begin. If the bride and groom will arrive separately, it is typical for the groom to be first on the scene. You both should arrive before or at the time the ceremony is scheduled to commence unless you have received word that many guests are still in transit. In order to allow for traffic, detours, and other unforeseen delays, add at least ten minutes to your anticipated travel time—more if you will be traveling on city streets or during a busy time of day. You can always make a few extra laps around the block if you are early, but there is no good solution for running late.

piece of cake

Don't guess how long it takes to get to your wedding site. Practice! You may be surprised that what you estimated to be a fifteen-minute trip is actually closer to thirty when you time your travel from door to outdoors.

As you establish departure times, keep in mind that getting to your wedding may not be as simple as hopping into the car or carriage and setting off, especially for the bride. If she has chosen a formal gown with a full skirt, climbing into a vehicle and disembarking can both take longer. If a lengthy walk will be required upon arrival, this may also take the bride some extra time. Err on the side of allowing more travel time than less. If your trip will exceed half an hour, you may want to locate the last available clean restroom on the route to your destination, particularly if there is no discreet way to make a last-minute pit stop at your ceremony site.

Together or Separately?

Traditionally, couples spend the early hours of their wedding day apart, journey separately to the ceremony site, and see each other only as the bride begins her march down the aisle. While making separate entrances is certainly an option, there are also advantages to arriving together. This approach may make sense for those who have already met prior to the ceremony for photographs. It is also appropriate for those who have lived together for a long time, who are sharing a room at their wedding destination, or who have been previously married, since these couples may wish to eschew the tradition of having a family member escort and give away the bride. Since your outdoor environment may provide few places for concealment, it is also a way to heighten the drama of your arrival and to eliminate the possibility that either of you will be visibly pacing around awaiting your beloved's appearance.

Horses and Other Antiquated Modes of Transportation

A stretch limousine in black or white is frequently the vehicle of choice for weddings. However, couples marrying outdoors are often attracted to alternative forms of transportation, particularly those with nostalgic appeal. Classic cars and horse-drawn carriages are both guaranteed head-turners. Before you hoist yourselves up onto a buckboard or rumble seat, however, carefully consider your options and ask plenty of questions.

Choosing Your Ride

As you think about arriving in style, keep in mind that your mode of transportation should be a good fit for the theme and location of your wedding. A wagon pulled by draught horses might be fitting for a barnyard wedding, whereas an antique coach drawn by a team of sleek horses might suit a celebration at a historic plantation home. Pulling up to a mansion backdrop in a vintage Rolls Royce oozes elegance, but if you're marrying at the beach, choose a classic convertible instead. Depending on the location, you may also be able to travel to your wedding destination via trolley, streetcar, rickshaw, train, or antique boat.

rain or shine

Galloping up on horseback to meet your beloved and then riding off into the sunset together is an exceedingly romantic image, but it is not something you should attempt unless you are both experienced riders. Equestrienne brides must also select their attire with safety in mind. A veil billowing in the wind may look lovely, but it could create serious problems if the sound or sight of it whipping in the wind spooks her mount.

Your transportation choice will also be driven, of course, by availability and price. If there is no horse farm near your wedding site, you may be able to find a service that is willing to truck horses and a carriage to your location, though this will add to the cost. If a vintage automobile is what you fancy and you don't know a car collector, check with local limousine services, as some may also have unique antiques in their fleets. You might also contact a local car club, as many proud owners love to show off their vehicles and may be willing to serve as your chauffeur for a reasonable fee. The Antique Automobile Club of America (online at *www.aaca.org*) has 400 regional clubs worldwide.

Questions to Ask

If a horse-drawn vehicle is your preference, it is a wise idea to visit farms that provide livery service to view available coaches, wagons, and carriages. While you may get an idea of their appearance via a Web site, there is no substitute for seeing the carriages and their condition up close. Ask if you can climb aboard to get a sense of the space and comfort each carriage provides. Meeting the people who will perform the all-important task of delivering you safely and dependably to your wedding ceremony is also prudent. Be prepared to ask a number of questions, including these:

- What horse-drawn vehicles are available on our wedding day, and how many people can each accommodate? Which horses will pull each vehicle?

- How many weddings do you provide transportation for annually? How experienced are the horses you use?

- How fast do the horses travel? What is the maximum distance they can cover? Are they able to navigate busy streets, or will we need to carefully consider the route?

- Where will you meet passengers prior to the wedding? Will the carriage be available after the ceremony for additional photos?

- Can we adorn the carriage with flowers, a "Just Married" sign, or other decorations?

- Will you supply a single driver? A driver and footman? How will they be attired?

- Do you carry necessary permits and insurance coverage?

- Under what conditions will the horses be unable to transport us as planned?

- What are your rates, and what is your payment policy? Can we view a sample of your contract?

If you have decided to hire a classic car for your celebration, it also makes sense to try to see the vehicle in person before your big day. Most owners of antique vehicles take great pride in keeping their cars in ship-shape condition, but you should verify for yourselves that the car is clean both inside and out. Go for a spin before you sign a contract if possible, as well, and listen for any troubling noises. Ask the car's owner questions like these:

- How reliable is the vehicle?

- How frequently is it operated and serviced?

- What is the car's maximum speed? How far are you willing to travel to pick up passengers and to transport wedding party members to wedding locations?

- Is the vehicle properly licensed, registered, and insured? Does the owner or driver have a chauffeur's license?

- How long will the car be available to us?

- Can we decorate the car? If it is a convertible, can the top be put up quickly?

- How will the driver be attired?

- Under what conditions will the car be unable to transport us as planned? Is the vehicle equipped with a spare tire? If the car breaks down, do you have a backup available on short notice?

- What rate do you charge, and does it include gasoline and tolls? What is your payment policy? Can we see a sample contract?

Potential Troubles

There are a number of potential hitches associated with choosing antiquated modes of transportation, the worst being that you may be left with no ride at all. In horribly inclement weather, both horse owners and antique-car aficionados may be reluctant to take their babies out in the storm, and an open carriage or convertible won't provide the dry ride you'll require. Of course, if bad weather forces your event inside, the effect of your grand arrival may be lost anyway. It is important to determine up front under what conditions you will be left stranded without a ride and to have a backup means of reaching your wedding site in place.

newlywed know-how

You may want to bring along an apple or carrots to reward horses for a job well done. While the bride and groom feeding the horses makes for a photogenic moment, don't get too close, or you could wind up with slobber on your skirt or slacks. Be sure to keep bouquets and boutonnières away from horses' mouths lest they be tempted to help themselves to an extra snack.

Even on a cloudless day, horses and antique vehicles will be more prone to mishap than a late-model limousine or your own car. Horses are usually obedient, but some circumstances may make them take off, rear up, or refuse to go. Old cars may be beautifully designed, but their outdated electrical and mechanical systems may be unreliable, and a breakdown could cause you to arrive late and anxious. Don't be dissuaded, though, if you dream of riding to your wedding in a charming horse and buggy or a vintage Bentley. There is a simple solution: Have a backup vehicle follow you.

Limo Limits

If the beautiful spot you have selected is situated far from the nearest parking area or access road, you will need to think through how you will cross that final distance. If the property has a utility vehicle, such as a four-wheel-drive truck or motorized cart, this may solve one problem while creating another. Though a ride may be tempting, the bride's and others' attire can be sullied if a work vehicle is not meticulously cleaned in advance or outfitted with sheets or protective seat covers. With a golf cart or other open vehicle, dirt can still be an issue if pathways are dry and dusty or puddles are prevalent.

piece of cake

Don't attempt to walk a great distance or over rough terrain in high heels, dainty slippers, or bare feet. If you will need to travel a distance on foot to reach your wedding site, choose sturdy footwear and carry the shoes that match your gown until you are close to your final destination.

Walking is sometimes the only solution. If you need to reach your wedding site on your own power, allow plenty of time to stroll at a leisurely pace. If the day is hot and humid or if the distance is substantial, enlist a volunteer to set up a way station at a point along the path so that you won't arrive at your ceremony panting and parched. Stop for a breather, a drink of cold water, a squirt of refreshing mist, and a look in the mirror before taking the final steps into the view of those who anxiously anticipate your arrival.

Aerial Arrivals

As dramatic entrances go, there truly is nothing that rivals dropping in from the sky. Of course, aerial nuptials are not for the faint of heart or the light of wallet. If you're feeling adventurous, however, beginning wedded life aloft is certainly an uplifting and memorable way to embark on the adventure that is marriage.

The Drama of Dropping In

A stretch limousine is classy. A horse and carriage is lovely. A vintage Rolls Royce is glamorous. But a hot air balloon, small private plane, or helicopter is literally over the top. Free-falling into marriage until your parachute catches is the ultimate in drama, though it's hardly original; the first parachute wedding took place in 1940.

newlywed know-how

Las Vegas is the helicopter-wedding capital of the world. Get married while flying over the Strip at night, or exchange promises at the bottom of the Grand Canyon. Other places where you will find companies that specialize in helicopter weddings include Arizona, Hawaii, New Zealand, Cancun, Niagara Falls, Tennessee, and the Canadian Rockies.

Though a fly-in affair isn't for every couple, a helicopter or other small craft can take you to wondrous spots that might otherwise be inaccessible. If you are planning to elope or to host a very small gathering, flying to a remote and spectacular place may be a real possibility. You can even marry in-flight with a beautiful scene stretched out below. Arriving by air is also a way to wow and surprise guests who have gathered for your wedding on a wide-open stretch of beach or countryside.

Before You Take Off

If you are intrigued by the idea of taking to the skies, you need to evaluate your budget, your stomach, and your ability to cope with disappointment.

For starters, it's not cheap to charter an aircraft. The more people you intend to bring along, the greater the cost.

Keep in mind, as well, that flying in a helicopter or small plane is nothing like being aboard a commercial airliner. The queasy feeling in the pit of your stomach may not be wedding jitters at all. It is best not to take chances unless you are an experienced flyer and know you will be comfortable in the air. Finally, you won't be able to leave terra firma behind if weather conditions do not cooperate, so a storm or other disturbance could force you to postpone your ceremony or make alternate arrangements. Hot air balloons in particular are easily grounded if conditions are less than optimal.

rain or shine

Ask aircraft operators about their experience level, safety record, and insurance coverage before making a reservation. Also inquire about the company's cancellation policy and determine whether you will incur charges in the event your flight must be cancelled or postponed due to bad weather.

Before you take off, you must also know exactly where you will land and obtain the necessary permission to do so. Helicopters and small planes can't land just anywhere, so the destination you choose must not only allow fly-ins but must have adequate space and clearance for a safe landing. While it is a somewhat more trivial matter, you should also determine in advance how much interior space the plane, balloon, or helicopter will offer, particularly if the bride's gown is voluminous.

Cleanup

It is a universal if inexplicable phenomenon that brides and grooms experience their weddings at warp speed. Before you know it, it will be time to clean up and say your good-byes. As your outdoor celebration draws to a close, remember to leave this place you cherish in the condition you found it or perhaps even a bit better. Before you depart for some well-deserved relaxation on your honeymoon, there are just a few final details to wrap up.

Delegate Responsibilities

Don't be afraid to delegate. The task of cleaning up after your celebration will seem much less daunting if chores are divided among a number of vendors and volunteers. Advance planning will ensure that all necessary tasks are assigned, that take-away items are safely stowed in designated vehicles, and that you leave your wedding site as pristine as ever.

Who Will Help?

Though you may be reluctant to ask for help, you will find that many friends and family members will be more than willing to give you a hand at the end of the day. Before you embark on a recruitment drive, however, first determine which cleanup responsibilities will be handled by your site's maintenance staff or by vendors you have hired. Your DJ, for example, should remove his own equipment; your catering staff should pack up and scrub down food preparation, cooking, and serving areas; and your rental company should handle breakdown and removal of tents, tables, chairs, and other items furnished for your event. Trash removal and restroom servicing may be provided by on-site employees. Read your contracts carefully and ask questions, however, rather than risking erroneous assumptions.

Even if your cleanup responsibilities will be few, it is a good idea to assign someone, such as your best man, the role of overseeing efforts and performing one final inspection of the site. Do this at the end of the night or on the following morning, if that is when your rental company has scheduled a pickup. Choose someone who is conscientious and responsible, particularly if you will be departing before cleanup is concluded. Assemble a core group of people in advance who you know will stick around to assist, but also accept offers to help from any other guests who volunteer to pitch in.

piece of cake

In order to minimize the mess, be sure that trash and recycling bins are prominently placed. If you expect guests to clear their tables, you may want to have your DJ or band leader make an announcement to this effect.

A Cleanup Checklist

You will know you have done a thorough cleaning job if a visitor to the site the day after your event would never guess that a wedding had occurred there. Though the list of required cleanup tasks will vary based on your venue's policies, any modifications you have made to the site, and the number of functional and decorative items you have brought in, here are some basic tasks you should be sure to include:

☐ Pick up any food, paper, or other litter.

☐ Clean all on-site cooking apparatus and remove any leftover food items from on-site refrigerators.

☐ Place all trash and recyclables in proper receptacles or carry them off-site if required.

☐ Wipe down all tables and chairs, and sweep the dance floor, walkways, and other surfaces.

☐ Return any items that were moved for the ceremony and reception to their original locations.

☐ Remove or dispose of all decorations that were brought in, including floral arrangements.

☐ Carry all cards and gifts to a secure vehicle that will transport them to a friend's or relative's home for safekeeping while you are away or to your own home if you will not be immediately departing for a honeymoon trip.

☐ Tidy up restroom facilities and remove any toiletry items supplied for the event.

☐ Fill any holes in the ground created by such things as tent or canopy poles, speaker or light stands, or chair and table legs.

Thanking the Crew

In your haste to finally be alone together after a long and exciting day, don't neglect one very important thing—thanking your cleanup crew. This includes not only friends and relatives who have agreed to help but those hired vendors who, though doing their job, worked diligently to make your event a success from start to finish. If you must race off to catch a ride to your honeymoon destination, ask the person in charge of cleanup to keep a list of helpers. In the thank-you notes you will write when you return, be sure to express your appreciation to these individuals for their generous assistance.

Clean As You Go

There is no hard-and-fast rule that says you must wait until the party is over to begin tidying up. In fact, asking volunteers to make periodic cleaning sweeps throughout your event is an efficient strategy. Jobs such as loading gifts in a getaway vehicle also need not wait until the end of your event. Especially if you have a deadline time for vacating the premises, it may be a good idea not to leave everything that needs to be accomplished for the last minute.

rain or shine

Be sure to alert service providers about any rules your venue has about the time the property will close. It may take your band, DJ, lighting company, or caterer longer to break down its equipment than you anticipated. Discuss timing with vendors in advance to ensure you won't violate the terms of your site rental contract or incur additional fees.

Try, if possible, to balance your inclination to minimize the time required to clean up at the conclusion of your celebration with consideration for your friends' and family members' desire to enjoy the festivities. While asking a bridesmaid to check the ladies' restroom once an hour might not be a huge imposition, expecting her to camp out there to pick up every piece of paper towel as it hits the floor certainly is. Try, as well, to fight any compulsion you may have to spend time cleaning up during the course of your reception. Your guests want to see you two dancing and smooching, not sweeping or scrubbing.

Do No Harm, Leave No Trace

This is a philosophy that resonates with those who cherish the outdoors and its recreational opportunities. The motto, "Do no harm, leave no trace," is also fitting for couples marrying in a place of natural beauty. As you make your commitment to each other in this scenic spot, vow, as well, to leave its splendid features undisturbed.

Respect Your Surroundings

Chances are good that use of the outdoor site you have selected comes with a set of regulations. Even if you have relatively unencumbered use of the property, make it a priority to avoid any actions that would irrevocably mar the landscape. Doing no harm even applies in your parents' backyard.

newlywed know-how

One of the basic "Do no harm" tenets is to leave anything you find in the outdoors in its place. That means you should not remove plants, flowers, rocks, berries, artifacts, or any other natural objects from the site. You will have plenty of fond memories and photographs to take away as souvenirs of your wedding day in the great outdoors.

One of the challenges you will face is communicating any mandatory or practical restrictions to your assembled guests. It is your responsibility to guarantee that no one tramples sensitive dune grass, plucks rare blossoms, disrupts nesting birds, wanders into restricted areas, pollutes waterways, or causes other property damage. If you have been provided with a list of rules for visitors to the site, you may want to send copies to guests in advance with their invitations. You can also include printed rules in your wedding program or have laminated sheets outlining these regulations available at tables. In some cases, you may want to have your DJ or band leader make an announcement to warn guests about serious fines that may be imposed for failing to comply with certain regulations. While it may seem heavy-handed, it is your job to instill in guests the same respect for your wedding site that the two of you have.

Better Than You Found It

Leaving no trace that your event transpired is an admirable goal. Leaving your wedding site in even better shape than you found it is truly commendable and often quite possible. You might undertake something as simple as bringing a team of volunteers to the property the day before your wedding to pick up litter. You might get involved with ongoing volunteer projects at the site to groom trails, weed gardens, or clean up beaches. You might even provide financial support for such things as removal of unhealthy trees, purchase of new plantings, restoration of historic structures, or repair of damaged stone walls.

Ask about opportunities to help. If you have a project in mind that you would like to undertake in order to beautify the site prior to your event, be sure to get the appropriate permission. Be realistic about what can be accomplished in the time available prior to your big day. Well-intentioned plans may fall by the wayside as you become overwhelmed by other wedding preparations, so be careful not to begin a project that you cannot finish.

Functional Favors

It is customary to present guests with token gifts in appreciation for their attendance at your wedding. In order to limit the number of items that must be carried into your outdoor reception site, you may want to consider favors that are functional or that serve a dual purpose. You can also ease your cleanup efforts by giving away much more than custom-imprinted matchbooks and votive candles.

Practical Take-Aways

While heart-shaped soaps and personalized tins of mints might make fine favors, couples marrying outdoors may want to consider more practical alternatives. Think about useful items that might come in handy during your event that would also serve as fine gifts, particularly if they are custom-imprinted or engraved in honor of your celebration. Possibilities include the following:

- Umbrellas
- Flashlights
- Champagne flutes
- Dessert plates
- Coasters
- Coffee mugs
- Decorative hand fans
- Sunscreen in pretty bottles
- Paperweights
- Napkin rings
- Bottle openers

piece of cake

Though plenty of companies specialize in customized wedding favors, you may actually get a better deal on imprinted gear from a promotional products company that primarily targets business customers. In general, for custom-imprinted or engraved items, the more you buy, the cheaper the price per piece.

Think, too, about favors that can play a dual role. Place-card frames, for example, might become take-home favors. Colorful beach balls or inflatable fish that served as decorations for your pool or beach wedding will be fun souvenirs for guests with children at home. Miniature potted plants, colorful glass bud vases, ornate candle holders, and themed salt-and-pepper shakers can all give tabletops pizzazz in addition to serving as gifts for guests.

Give It Away

Decorating for your wedding can be exciting and fun, even if it involves making many trips to and from the car to haul supplies. Tearing down and packing up is not nearly as enjoyable. Here's a tip: The more you give away, the less you will have to toss or take away. If you feel a twinge of reluctance to part with the centerpieces you spent hours crafting or those adorable heart-shaped candy dishes you found at a flea market, try not to let sentimentality win out over practicality. After all, do you really need a dozen fishbowls filled with glass marbles and half-melted floating candles cluttering up your home?

Once you have decided to give guests more than they bargained for, it is important to come up with a strategy for disbursing coveted items that will not incite jealous riots. Hiding a penny under one plate or attaching a sticker to the bottom of one chair are common methods for giving away objects, such as centerpieces, to one person at each table. You might also award these items to the couple that has been together longest, the person whose birthday is closest, or the guest who traveled the longest distance. If you'd rather distribute rewards based on skill rather than luck, you might devise a trivia game with questions about your courtship or your wedding location.

Larger decorative items can also be given away, such as wreaths, pumpkins, candelabras, canopies, tiki torches, or serving baskets. You might want to offer them first to your parents, grandparents, or bridal party members who have been helpful throughout your wedding planning process. If you do not find takers, invite guests to enter their names in a drawing or to bid for the items in a silent auction, with the proceeds going to your favorite charity. You can also enlist the assistance of your DJ or band to choose the party's best dancers and award them prizes.

rain or shine

If your catering crew will be packaging up leftovers, don't forget to ask them to set aside sandwiches or a snack for the two of you. You may find yourselves ravenous later in the evening if you didn't get much of a chance to eat during the wedding.

If you have not made arrangements to donate leftovers to a food pantry or shelter, you should also plan to give away as many of the edibles that remain at the end of the party as possible. Stock up on plastic bowls with lids, or ask your caterer to supply plastic bags and take-away containers. Many guests will be happy to take food home, and you may need to again employ creative methods for choosing who will leave with bags of rolls, frozen steaks, and other premium leftovers.

Saying "Farewell" to People and Place

Good-byes are never easy. When you have had an absolutely amazing time with an incredible group of people in a phenomenal spot, saying farewell can be downright dismal. You can ease the pain of separation from the people and a place that you love by carefully choreographing your departure, keeping the party going at scheduled post-wedding activities, and vowing to regularly reconnect with the enchanting location where your life as husband and wife began.

Good-bye and Thank You

You will know that you have hosted a wonderful party if the end arrives and no one is quite ready to leave. Still, depart you must. At most weddings, the festivities gradually wind down until few guests are left and the bride and groom unceremoniously take their leave. You can make the final moments of your wedding celebration something special, however, by creating your own farewell ritual or planning for a dramatic departure.

piece of cake

Before you go, make the rounds and thank all of the people who contributed to the success of your day. If possible, have a batch of thank-you notes written and ready for mailing the morning after your wedding. Arranging for flowers to be delivered to your parents and other key people the day after or upon their return home is also a thoughtful gesture.

How you take your leave will depend in part on the location you have selected. At a beach wedding, you might say good-bye by turning to wave to the assembled crowd at intervals as you walk hand-in-hand beside the moonlit sea until you fade from view. At a garden affair, guests might shower the two of you with rose petals as you dash off to meet your flower-decorated getaway vehicle. If you are marrying at a historic home with a balcony or verandah, wave jubilantly to guests from this high perch before kissing and vanishing.

You can also invite your guests to join in a ceremonial or celebratory farewell. Gather in a circle on the beach and pass a flame until everyone is holding a lit candle, then offer a final word of thanks for a glorious day. Ask your photographer to compose a group photo that captures everyone waving good-bye. Invite guests to pile aboard a hay wagon for a ride around the property before they are returned to their cars as the sun sets. Have your musicians lead a conga line all the way to the parking lot.

Post-Wedding Events

While some couples are anxious to race straight from their wedding to their honeymoon destination, others prefer to spend additional time with friends and loved ones whom they don't see often enough. You can buy yourselves a longer good-bye by inviting all or a select group of your guests to an after-wedding event. Whether you choose to get together with just a small group of close relatives and wedding party members at a family home directly following your formal celebration or to invite everyone to a catered brunch the next morning, a post-wedding event can be a casual and relaxed time for enjoying the company of your near and dear. If you have hosted a destination wedding, a final breakfast, luncheon, or picnic can be a nice opportunity for everyone to gather one last time to toast your union and their own new friendships.

An Ongoing Commitment

The outdoor location that you selected for your wedding will live in your hearts and memories. Many couples also choose to make their scenic wedding spot a place that they support financially and visit regularly. If you married at a facility operated by a nonprofit or governmental organization, you may want to explore opportunities to become a member or supporter of the property. Making a contribution toward preserving the site for enjoyment by others on your anniversary each year is a generous way to honor your ongoing commitment to each other. Volunteering your time and talents on a regular basis is another gesture that you might consider.

newlywed know-how

If you married at a zoo, aquarium, or wildlife sanctuary, a fun way to continue your involvement with the place is to adopt an inhabitant. Most organizations dedicated to wildlife preservation welcome adoptions, which help to feed and house individual creatures. These often come with fun perks for the donor, such as photos of the adopted animal or free admission to the facility.

Visiting your wedding site together will always provide an opportunity to reminisce and to reaffirm the vows you made. If you had a destination wedding and won't be able to return any time soon, make a promise to each other that you will revisit the spot on your fifth or tenth wedding anniversary. Then, take action by setting up a payroll deduction plan at work or having a small amount transferred each month into a vacation fund so that you will be able to make that dream a reality.

Final Practicalities

When you return from your honeymoon, there will be a plethora of things to do: grocery shopping, opening cards and gifts, writing thank-you notes, having honeymoon photos printed, viewing wedding proofs from the professional photographer, maybe changing your name and address. There is one chore, however, that should not wait until your return. If you will be embarking straight away on your honeymoon, be sure to enlist the aid of a friend or family member to return the groom's tuxedo (if it was rented) or to take his suit and the bride's gown to a dry cleaner. Those who marry outdoors subject their fine attire to a variety of perils, and you won't want to allow stains to set in while you're lounging in a hammock or dancing the nights away on your honeymoon.

ask the wedding planner ?

What is wedding gown preservation?

Offered by most dry cleaners, wedding gown preservation is a process by which a cherished gown is thoroughly cleaned and any spots are removed. The dress is then pressed, shaped, and packaged using durable, archival-quality materials to ensure that its beauty will be preserved for years or even decades.

While having a suit cleaned and pressed is not terribly expensive, you may be dismayed by the costs involved in cleaning and preserving a gown that you are unlikely to wear again. Even if your gown miraculously appears to be spotless, it is still important to have it professionally cleaned, as sweat and champagne stains that may be invisible at first will cause fabric to become discolored over time. Consider the costs of cleaning and preserving your gown an investment in creating an heirloom that will always remind you of one of your life's happiest days and may someday make another bride appear as ravishing as you did on your wedding day.

State-by-State Directory of Suggested Outdoor Venues

If you are intrigued by the idea of marrying outdoors, one of your first questions may be, "Where can we do this?" Though not a comprehensive directory, this list is a starting point for exploring outdoor wedding venues. You will find a diverse lineup of properties included here, and while they differ vastly in size, type of setting, and price range, they all have served as the backdrop for brides and grooms who have chosen to marry outdoors. For more possible outdoor wedding venues, visit *www.outdoorweddingguide.com*.

Alabama

Bragg-Mitchell Mansion, Mobile, AL
www.braggmitchellmansion.com

USS ALABAMA Battleship Memorial Park, Mobile, AL
www.ussalabama.com

Alaska

Pearson's Pond Luxury Suites & Garden Spa, Juneau, AK
www.pearsonspond.com

Arizona

Full Circle Ranch, Cave Creek, AZ
www.fullcircleranch.com

Pointe Hilton Tapatio Cliffs and Squaw Peak Resorts, Phoenix, AZ
www.pointehilton.com

Verde Canyon Railroad, Clarkdale, AZ
www.verdecanyonrr.com

Arkansas

Cliff Cottage Inn, Eureka Springs, AR
www.cliffcottage.com

California

Disneyland Resort, Anaheim, CA
www.disneyland.com

Estancia La Jolla Hotel & Spa, La Jolla, CA
www.estancialajolla.com

Granlibakken Conference Center Lodge, Lake Tahoe, CA
www.granlibakken.com

The Jones Victorian Estate, Orange, CA
www.thejonesvictorianestate.com

The Lodge at Rancho Mirage, Rancho Mirage, CA
www.ranchomirage.rockresorts.com

Lover's Point Park & Beach, Pacific Grove, CA
www.pacificgroverecreation.org/loverspoint.html

Ritz-Carlton Half Moon Bay, Half Moon Bay, CA
www.ritzcarlton.com/resorts/half_moon_bay

Sequoia National Park, Fresno, CA
www.visitsequoia.com

Ventana Inn & Spa, Big Sur, CA
www.ventanainn.com

Colorado

Anschutz Family Sky Terrace at the Denver Museum of Nature & Science, Denver, CO
www.dmns.org

Chipeta Sun Lodge & Spa, Ridgway, CO
www.chipeta.com

The Inverness Hotel and Conference Center, Englewood, CO
www.invernesshotel.com

Powderhorn Resort, Mesa, CO
www.powderhorn.com

Redstone Inn, Redstone, CO
www.redstoneinn.com

Rocky Mountain National Park, Estes Park, CO
www.nps.gov/romo

Vista Verde Ranch, Steamboat Springs, CO
www.vistaverde.com

Connecticut

Eolia Mansion at Harkness Memorial State Park, Waterford, CT
www.dep.state.ct.us/stateparks/parks/eolia.htm

The Inn at Harbor Hill Marina, Niantic, CT
www.innharborhill.com

Inn at Mystic, Mystic, CT
www.innatmystic.com

Mystic Seaport, Mystic, CT
www.mysticseaport.com

Stonington Vineyards, Stonington, CT
www.stoningtonvineyards.com

The Webb House Barn at the Webb-Deane-Stevens Museum,
Wethersfield, CT
www.webb-deane-stevens.org

Delaware

Read House & Gardens, New Castle, DE
www.hsd.org/read.htm

Florida

Alfred B. Maclay Gardens State Park, Tallahassee, FL
www.floridastateparks.org/maclaygardens

Bob's Balloon Charters, Orlando, FL
www.bobsballoons.com

The Colony Beach & Tennis Resort, Longboat Key, FL
www.colonybeachresort.com

Jupiter Inlet Lighthouse, Jupiter, FL
www.lrhs.org

Miami Seaquarium, Miami, FL
www.miamiseaquarium.com

The Naples Beach Hotel & Golf Club, Naples, FL
www.naplesbeachhotel.com

Steinhatchee Landing Resort, Steinhatchee, FL
www.steinhatcheelanding.com

Trump International Sonesta Beach Resort, Miami, FL
www.sonesta.com/SunnyIsles

Vizcaya Museum and Gardens, Coconut Grove, FL
www.vizcayamuseum.org

Georgia

Chota Falls, Clayton, GA
www.chotafalls.com

Hawaii

The Bayer Estate, Honolulu, HI
www.bayerestate.com

Hawaii Volcanoes National Park, HI
www.nps.gov/havo

Hilton Hawaiian Village, Honolulu, HI
www.hiltonhawaiianvillage.com

Limahuli Garden and Preserve, Kalaheo, HI
www.ntbg.org/gardens/limahuli.html

Maui Tropical Plantation, Wailuku, HI
www.mauitropicalplantation.com

Idaho

The Coeur d'Alene Resort, Coeur d'Alene, ID
www.cdaresort.com

Trail Creek Grounds, Sun Valley Ski Resort, Sun Valley, ID
www.sunvalley.com

Illinois

Arabian Knights Farm, Willowbrook, IL
www.akfentertainment.com

Chicago Botanic Garden, Chicago, IL
www.chicago-botanic.org

Luthy Botanical Garden, Peoria, IL
www.peoriaparks.org/luthy/luthymain.html

Indiana

Brown County Indiana Wedding Gazebo, Nashville, IN
www.browncountyindianaweddingchapel.com/gazebo.html

Oak Hill Mansion, Carmel, IN
www.oakhillmansion.com

Iowa

Garst Farm Resort, Coon Rapids, IA
www.farmresort.com

Kansas

Circle S Ranch & Country Inn, Lawrence, KS
www.circlesranch.com

Glencliff Farm Bed, Breakfast & Spa, Independence, KS
www.glencliff.com

Sun Rock Ranch, Junction City, KS
www.sunrockranch.com

Kentucky

Pine Knob Theatre, Caneyville, KY
www.pineknob.com

Pinecrest Cottage & Gardens, Louisville, KY
www.pinecrestcottageandgardens.com

Louisiana

Houmas House Plantation and Gardens, Darrow, LA
www.houmashouse.com

Nottoway Plantation, Restaurant & Inn, White Castle, LA
www.nottoway.com

Oak Alley Plantation, Restaurant & Inn, Vacherie, LA
www.oakalleyplantation.com

Maine

The Asticou Inn, Northeast Harbor, ME
www.asticou.com

The Grey Havens Inn, Georgetown Island, ME
www.greyhavens.com

The Nonantum Resort, Kennebunkport, ME
www.nonantumresort.com

Maryland

Antrim 1844, Taneytown, MD
www.antrim1844.com

Glenview Mansion, Rockville, MD
www.rockvillemd.gov/glenview

The Inn at Perry Cabin, St. Michaels, MD
www.perrycabin.com

Massachusetts

Castle Hill and Steep Hill Beach, The Crane Estate, Ipswich, MA
castlehillfunctions.thetrustees.org

Cranwell Resort, Spa & Golf Club, Lenox, MA
www.cranwell.com

Lynch Park, Beverly, MA
www.bevrec.com/lynchpark.html

Ocean Edge Resort, Cape Cod, Brewster, MA
www.oceanedge.com

Thompson Island Conference Center, Thompson Island, Boston, MA
www.thompsonisland.org

Michigan

Castle Farms, Charlevoix, MI
www.castlefarms.com

Infinity Yacht Charters, St. Clair Shores, MI
www.infinityyacht.com

Lighthouse Point, St. Ignace, MI
www.lighthousepte.com

Mission Point Resort, Mackinac Island, MI
www.missionpoint.com

Minnesota

Como Park Zoo and Conservatory, St. Paul, MN
www.comozooconservatory.org

Loghouse & Homestead on Spirit Lake, Vergas, MN
www.loghousebb.com

Noerenberg Gardens, Orono, MN
www.threeriversparkdistrict.org/parks/norenburgmemorial.cfm

Mississippi

Monmouth Plantation, Natchez, MS
www.monmouthplantation.com

Missouri

Bridal Cave, Camdenton, MO
www.bridalcave.com

Chateau on the Lake Resort and Convention Center, Branson, MO
www.chateauonthelakebranson.com

Montana

Chico Hot Springs Resort and Day Spa, Pray, MT
www.chicohotsprings.com

Runamuk Guest Ranch, Roundup, MT
www.runamukguestranch.com

Nebraska

Lauritzen Gardens, Omaha, NE
www.omahabotanicalgardens.org

Nevada

Cal-Neva Resort Spa & Casino, Crystal Bay, NV
www.calnevaresort.com

Flamingo Hilton, Las Vegas
www.caesars.com/flamingo/lasvegas

The Grove, Las Vegas, NV
www.lasvegasweddingsatthegrove.com

Lake Mead Cruises, Boulder City, NV
www.lakemeadcruises.com

Sunset Gardens, Las Vegas, NV
www.sunsetgardens.com

New Hampshire

Cathedral of the Pines, Rindge, NH
www.cathedralpines.com

Mount Washington Hotel, Bretton Woods, NH
www.mtwashington.com

Sunset Hill House, Sugar Hill, NH
www.sunsethillhouse.com

New Jersey

Indian Trail Club, Franklin Lakes, NJ
www.indiantrailclub.com

Ocean Place Resort & Spa, Long Branch, NJ
www.oceanplaceresort.com

The Park Savoy, Florham Park, NJ
www.theparksavoy.com

Windows on the Water, Sea Bright, NJ
www.njwindowsonthewater.com

New Mexico

Casa del Granjero, Albuquerque, NM
www.innewmexico.com

Hacienda Doña Andrea de Santa Fe, Cerrillos, NM
www.hdasantafe.com

Rancho Manzana, Chimayo, NM
www.ranchomanzana.com

New York

La Tourelle Country Inn, Ithaca, NY
www.latourelleinn.com

The New York Botanical Garden, Bronx, NY
www.nybg.org

Tavern on the Green, New York, NY
www.tavernonthegreen.com

Wölffer Estate Vineyard & Stables, Sagaponack, NY
www.wolffer.com

Yaddo Mansion & Rose Garden, Saratoga Springs, NY
www.yaddo.org

North Carolina

Biltmore Estate, Asheville, NC
www.biltmore.com

Cape Hatteras National Seashore, Hatteras Island, Manteo, NC
www.nps.gov/caha/capehatteras.htm

The Elizabethan Gardens, Roanoke Island, Manteo, NC
www.elizabethangardens.org

The Inn at Yonahlossee, Boone, NC
www.yonahlossee.com

Sarah P. Duke Gardens, Duke University, Durham, NC
www.hr.duke.edu/dukegardens

North Dakota

Badlands Bliss, Medora, ND
www.badlandsbliss.com

Ohio

Hocking Hills Resort, South Bloomingville, OH
www.ashcave.com

Cuyahoga Valley National Park, Brecksville, OH
www.nps.gov/cuva

A Georgian Manner, Logan, OH
www.ohioweddings.net

Oklahoma

Lakeside Bed & Breakfast, Wagoner, OK
www.lakesidebed.com

Myriad Botanical Gardens & Crystal Bridge, Oklahoma City, OK
www.myriadgardens.com

Oregon

Gentle House, Western Oregon University, Monmouth, OR
www.wou.edu/president/advancement/gentle/rental.html

The Resort at the Mountain, Welches, OR
www.theresort.com

Pennsylvania

The Hotel Hershey, Hershey, PA
www.hotelhershey.com

The Pennsbury Inn, Chadds Ford, PA
www.pennsburyinn.com

Stroudsmoor Country Inn, Stroudsburg, PA
www.stroudsmoor.com

Rhode Island

Astors' Beechwood Mansion, Newport, RI
www.astorsbeechwood.com

Blithewold Mansion, Gardens & Arboretum, Bristol, RI
www.blithewold.org

Castle Hill Inn & Resort, Newport, RI
www.castlehillinn.com

Watch Hill Inn, Watch Hill, RI
www.watchhillinn.com

South Carolina

Daufuskie Island Resort & Breathe Spa, Hilton Head, SC
www.daufuskieislandresort.com

Magnolia Plantation and Its Gardens, Charleston, SC
www.magnoliaplantation.com

Market Pavilion Hotel Pavilion Level, Charleston, SC
www.marketpavilion.com

Marriott Hilton Head Beach & Golf Resort, Hilton Head Island, SC
www.hiltonheadmarriott.com

Middleton Place, Charleston, SC
www.middletonplace.org

South Dakota

McKennan Park Sunken Gardens, Sioux Falls, SD
www.siouxfalls.org/parks

Sylvan Lake Resort, Custer, SD
www.custerresorts.com

Tennessee

Cades Cove, Great Smoky Mountains National Park, Townsend, TN
www.nps.gov/grsm

Christopher Place, Newport, TN
www.christopherplace.com

Golden Valley Weddings, Pigeon Forge, TN
www.goldenvalleyweddings.com

Von Bryan Mountaintop Inn Bed and Breakfast, Sevierville, TN
www.vonbryan.com

Texas

Blisswood, Cat Spring, TX
www.blisswood.net

Dallas Arboretum, Dallas, TX
www.dallasarboretum.org

The House of the Seasons, Jefferson, TX
www.houseoftheseasons.com

Kali-Kate Farm, Buda, TX
www.kali-kate.com

Lady Bird Johnson Wildflower Center, Austin, TX
www.wildflower.org

The Parklands, Austin, TX
www.carolscatering.com/parklands.htm

Three Falls Cove, Sanford, TX
www.threefallscove.com

Utah

Park City Mountain Resort, Park City, UT
www.parkcitymountain.com

Wolf Creek Resort, Eden, UT
www.wolfcreekresort.com

Vermont

The Equinox Resort & Spa, Manchester Village, VT
www.equinox.rockresorts.com

Inn at the Round Barn B&B, Waitsfield, VT
www.innattheroundbarn.com

The Inn at Weston, Weston, VT
www.innweston.com

Robert Todd Lincoln's Hildene, Manchester, VT
www.hildene.org

The Wildflower Inn, Lyndonville, VT
www.wildflowerinn.com

Virginia

Keswick Hall at Monticello, Charlottesville, VA
www.keswick.com

Norfolk Botanical Garden, Norfolk, VA
www.norfolkbotanicalgarden.org

Royal Oaks Wedding Garden, Love, VA
www.vacabins.com

Willow Grove Inn, Orange, VA
www.willowgroveinn.com

Washington

The Cutting Garden, Sequim, WA
www.cuttinggarden.com

Freestone Inn at Wilson Ranch, Mazama, WA
www.freestoneinn.com

Llama Rose Farm & Gardens, Poulsbo, WA
www.llamarose.com

Mountain Springs Lodge, Leavenworth, WA
www.mtsprings.com

Ohme Gardens, Wenatchee, WA
www.ohmegardens.com

The Woodmark Hotel, Kirkland, WA
www.thewoodmark.com

West Virginia

Cass Scenic Railroad State Park, Cass, WV
www.cassrailroad.com

Creekside Resort, Greenville, WV
www.creeksideresort.net

Ritter Park Rose Garden, Huntington, WV
www.ghprd.org/ritter.html

Valley Falls State Park, Fairmont, WV
www.valleyfallsstatepark.com

Wisconsin

Country Inn Hotel Conference Center, Waukesha, WI
www.countryinnhotel.com

Victorian Treasure Inn, Lodi, WI
www.victoriantreasure.com

Wyoming

Cheyenne Botanic Gardens, Cheyenne, WY
www.botanic.org

Terry Bison Ranch, Cheyenne, WY
www.terrybisonranch.com

Teton Mountain Lodge, Teton Village, WY
www.tetonlodge.com

Wedding Day Emergency Contact Sheet

When your outdoor wedding day finally arrives, you will want to have all important phone numbers at your fingertips. Complete this contact list in advance, and distribute copies to key wedding participants. It is a good idea to include not only home or business telephone numbers but cell phone or pager numbers as well. For participants who will be arriving from out of town, be sure to obtain a local number where they can be reached.

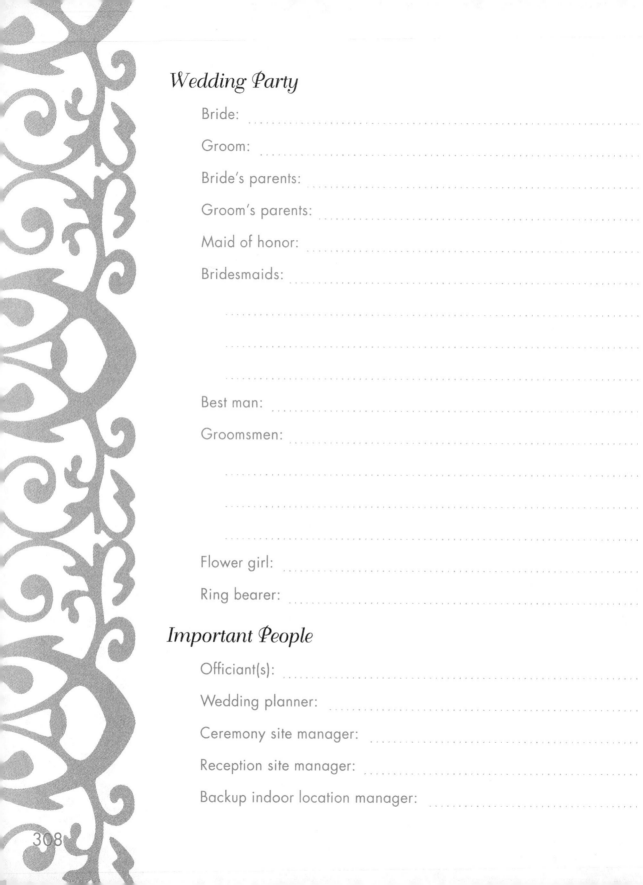

Wedding Party

Bride: ....

Groom: ....

Bride's parents: ....

Groom's parents: ....

Maid of honor: ....

Bridesmaids: ....

....

....

....

Best man: ....

Groomsmen: ....

....

....

....

Flower girl: ....

Ring bearer: ....

Important People

Officiant(s): ....

Wedding planner: ....

Ceremony site manager: ....

Reception site manager: ....

Backup indoor location manager: ....

Photographer: ....

Videographer: ....

Florist: ....

Food and Drink

Caterer: ....

Alcohol/beverage provider: ....

Cake baker: ....

Music

Ceremony musicians: ....

Reception musicians: ....

DJ: ....

Clothing, Hair, and Makeup

Tuxedo shop: ....

Seamstress: ....

Salon: ....

Makeup artist: ....

Transportation

Taxi service: ....

Transportation provider(s): ....

....

....

Equipment

Rental company: ....

Tent company: ....

Lighting company: ....

Preparation and Cleanup

Setup volunteers: ....

....

....

Cleanup volunteers: ....

....

....

Cleaning service: ....

Flights and Accommodations

Wedding night accommodations: ....

Airline: ....

Honeymoon accommodations: ....

Emergency Contacts

Local ambulance service: ....

Nearest hospital: ....

Local or state police: ....

Babysitter: ....

Photo Credits

1 Tracy Rousseau
11 Rousseau Drive
Bowdoin, ME 04287
www.tracyrousseau.com

2 Oak Alley Plantation
Vacherie, LA
www.OakAlleyPlantation.com

George Long Photography
New Orleans, LA
www.GeorgeLong.com

3 Powderhorn Resort
P.O. Box 370
Mesa, CO 81643

4 Stroudsmoor Country Inn
P.O. Box 153
Stroudsburg, PA 18360

5 Inn at Harbor Hill Marina
Niantic, CT 06357
Sally Keefe
860-739-0331
info@innharborhill.com

6 The Woodmark Hotel
and Spa
1411 4th Avenue, Suite 610
Seattle, WA 98101

7 The Inn at Celebrity Dairy
Silk Hope, NC
www.celebritydairy.com

8 Sunset Hill House
Sunset Hill Road
Sugar Hill, NH 03585
Photo by Todd Caverly

9 Trump International
Sonesta Beach Resort
18001 Collins Avenue
Sunny Isles Beach, FL 33160

10 Naples Beach Hotel
and Golf Club
851 Gulf Shore Blvd.
North Naples, FL 34102
239-435-4361

Index

A

Accidents, 84–86

Adams, John Quincy, 60

Aerial nuptials, 274–76

Air conditioners, 45–46, 48–49, 156

Aisle, 127–28, 221–22

Aisle runner, 128, 221–22

Alcoholic beverages, 86–87, 112–13, 172, 177–78, 265

Allergies, 64

Altar, 127–28

Alternate sites, 49–51, 64–65, 236

American Rental Association, 48

Antique automobiles, 268–73

Appointments, keeping, 256–57

Arches, 124–25, 127–28

Architectural elements, 124–25, 127–28

Autumn weddings, 22

B

Backup plans
for backyard weddings, 76
for beach weddings, 62
for foul weather, 43–58, 236–38, 252–54, 261

Backyard weddings, 75–89

Bands, 162–65

Bartender, 172

Beach pests, 35

Beach weddings, 60–62

Beauty appointments, 256–57

Beauty emergencies, 248–49

Beauty tips, 40–41

Bees, 33–34, 64

Beverages, 86–87, 112–13, 172, 177–78, 265

Birds, 35–36, 62

Birdseed, 70

Bridal attire, 67, 101, 111, 217–34

Bridal boutiques, 219

Bridal consignment stores, 220

Bridal gown, 218–22, 288
Bridal gown preservation, 288
Bridal train, 221–22
Bridesmaids, 226–28
Bridges, 124
Budget, 8–10, 76–78, 94, 185–86
Buffet, 176, 178
Bugs, 33–35

C

Casual attire, 226, 230–31, 233. *See also* Informal weddings
Caterers, 67, 89, 169–75
Cell phones, 30, 247
Ceremony
    day of, 141–51, 251–68
    focus of, 144
    involving guests in, 149–51
    length of, 141–42
    music for, 146–49
    officiant for, 138–41, 244
    readings for, 142–43
    rituals for, 142–43
    sites for, 3–4, 12–13, 289–305
    sound system for, 144–46
    style of, 138–39, 141–43
Children, 151, 228, 246

Civil ceremony, 139
Civil twilight, 166
Cleanup, 87–89, 277–88
Clergy members, 139
Cocktails, 112–13. *See also* Alcoholic beverages
Cold weather, 22–24, 26
Commitment, 287
Confetti, 70
Contingency plans
    for backyard weddings, 76
    for beach weddings, 62
    for foul weather, 9, 43–58, 236–38, 252–54, 261
Contracts, 70–71
Costs, 8–10, 76–78, 94, 185–86
Countdown, 235–50
Craft ideas, 132–35
Cruise-ship weddings, 97–99

D

Dance floors, 161–62
Dancing, 161–65
Decorations, 10, 121–35, 168, 248
Desserts, 180. *See also* Wedding cake
Destination weddings
    advantages of, 92–93

    cruise-ship weddings, 97–99
    disadvantages of, 94
    events surrounding, 103–5
    guests at, 99–100
    planning for, 100–103
    popular choices for, 91, 95, 101, 275
    possibilities for, 91–92
    selecting, 95–97
Digital photography, 6, 194–95
Dining outdoors, 170–71
Dinnerware, 171
Directions to site, 30–31, 210, 212
Disney theme parks, 65, 66
Distractions, 33–37, 144
DJs, 145, 162–65
Do-it-yourself event, 78–84
Dogs, 36
DRYDAY Planning Forecasts, 20

E

E-mail guest list, 55–56, 250
Egan, Carolyn, 20–21
Electrical power, 10, 45–46, 145–46, 156
Elopement, 93, 94

Emergency contact sheet, 245, 247, 307–10
Emergency kit, 247–49
Emergency precaution checklist, 85
Emotions, 150, 238, 258
Entrances, 263–76
Evening reception, 165–67
Event coordinators, 78, 80

F

Fall weddings, 22
Fans, 46, 156
Faraway weddings. See Destination weddings
Favors, 88, 104, 132, 134–35, 282–85
Feng shui, 123–24
Final countdown, 235–50
Final decisions, 252–54
Final details, 238–42, 288
Final preparations, 257–58
Flies, 34–35
Floods, 27
Floral arrangements, 10, 63–64
Flower girl, 228, 246
Focus, 144
Folklore, 19–20
Food safety, 176–77

Foreign locations, 91, 95, 102. *See also* Destination weddings
Foul weather, 15–16, 25–28, 52–54. *See also* Weather concerns
Foul-weather gear, 44–46, 247–48

G

Garden weddings, 63–65
Gazebos, 124, 127, 155
Getaway wedding, 92–94. *See also* Destination weddings
Good-byes, 285–86
Grand entrance, 263–76
Groom's attire, 228–32
Groomsmen, 230–31
Guests
    arrival of, 266
    attire for, 39, 232–33
    comfort of, 37–40
    communicating with, 54–57, 117–18, 208–12, 249–50, 255–56
    and destination weddings, 99–100
    e-mailing, 55–56, 250
    forewarning, 38–39

invitations for, 54–55, 111–12, 117–18, 201–15
involving, 149–51
number to invite, 37–38
thanking, 285–86
transportation for, 30–33, 264–68

H

Hair-care supplies, 223, 248
Hair styles, 222–25
Heat waves, 21, 24, 26
Heaters, 45–46, 48–49
Historic properties, 65–67
Home weddings, 75–89
Honeymoon, 88, 262
Horoscopes, 20–21
Horse-drawn carriages, 268–73
Hot weather, 21, 24, 26
Hurricanes, 27

I

Illumination, 166–67
Inclement weather, 15–16, 25–28, 52–54. *See also* Weather concerns
Inclement-weather gear, 44–46, 247–48

Indoor reception, 168
Informal weddings, 10, 12, 39. *See also* Casual attire
Injuries, 84–86
Insects, 33–35, 64
Instruments, 147–49
Insurance, 9, 57, 86
Interactive invitations, 214–15
Interfaith marriages, 7, 141
Intimate atmospheres, 158–60
Invitation enclosures, 210–12
Invitation themes, 111–12, 117–18, 201, 204–8
Invitations, 54–57, 111–12, 117–18, 201–15

J, K, L

Joining Hands and Hearts, 7
Keepsakes, 133, 142–43
Lake settings, 98–99
Las Vegas, 91, 95, 101, 275
Last-minute decisions, 252–54
Leaf pressings, 134, 142
Leftovers, 89, 285
Legalities, 71, 101–2, 138–39, 141, 261
Liability, 84–86

Lighting, 166–67
Limited-access sites, 31–33
Limousines, 268, 273–74
Liquor liability, 86
Live music, 146–49, 162–65
Local lore, 111–12
Locations
  beach weddings, 60–62
  destination weddings, 91–105
  garden weddings, 63–65
  historic properties, 65–67
  permission for using, 4, 69–71
  public places, 12–13, 67–69
  questions to ask, 71–74
  selecting, 3–4, 58–74
  by state, 289–305

M

Macomb, Susanna Stefanachi, 7
Maps, 30–31, 210, 212
Marriage laws, 101–2, 138–39
Marriage license, 71, 141, 261
Memories, 4–6, 196–97, 262
Menus, 175–78
Microphones, 145–46

Mosquitoes, 34
Music, at ceremony, 146–49
Music, at reception, 161–65
Musical selections, 148

N

National Park Service, 66
Natural elements, 132–33
Nervousness, 258
Night-time receptions, 165–67

O

Officiants, 138–41, 244
Old Farmer's Almanac, 20
Onlookers, 36–37
Outdoor conditions, 40–41. *See also* Weather concerns
Outdoor dining, 170–71
Outdoor pests, 33–36
Outdoor rooms, 158–60

P

Parking concerns, 31–33, 83, 167, 264–65
Parking illumination, 167
Passersby, 36–37

Paths, 127–28. *See also* Aisle

Patio, 155, 158–59

Peak wedding months, 9, 21–22

Period costumes, 67. *See also* Theme weddings

Permissions, 4, 69–71

Permits, 68, 69

Pests, 33–36

Pets, 36

Photography

  of altar space, 129

  black-and-white photos, 192–93

  costs for, 185–86

  creative effects for, 192–95

  digital photography, 194–95

  family photos, 5, 190, 195

  and foul weather, 52–54

  informal photos, 5

  and makeup, 191–92

  natural light for, 5–6

  poses for, 5, 188–89

  professional photographers, 52, 183–87

  proofs, 188

  scheduling, 188–90

  and shadows, 190–91

  shot list for, 195–96

  special effects, 193–94

  and sunlight, 129

  and videography, 196–200

  and wedding memories, 4–6

Photojournalism, 52, 184

Pitfalls to avoid, 29–42

Place cards, 134

Planning wedding events, 78–84, 100–103. *See also* Wedding planners

Planting ceremony, 142

Popular destination locations, 91, 95, 101, 275

Popular wedding months, 9, 21–22

Popular wedding themes, 108

Popularity of outdoor weddings, 11–12

Post-wedding events, 14, 87–89, 103–4, 277–88

Postponing wedding, 27, 51–52

Pre-wedding details, 238–42

Pre-wedding events, 14, 103–4

Precipitation averages, 24

Private moments, 259–60

Professional help, 80–81. *See also* Wedding planners

Property insurance, 86

Public places, 12–13, 67–69

R

Radio communication, 30, 247

Rain date, 27, 51–52

Rainy weather, 15, 16, 25, 27–28. *See also* Weather concerns

Reasons for outdoor weddings, xi, 1–14

Reception

  dancing at, 161–65

  evening reception, 165–67

  indoor reception, 168

  intimate reception, 158–60

  music for, 161–65

  restrooms for, 156–58

  shelters for, 154–56

  sites for, 7, 10, 153–68

  and weather concerns, 154–55

Rehearsals, 243–47

Relaxation, 242, 262

Religious ceremony, 139, 141

Remembrances, 150

Remote sites, 30–33

Rental equipment, 8–9, 32, 41, 45, 48–51

Rental equi[...] 81–82

Rental fac[...]

318

Renting transportation, 32
Restrictions, 31–32, 70
Restroom facilities, 156–58
Rice-throwing, 70
Ring bearer, 246
River settings, 98–99
RSVPs, 213, 214

S

Save-the-date cards, 8, 54, 117, 201–4
Seasonal changes, 130–32
Seasonal weddings, 21–23
Seating arrangements, 125–27, 178
Settings
    beach weddings, 60–62
    garden weddings, 63–65
    historic properties, 65–67
    permission for using, 4, 69–71
    public places, 12–13, 67–69
    questions to ask, 71–74
    selecting, 58–74
    types of, 60–69
Severe weather, 27. See also
Weather concerns
Shelters, 9, 45–50, 64–65, 54–56
    es, 44–45

Shuttles, 264–65
Site possibilities
    beach weddings, 60–62
    destination weddings, 91–105
    garden weddings, 63–65
    historic properties, 65–67
    permission for using, 4, 69–71
    public places, 12–13, 67–69
    questions to ask, 71–74
    selecting, 3–4, 58–74
    by state, 289–305
Site preparation, 240
Site restrictions, 31–32, 70
Site usage contract, 70–71
Site usage fees, 9, 10, 68
Site usage permissions, 4, 69–71
Smiling, 27–28, 242, 259
Snakes, 36
"Something blue," 60
Song selections, 148. See also Music
Sound issues, 41–42, 62, 144–49
Sound systems, 145–46
Special-needs guests, 32–33
Spring weddings, 22
Stormy weather, 15, 16, 27. See also Weather concerns
Stress, 242, 258
Summer weddings, 21–22

Sunlight, 129, 190–91
Sunrise, 130
Sunset, 130, 166
Superstitions, 20, 188–89

T

Table centerpieces, 88, 134–35
Table lighting, 134, 167
Tarps, 45
Taxi service, 87
Temperatures, 21–24, 26. See also Weather concerns
Tents, 9, 45–50, 64–65, 155, 168
Thank-you notes, 88, 135, 280, 286
Theme accessories, 113–15
Theme conflicts, 115–17
Theme foods, 112–13
Theme invitations, 111–12, 117–18, 201, 204–8
Theme parks, 65, 66
Theme weddings, 7–8, 67, 108–19
Thomas, Robert B., 20
Toasts, 177, 195
Tornadoes, 27
Trains, 221–22
Transportation, 30–33, 94, 96, 99–100, 264–68

Transportation timeline, 268
Travel, 94, 96, 99–100
Trellises, 124
Tuxedos, 228–31, 288
Twain, Mark, 16
Twilight, 166

U, V

Umbrellas, 44–45
Veils, 224–25
Videography, 196–200
Vows, exchanging, 144–46
Vows, writing, 143

W

Walkie-talkies, 30, 247
Weather and seasons, 21–24
Weather concerns
   conquering fears over,
   16–17
   and contingency plans, 9,
   43–58, 236–38, 252–54,
   261
   and destination weddings,
   102–3
   and dining outdoors, 171,
   178–79
   emergency kit for, 247–48

and extreme weather,
25–27
gear for, 44–46, 247–48
obsession with, 243
and photographs, 52–54
and rain dates, 27, 51–52
for reception, 154–55
and seasons, 21–23
and unpredictable
weather, 15, 27–28
and wedding day, 252–54
Weather forecasting, 17–21
Weather gear, 44–46, 247–
48
Weather statistics, 23–24
Wedding announcements, 93
Wedding attire, 67, 101,
111, 217–34
Wedding cake, 179–81
Wedding ceremony, 138–51.
See also Ceremony
Wedding colors, 63, 116–17
Wedding day, 251–68. See
also Ceremony
Wedding day supplies,
247–49
Wedding gown, 218–22, 288
Wedding gown preservation,
288
Wedding insurance, 9, 57,
86
Wedding night, 262
Wedding planners, 78, 80

Wedding reception. See
Reception
Wedding themes. See Theme
weddings
Wedding trends, 11–14
Windy weather, 25, 27, 171,
223–24. See also Weather
concerns
Winter weddings, 22–23
Written permissions, 70–71
Written plans, 244–45

THE **EVERYTHING** SERIES!

BUSINESS & PERSONAL FINANCE

Everything® Budgeting Book
Everything® Business Planning Book
Everything® Coaching and Mentoring Book
Everything® Fundraising Book
Everything® Get Out of Debt Book
Everything® Grant Writing Book
Everything® Home-Based Business Book
Everything® Homebuying Book, 2nd Ed.
Everything® Homeselling Book, 2nd Ed.
Everything® Investing Book, 2nd Ed.
Everything® Landlording Book
Everything® Leadership Book
Everything® Managing People Book
Everything® Negotiating Book
Everything® Online Business Book
Everything® Personal Finance Book
Everything® Personal Finance in Your 20s and 30s Book
Everything® Project Management Book
Everything® Real Estate Investing Book
Everything® Robert's Rules Book, $7.95
Everything® Selling Book
Everything® Start Your Own Business Book
Everything® Wills & Estate Planning Book

COOKING

Everything® Barbecue Cookbook
Everything® Bartender's Book, $9.95
Everything® Chinese Cookbook
Everything® Cocktail Parties and Drinks Book
Everything® College Cookbook
Everything® Cookbook
Everything® Cooking for Two Cookbook
Everything® Diabetes Cookbook
Everything® Easy Gourmet Cookbook
Everything® Fondue Cookbook
Everything® Gluten-Free Cookbook

Everything® Grilling Cookbook
Everything® Healthy Meals in Minutes Cookbook
Everything® Holiday Cookbook
Everything® Indian Cookbook
Everything® Italian Cookbook
Everything® Low-Carb Cookbook
Everything® Low-Fat High-Flavor Cookbook
Everything® Low-Salt Cookbook
Everything® Meals for a Month Cookbook
Everything® Mediterranean Cookbook
Everything® Mexican Cookbook
Everything® One-Pot Cookbook
Everything® Pasta Cookbook
Everything® Quick Meals Cookbook
Everything® Slow Cooker Cookbook
Everything® Slow Cooking for a Crowd Cookbook
Everything® Soup Cookbook
Everything® Thai Cookbook
Everything® Vegetarian Cookbook
Everything® Wine Book, 2nd Ed.

CRAFT SERIES

Everything® Crafts—Baby Scrapbooking
Everything® Crafts—Bead Your Own Jewelry
Everything® Crafts—Create Your Own Greeting Cards
Everything® Crafts—Easy Projects
Everything® Crafts—Polymer Clay for Beginners
Everything® Crafts—Rubber Stamping Made Easy
Everything® Crafts—Wedding Decorations and Keepsakes

HEALTH

Everything® Alzheimer's Book
Everything® Diabetes Book
Everything® Health Guide to Controlling Anxiety

Everything® Hypnosis Book
Everything® Low Cholesterol Book
Everything® Massage Book
Everything® Menopause Book
Everything® Nutrition Book
Everything® Reflexology Book
Everything® Stress Management Book

HISTORY

Everything® American Government Book
Everything® American History Book
Everything® Civil War Book
Everything® Irish History & Heritage Book
Everything® Middle East Book

HOBBIES & GAMES

Everything® Blackjack Strategy Book
Everything® Brain Strain Book, $9.95
Everything® Bridge Book
Everything® Candlemaking Book
Everything® Card Games Book
Everything® Card Tricks Book, $9.95
Everything® Cartooning Book
Everything® Casino Gambling Book, 2nd Ed.
Everything® Chess Basics Book
Everything® Craps Strategy Book
Everything® Crossword and Puzzle Book
Everything® Crossword Challenge Book
Everything® Cryptograms Book, $9.95
Everything® Digital Photography Book
Everything® Drawing Book
Everything® Easy Crosswords Book
Everything® Family Tree Book, 2nd Ed.
Everything® Games Book, 2nd Ed.
Everything® Knitting Book
Everything® Knots Book
Everything® Photography Book
Everything® Poker Strategy Book
Everything® Pool & Billiards Book
Everything® Quilting Book
Everything® Scrapbooking Book

All Everything® books are priced at $12.95 or $14.95, unless otherwise stated. Prices subject to change without notice.

Everything® Sewing Book
Everything® Test Your IQ Book, $9.95
Everything® Travel Crosswords Book, $9.95
Everything® Woodworking Book
Everything® Word Games Challenge Book
Everything® Word Search Book

HOME IMPROVEMENT

Everything® Feng Shui Book
Everything® Feng Shui Decluttering Book,
  $9.95
Everything® Fix-It Book
Everything® Homebuilding Book
Everything® Lawn Care Book
Everything® Organize Your Home Book

EVERYTHING® KIDS' BOOKS

All titles are $6.95
Everything® Kids' Animal Puzzle & Activity
  Book
Everything® Kids' Baseball Book, 3rd Ed.
Everything® Kids' Bible Trivia Book
Everything® Kids' Bugs Book
Everything® Kids' Christmas Puzzle
  & Activity Book
Everything® Kids' Cookbook
Everything® Kids' Crazy Puzzles Book
Everything® Kids' Dinosaurs Book
Everything® Kids' Gross Jokes Book
Everything® Kids' Gross Puzzle and
  Activity Book
Everything® Kids' Halloween Puzzle
  & Activity Book
Everything® Kids' Hidden Pictures Book
Everything® Kids' Joke Book
Everything® Kids' Knock Knock Book
Everything® Kids' Math Puzzles Book
Everything® Kids' Mazes Book
Everything® Kids' Money Book
Everything® Kids' Nature Book
Everything® Kids' Puzzle Book
Everything® Kids' Riddles & Brain Teasers Book
Everything® Kids' Science Experiments Book
Everything® Kids' Sharks Book
Everything® Kids' Soccer Book
Everything® Kids' Travel Activity Book

KIDS' STORY BOOKS

Everything® Fairy Tales Book

LANGUAGE

Everything® Conversational Japanese Book
  (with CD), $19.95
Everything® French Phrase Book, $9.95
Everything® French Verb Book, $9.95
Everything® Inglés Book
Everything® Learning French Book
Everything® Learning German Book
Everything® Learning Italian Book
Everything® Learning Latin Book
Everything® Learning Spanish Book
Everything® Sign Language Book
Everything® Spanish Grammar Book
Everything® Spanish Practice Book
  (with CD), $19.95
Everything® Spanish Phrase Book, $9.95
Everything® Spanish Verb Book, $9.95

MUSIC

Everything® Drums Book (with CD), $19.95
Everything® Guitar Book
Everything® Home Recording Book
Everything® Playing Piano and Keyboards
  Book
Everything® Reading Music Book (with CD),
  $19.95
Everything® Rock & Blues Guitar Book
  (with CD), $19.95
Everything® Songwriting Book

NEW AGE

Everything® Astrology Book, 2nd Ed.
Everything® Dreams Book, 2nd Ed.
Everything® Ghost Book
Everything® Love Signs Book, $9.95
Everything® Numerology Book
Everything® Paganism Book
Everything® Palmistry Book
Everything® Psychic Book
Everything® Reiki Book
Everything® Tarot Book
Everything® Wicca and Witchcraft Book

PARENTING

Everything® Baby Names Book
Everything® Baby Shower Book
Everything® Baby's First Food Book
Everything® Baby's First Year Book
Everything® Birthing Book
Everything® Breastfeeding Book
Everything® Father-to-Be Book
Everything® Father's First Year Book
Everything® Get Ready for Baby Book
Everything® Get Your Baby to Sleep Book,
  $9.95
Everything® Getting Pregnant Book
Everything® Homeschooling Book
Everything® Mother's First Year Book
Everything® Parent's Guide to Children
  and Divorce
Everything® Parent's Guide to Children
  with ADD/ADHD
Everything® Parent's Guide to Children
  with Asperger's Syndrome
Everything® Parent's Guide to Children
  with Autism
Everything® Parent's Guide to Children with
  Bipolar Disorder
Everything® Parent's Guide to Children
  with Dyslexia
Everything® Parent's Guide to Positive
  Discipline
Everything® Parent's Guide to Raising a
  Successful Child
Everything® Parent's Guide to Tantrums
Everything® Parent's Guide to the Overweight
  Child
Everything® Parent's Guide to the Strong-
  Willed Child
Everything® Parenting a Teenager Book
Everything® Potty Training Book, $9.95
Everything® Pregnancy Book, 2nd Ed.
Everything® Pregnancy Fitness Book
Everything® Pregnancy Nutrition Book
Everything® Pregnancy Organizer, $15.00
Everything® Toddler Book
Everything® Tween Book
Everything® Twins, Triplets, and More Book

All Everything® books are priced at $12.95 or $14.95, unless otherwise stated. Prices subject to change without notice.

PETS

Everything® Cat Book
Everything® Dachshund Book
Everything® Dog Book
Everything® Dog Health Book
Everything® Dog Training and Tricks Book
Everything® German Shepherd Book
Everything® Golden Retriever Book
Everything® Horse Book
Everything® Horseback Riding Book
Everything® Labrador Retriever Book
Everything® Poodle Book
Everything® Pug Book
Everything® Puppy Book
Everything® Rottweiler Book
Everything® Small Dogs Book
Everything® Tropical Fish Book
Everything® Yorkshire Terrier Book

REFERENCE

Everything® Car Care Book
Everything® Classical Mythology Book
Everything® Computer Book
Everything® Divorce Book
Everything® Einstein Book
Everything® Etiquette Book, 2nd Ed.
Everything® Inventions and Patents Book
Everything® Mafia Book
Everything® Philosophy Book
Everything® Psychology Book
Everything® Shakespeare Book

RELIGION

Everything® Angels Book
Everything® Bible Book
Everything® Buddhism Book
Everything® Catholicism Book
Everything® Christianity Book
Everything® Jewish History & Heritage Book
Everything® Judaism Book
Everything® Koran Book
Everything® Prayer Book
Everything® Saints Book

Everything® Torah Book
Everything® Understanding Islam Book
Everything® World's Religions Book
Everything® Zen Book

SCHOOL & CAREERS

Everything® Alternative Careers Book
Everything® College Survival Book, 2nd Ed.
Everything® Cover Letter Book, 2nd Ed.
Everything® Get-a-Job Book
Everything® Guide to Starting and Running
    a Restaurant
Everything® Job Interview Book
Everything® New Teacher Book
Everything® Online Job Search Book
Everything® Paying for College Book
Everything® Practice Interview Book
Everything® Resume Book, 2nd Ed.
Everything® Study Book

SELF-HELP

Everything® Dating Book, 2nd Ed.
Everything® Great Sex Book
Everything® Kama Sutra Book
Everything® Self-Esteem Book

SPORTS & FITNESS

Everything® Fishing Book
Everything® Golf Instruction Book
Everything® Pilates Book
Everything® Running Book
Everything® Total Fitness Book
Everything® Weight Training Book
Everything® Yoga Book

TRAVEL

Everything® Family Guide to Hawaii
Everything® Family Guide to Las Vegas,
    2nd Ed.
Everything® Family Guide to New York City,
    2nd Ed.
Everything® Family Guide to RV Travel &
    Campgrounds

Everything® Family Guide to the Walt Disney
    World Resort®, Universal Studios®,
    and Greater Orlando, 4th Ed.
Everything® Family Guide to Cruise Vacations
Everything® Family Guide to the Caribbean
Everything® Family Guide to Washington
    D.C., 2nd Ed.
Everything® Guide to New England
Everything® Travel Guide to the Disneyland
    Resort®, California Adventure®,
    Universal Studios®, and the
    Anaheim Area

WEDDINGS

Everything® Bachelorette Party Book, $9.95
Everything® Bridesmaid Book, $9.95
Everything® Elopement Book, $9.95
Everything® Father of the Bride Book, $9.95
Everything® Groom Book, $9.95
Everything® Mother of the Bride Book, $9.95
Everything® Outdoor Wedding Book
Everything® Wedding Book, 3rd Ed.
Everything® Wedding Checklist, $9.95
Everything® Wedding Etiquette Book, $9.95
Everything® Wedding Organizer, $15.00
Everything® Wedding Shower Book, $9.95
Everything® Wedding Vows Book, $9.95
Everything® Weddings on a Budget Book,
    $9.95

WRITING

Everything® Creative Writing Book
Everything® Get Published Book
Everything® Grammar and Style Book
Everything® Guide to Writing a Book Proposal
Everything® Guide to Writing a Novel
Everything® Guide to Writing Children's Books
Everything® Guide to Writing Research Papers
Everything® Screenwriting Book
Everything® Writing Poetry Book
Everything® Writing Well Book

Available wherever books are sold!
To order, call 800-258-0929, or visit us at *www.everything.com*
Everything® and everything.com® are registered trademarks of F+W Publications, Inc.